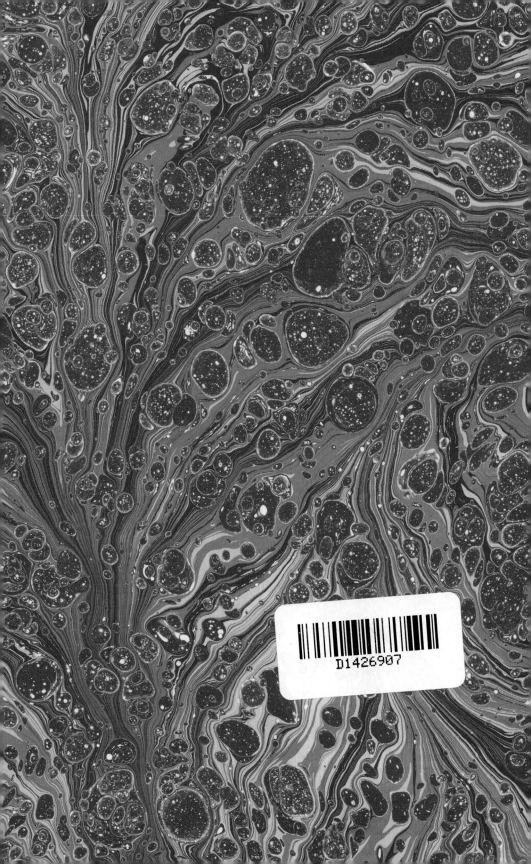

The Black Bats

The
Black Bats
CIA Spy Flights
over China from Taiwan
1951-1969

Chris Pocock
with Clarence Fu

Schiffer Military History
Atglen, PA

Book Design by Ian Robertson.

Copyright © 2010 by Schiffer Publishing.
Library of Congress Control Number: 2010921406

Printed in Hong Kong.
ISBN: 978-0-7643-3513-6

We are interested in hearing from authors with book ideas on related topics.

Published by Schiffer Publishing Ltd.
4880 Lower Valley Road
Atglen, PA 19310
Phone: (610) 593-1777
FAX: (610) 593-2002
E-mail: Info@schifferbooks.com.
Visit our web site at: www.schifferbooks.com
Please write for a free catalog.
This book may be purchased from the publisher.
Please include $5.00 postage.
Try your bookstore first.

In Europe, Schiffer books are distributed by:
Bushwood Books
6 Marksbury Avenue
Kew Gardens
Surrey TW9 4JF, England
Phone: 44 (0) 20 8392-8585
FAX: 44 (0) 20 8392-9876
E-mail: Info@bushwoodbooks.co.uk.
Visit our website at: www.bushwoodbooks.co.uk

Contents

Author's Note

Although many U.S. government documents of the period refer to the GRC (Government of the Republic of China), I have chosen to use ROC throughout. Similarly, I use PRC when formally referring to The People's Republic of China on the mainland. However, the informal term 'ChiComs' (for Chinese Communists) also appears in many U.S. documents. Since this term was commonly used by Americans during the period under discussion I have also chosen to use it freely. I hope that this does not offend any readers of this book in the PRC.

The problem of how to romanize the Chinese language has vexed many an author, not least this one. In the case of Taiwan, the problem is compounded because the ROC officially refused to follow the PRC's adoption of Hanyu Pinyin as the method of romanization. But neither did the ROC stick rigidly to the previous Wade-Giles method. Instead, a hybrid 'system' known as Tongyong Pinyin has evolved in Taiwan which confuses the locals as well as visitors!

In this book, I have used the Hanyu Pinyin method with only a few exceptions, where the alternative romanizations are so well established in the West. For instance, Taiwan or Wade-Giles romanization is used for the names of prominent personalities, such as Mao, Chou, and the Chiangs, and for Hsinchu airbase, the scene of much of the narrative. I am grateful to Clarence Fu for providing the romanization, and also for inserting the Chinese characters for names and places into my narrative. Therefore, at least those of you who can read Chinese will not suffer any confusion!

I have chosen to use the title Chinese Air Force (CAF) when referring to the air arm on Taiwan. Today it is formally known as the Republic of China Air Force (ROCAF), but in the period under discussion 'CAF' was in common use in Taiwan and the U.S.

I have also chosen to use the Russian designations of the aircraft flown by the People's Liberation Army Air Force (PLAAF). The relevant Chinese designations were J-5 (MiG-17), and H-5 (Il-28).

Foreword

by Major General Lu De Qi, RoCAF (retired)

The special operations of the Republic of China Air Force (RoCAF) can be traced back to the Korean War era. They ended some 20 years later when the Vietnam War was winding down. During this period, the CIA and the USAF provided aircraft and equipment while the ROCAF provided air and ground crew. In the beginning, the mission was to drop propaganda leaflets and agents. Later an ELINT mission was added and became the most important aspect. The operations area was over mainland China in the beginning, but later the crews also flew over the skies of Indochina.

I was personally involved in the special operations on three separate occasions. The first period was in 1952, when I was one of seven crew members chosen to be secretly trained at Tachikawa in Japan to fly the B-26 and the B-17. We flew over the western Pacific, but were never told the purpose of our training.

The second period was in 1955, when I was chosen to carry out the top-secret Fox Hunt missions. We flew a converted P4Y-2 to penetrate China's airspace in the night to collect radar and communication information. It was the beginning of ROCAF's ELINT missions.

The third period started in 1961 when I was assigned to join the 34th Squadron. I flew mainland China overflight missions in the C-54 and the P2V. The casualty rate was high and I was promoted to deputy commander in half a year. Later I was promoted to Commander and supervised the Operations Magic Dragon and Operation South Star.

Aviation historian Fu Jing Ping spent lots of time and energy to discover the real histories of special operations in the ROCAF. It took him two years to complete a book on this subject in Chinese. I am very glad that Mr. Fu has worked with noted aviation writer Chris Pocock on an English version of the book. I hope this will bring to a larger audience in the western world, the stories of those brave aircrew who flew hundreds of missions into the dangerous skies over in China.

A total of 142 aircrew perished in 20 years. I hope that their heroic stories can be properly recorded in history. May their souls rest in peace.

Foreword

by Donald A. Jackson, CIA, US NACC in Taiwan 1959-62

Chris Pocock has been working on this story for ten years and has written a book that should be of interest to very many people. It is about the Republic of China Air Force and the American men and women - Officers, Enlisted, and Civilian - that supported the intelligence collection operations over the China mainland. Very few people in Taiwan, the U.S., or elsewhere are aware of this story. It is a small snapshot of what was happening during the Cold War Years in East and Southeast Asia.

The heroics of the brave ROCAF crews that flew these reconnaissance missions, many 14 hours in duration, over the China mainland and elsewhere should have been recognised many years ago. The flights of the Black Bat Squadron never penetrated the air defenses of mainland China without being detected. Almost all of them were attacked by fighter aircraft, by ground air defenses, and by specially-modified bomber aircraft. The U.S. derived great benefit from the intelligence information collected.

Both myself and the other American civilians, together with the officers and enlisted men of the U.S. Air Force and U.S. Navy, were all very proud to have been involved in a technical and operational supporting role. It was indeed an honor to work with those dedicated, daring and courageous ROCAF airmen.

Prologue

When the Chinese nationalists retreated to Taiwan in 1949 after losing the civil war, their long-term prospects of defending the island seemed poor. The U.S. government had already washed its hands of Generalissimo ('Gimo') Chiang Kai Shek (蔣介石) and his Kuomintang (KMT) forces. In August 1949 Washington published a White Paper that blamed the nationalists for their defeat at the hands of Mao Tse Tung's (毛澤東) communists in China's civil war, despite the U.S. having provided aid worth $2 billion to the KMT. In October 1949, the CIA estimated that the Republic of China (ROC) on Taiwan could survive for "at best...three years." In January 1950, President Truman declared that the U.S. "would not provide military aid or advice to the Chinese forces on Formosa."[1]

Two million KMT soldiers and dependents escaped to Taiwan. About 160 aircraft of the Chinese Air Force (the CAF) made it to the island, mostly P-47 and P-51 fighters and B-24 and B-25 bombers, all supplied by the U.S. From Taiwan the CAF bombed mainland ports, trying to disrupt communist preparations for an invasion. The CAF also helped to defend some fifty islands along the mainland coast that were still under nationalist control. Against the odds KMT forces did repel a communist attack on Quemoy, one of the largest islands.

Meanwhile, in the newly-declared People's Republic of China (PRC), Mao began to consolidate his victory. Remnants of the KMT army were rounded up for elimination or re-education. The families of those who had fled to Taiwan were interrogated about their recently-departed relatives. They faced years of discrimination and deprivation. The KMT suffered another rout when communists successfully took Hainan Island in April 1950. Taiwan would be next. It was only 90 miles from the mainland.

Then, on 25 June 1950 everything changed. Communist North Korea invaded the South. Kim Il Sung got tacit approval from Stalin and Mao. All three calculated that the U.S. would not respond.

They were wrong. The U.S. interpreted the invasion as part of a general Communist offensive in Asia. America enlisted the support of the United Nations. The Soviet Union was boycotting the Security Council over the UN decision to prevent the PRC from joining. Within two days the Council voted to send military forces, led by the U.S., to defend South Korea.

The outbreak of the Korean War saved the Chinese nationalists on Taiwan. President Truman sent an aircraft carrier, a heavy cruiser, and eight destroyers into the Taiwan Strait to repel any attack from the mainland. Within days the PRC halted its preparations to invade Taiwan. Mao eventually committed communist forces to the Korean conflict instead, in late October 1950.

But the U.S. intervention in the Taiwan Strait came with strings attached. Truman declared that "the determination of the future status of Formosa must await the restoration of security in the Pacific." He demanded that the nationalists stop all air and naval operations against the mainland. The nationalists acquiesced. But this public injunction by Truman did not prevent his administration from sponsoring covert action against the PRC launched from Taiwan.[2]

And so the scene was set for more than two decades of uneasy partnership between the U.S. and the ROC in the anti-communist struggle. Chiang Kai Shek was officially committed to retaking the mainland – but the Gimo's actions rarely spoke as loud as his words. The U.S. officially opposed this nationalist dream, but sometimes covertly encouraged it in order to keep Mao's China on the defensive.

Chapter One

1951-1953

By early 1951, the U.S. government was making secret preparations to make Taiwan a significant base in the fight against communist expansion. The see-saw battle for territory in Korea had turned against the UN forces led by U.S. General Douglas MacArthur. He pushed for U.S. military support to the nationalists on Taiwan, hoping that this would dissuade communist China from throwing all its forces into support for North Korea. He even argued for the bombing of mainland Chinese cities.

This was a step too far for President Truman, who feared that this would provoke the Soviet Union to enter the conflict in Korea. But there was another way.

In mid-January 1951, a CIA analysis suggested that "by supplying the active anti-Communist forces already present in mainland China with effective communications, military equipment and logistic support, Communist military strength could be sapped, and their capabilities for operations elsewhere could be reduced."[3]

Frank Wisner was the architect of U.S. covert action in the early years of the Cold War. He ran the innocuous-sounding Office of Policy Coordination (OPC), which was absorbed into the young Central Intelligence Agency (CIA). OPC was the organization that encouraged anti-communist resistance behind the Iron Curtain in Europe. All the way from the Baltic States in the north to Albania in the south, OPC trained and inserted nationalist exiles who opposed the new regimes in their home countries. Carrying radios and weapons, many of them were air-dropped at night.

With the active encouragement of Madam Chiang Kai-Shek, who spent much time in the U.S. rallying support for her husband's regime, OPC formed Western Enterprises Inc (WEI) in February 1951. Ostensibly a Pittsburgh-based company, in reality WEI was a 'cover' for U.S.-inspired paramilitary operations against mainland China from Taiwan. As one participant explained with some irony, "having already been trained in parachuting, explosives and other appropriate aspects of commercial life, WEI's first employees appeared on Taiwan the following month, March 1951."[4]

WEI set up its headquarters and living quarters in the Taipei Guest House, off the Zhong Shan North Road. Over the next four years WEI trained and equipped nationalist guerilla troops who made various forays into the mainland. Most of the actions were small-scale raids on coastal areas launched by landing craft from the offshore islands that were still under nationalist control. In addition, ships plying between mainland China's ports were attacked. But for true believers in covert action like Frank Wisner, the focus had to extend much further inland, where pockets of resistance to the Chinese communists (Chicoms) should be encouraged. That required dropping agents from the air.

Civil Air Transport (CAT)
In May 1951 a U.S. Military Aid and Assistance Group (MAAG) was established in Taipei
to provide training and equipment to the Republic of China's military forces. But the
poorly-trained and equipped CAF did not receive a new supply of American fighters and
bombers until 1953. Moreover, in 1951-52 it remained official U.S. policy that military aid
to the nationalists could only be used for internal security and the defense of Taiwan itself.
Therefore, although the CAF already had a large fleet of C-46 and C-47 transports, WEI
could not entrust it with specialised, covert air support operations.[5]

However, Wisner persuaded the CIA to become the owner of an airline that could
do the job instead. This was Civil Air Transport (CAT), the outfit formed in Shanghai in
1946 and led by former U.S. General Claire Chennault of 'Flying Tigers' fame. Chennault
enjoyed an enduring friendship with Chiang Kai-shek. CAT provided loyal support to
the KMT regime during the Chinese civil war, with its gung-ho American pilots flying
airlift and airdrop missions under communist fire. In 1949 CAT followed the nationalists
in defeat to Taiwan. In June 1950 the CIA secretly acquired the bankrupt CAT, which
began flying its C-46s and C-47s from Japan to Korea on airlift missions supporting the
UN force. Covert airdrops by CAT behind the communist lines in Korea, and into Chinese
Manchuria, followed.

In February 1951, CAT flew its first sorties in support of nationalist Chinese forces.
Operation Paper was a covert airlift of weapons to a large KMT force that had survived
the communist victory by fleeing into Burma. The 'Yunnan Anti-Communist National
Salvation Army' led by General Li Mi (李彌) was based in the remote mountains of eastern
Burma. CAT picked up arms and ammunition from the CIA depot on Okinawa and flew
them to northern Thailand, from where they were delivered to the KMT across the border
by land. When Li Mi's troops invaded Yunnan in May 1951 CAT airdropped more supplies
to them. But in a portent of things to come, the nationalist troops were routed by communist
forces. The survivors retreated to their mountain refuge in Burma.[6]

The first major action against the mainland organised by WEI met with no greater
success. A 200-strong raid from Jinmen by sea in September 1951 was easily defeated by
the People's Liberation Army (PLA).

By that time CAT was already performing regular airdrops from Taoyuan airbase, near
Taipei, over the Chinese coastal provinces, as far south as Hainan Island. Propaganda leaflets
were dropped and individual agents or small communications teams were inserted. The
flights were usually unopposed, since the mainland's air defences were still rudimentary,
based on obsolete aircraft captured from the KMT. Soviet-supplied air defence artillery
was beginning to appear, but the most advanced Soviet equipment – radar and jet fighters
– was only to be found in the far north of China, supporting the Korean War.[7]

For the airdrop missions that supported WEI actions, CAT's chief pilot, Robert
Rousselot, selected a small cadre of aircrew. They were still mostly Americans; brave
and ideologically committed characters who volunteered for only a small hazardous pay
supplement. CAT also employed Chinese as copilots, radio operators, and parachute
dispatch officers, or PDOs (colloquially called 'kickers'), who supervised the airdrop
procedure. CAT flew a total of 12 airdrops in 1951 using the C-46s to insert 110 agents. In
1952 there were 23 missions to insert 150 agents.[8]

But medium-range aircraft such as CAT's C-46s did not have the range to reach northwest China, where anti-communist resistance forces led by former warlords and KMT generals were still active. OPC decided to support these forces which were optimistically characterized by the nationalists as "Taiwan Inside the Mainland." Small teams of Chinese were trained by WEI in secure radio communication and encryption ('commo'); weather observation; and parachuting. They would be dropped into the remote deserts and mountains of Qinghai, Gansu, and Sichuan provinces together with radios, guns, ammunition, and fake currency.[9]

In 1952 CAT acquired a B-17 bomber from the U.S. airbase at Kadena, on Okinawa. CAT also acquired a C-54 (DC-4) transport that could carry airline passengers but could be temporarily converted for airdrop missions. These aircraft had the range to fly from Taiwan to northwest China and back – a roundtrip of up to 14 hours.[10]

The airline's chief pilot Rousselot himself led an all-American crew of six on the first long range airdrop sortie – all the way to Lake Kokonor, in Qinghai, in March 1952. His crew comprised a co-pilot, a navigator, two PDOs, and an inflight interpreter. The latter would handle communications with the commo team to be dropped and, on subsequent airdrop missions, would talk by radio to the resistance fighters on the ground. Navigation was a major problem on these flights. There were no aids such as LORAN to rely on, so the dead-reckoning skills of the crew were vital. Maps of inland China were out-of-date and unreliable. So the airdrop missions were usually scheduled for nights with a full moon, to aid identification of features on the ground. Still, there was sometimes confusion over the exact location of the drop zones. Or they would be obscured by clouds – there was no reliable way to forecast the weather so far inland.[11]

One epic flight in the C-54 lasted just five minutes short of 16 hours, according to CAT pilot Erik Shilling. The drop zone was 200 miles northwest of Chengdu, high in the Himalayas, and therefore had to be done in daylight. The aircraft took off from Clark airbase, in the Philippines, and landed at Kadena airbase on Okinawa.[12]

A total of 27 airdrop missions were staged to northwest China in 1952-53. The flights would be planned to enter the mainland's airspace at known 'blind spots' in the early warning radar coverage along the coast. The PRC was using Soviet-supplied P-3 'Dumbo' radar units; some old SCR-270s supplied by the U.S. in 1940; and some radars that had been

NIGHT PHOTO MISSIONS IN THE B-25

Qi Rong Chun (戚榮春), who later became deputy commander of the CAF, flew night recon missions to Luqiao and Zhangqiao airfields in Zhejiang province. He remembered handing the B-25 over to the co-pilot when nearing the target, and went into the bombardier's position in the nose, from where he gave course corrections to the co-pilot and then released the photoflash bomb when they were over the target.

Qi said this kind of mission was very dangerous, because they flew at only 8,000 feet, so that even small-calibre anti-aircraft weapons could hit the aircraft. Moreover, the M46 photoflash bombs that they carried were very flammable. If they were hit by anti-aircraft fire they would soon destroy the aircraft.

Because the M46s were so dangerous, the flight engineer had to climb above the bomb bay to observe that each one had been dropped and, if not, to manually drop it. Otherwise the timer would detonate the bomb in the aircraft. The timer was set to detonate at 1,500 feet and provide 1/5th second of light @ 500 million candlelight. A sensor in the B-25 belly detected the strong light and activated the aircraft's cameras.

One of the first B-25 photo missions in 1952 flew over Zhangqiao airbase. On the film a number of wooden crates were visible. It was later confirmed that these contained the first Il-28 jet bombers sent to China by the USSR. - *Fu, p17*

SECRET SCENES AT TAOYUAN AIRBASE

Whenever the Western Company performed its missions local martial law was imposed at Taoyuan airfield, and army guards were stationed in the area. The takeoff time was usually dusk, using night cover to penetrate mainland China, and the return back was the next morning. People wearing PLA uniforms were seen shaking hands with intelligence officers before boarding the aircraft.

When the Chinese Air Force began flying special missions, the briefings were not held in the 5th Fighter Group or 12th Recon Squadron facilities, but in a tent. The agents to be dropped also waited in the tent. They wore a special uniform, and each carried an automatic rifle, plus two handguns in their waist, a torchlight, and a small knife tied to their feet. On one occasion there were three tough-looking females in the agent team. - *Fu, p20*

captured from the defeated Japanese forces. The positions of these radars were mapped by ELINT missions flown along the China coast by USAF or U.S. Navy aircraft.

These deep and daring penetrations by CAT were not prevented by the rudimentary air defenses on the mainland. And there were no technical malfunctions. What would have happened if the C-54 or the B-17 had been forced to land? With no chance of rescue, the crew carried gold bars with which they might bribe their way home. Alternatively, there was the option of committing suicide by taking cyanide capsules.

But even if the long flights went undetected they were seldom successful. On only 10 of the missions did airdrops actually proceed. Moreover, the commo teams and guerillas who parachuted onto the mainland were steadily rounded up by the PLA.[13]

Meanwhile, the U.S. decided to train nationalist aircrews to fly night missions over the mainland. Four pilots from the 12th Reconnaissance Squadron of the CAF were selected, plus two navigators, two radio operators, and two chief mechanics from other CAF units. American advisors on Taiwan taught these two crews to fly at night on a pair of B-25C bombers that were converted for reconnaissance. Supervised from CAF headquarters in Taipei by Major General Luo Ying De (羅英德), they flew a number of photo missions over the mainland in mid-1952.[14]

CAF aircrews were also sent to Japan for training on the B-17 by instructors from the WEI, led by James Lassiter. The first B-17 mission over the mainland by an all-Chinese crew of seven took place on 24 August 1952. From October 1952 Maj. Han Cai Sheng (韓采生) was put in charge of these CAF special mission crews.

Between December 1952 and April 1953 these crews flew another 12 of the airdrop missions to northwest China. It was an uncomfortable and exhausting experience. The B-17 could fly higher than CAT's DC-4, cruising at up to 20,000 feet. To stretch the range two extra fuel tanks were added in the fuselage. But to save weight so that the maximum takeoff weight was not exceeded some standard equipment was stripped from the aircraft, including the autopilot, the cabin heaters, and the permanent oxygen system.

The two pilots took turns to hand-fly the unpressurized plane, battling fatigue with amphetamine pills supplied by WEI. All the Chinese aircrew shivered despite their uncomfortably thick flying suits, and they had to breathe oxygen in turn from portable cylinders. We must take turns to faint, they joked amongst themselves! Navigators found that their sextant shots were messed up by the ice that kept forming on the overhead window. They carried a thermos flask with hot water that they poured onto a towel in order to clear it. Agents and supplies were despatched through a 54-inch diameter hatch cut into the belly of the B-17. American instructors called it 'The Joe Hole.' The kickers

LIMPING HOME WITH ENGINE FAILURES

None of the airdrop missions to northwest China in 1952-53 came to grief because of mechanical failure, but there were some close calls. On one of the CAT C-54 missions, an engine failed fours hours after crossing the mainland coast. Captain Roy Watts feathered it and pressed on successfully. A Chinese B-17 crew led by Qi Rong Chun was returning over the Taiwan Strait when all four engines began misbehaving. Two had failed completely by the time they reached Taoyuan, where bad weather forced them to divert to Taipei. A third engine quit on the way there, so they landed at Sungshan airport, on the city's northern side, with only one prop turning. The cause? No one had thought to increase the B-17's oil capacity to cater for the extra running time on a 13-hour-plus flight!

An extra tank of oil was then added in the fuselage of the B-17, but the contents had to be manually pumped to the engines by the inflight mechanic. At cruising altitude in the unpressurized plane the effort required was sometimes just too much, and the mechanic fainted.

- Leary, p137; Fu, p20

had to manhandle the supplies towards the hatch and secure them until the pilots gave the command to release them.[15]

C-47 Shot Down in China

During the Korean War CAT flew another series of covert missions over mainland China - but not from Taiwan. The U.S. aimed to encourage subversion across the border from North Korea. There were said to be anticommunist dissidents in Manchuria who could be encouraged and supported. But this so-called 'Third Force' was judged by OPC to hold no loyalty for Chiang Kai-Shek's regime on Taiwan. The American airmen of CAT were tasked to insert OPC-trained agents to support these dissidents in an operation codenamed Tropic. The flights were staged out of Japan and Korea.

To fly the missions, CAT acquired three C-47s that were painted olive drab and equipped with engine flame suppressors. Operation Tropic was kept secret from Chennault, who was still the chairman of CAT, in case he blabbed to the Gimo.[16]

The nighttime, low-level airdrops into Manchuria began in spring 1952. On 29 November that year, a C-47 returned to Jilin province to pick up a previously-inserted agent who radioed that he was ready to come out with some secret documents. The exfiltration would use a pick-up system in which the agent erected two poles and strung a wire between them. He would then don his parachute harness, attach it to the wire, and sit down on the ground. Dangling a grapple attached to a winch, the C-47 would descend to tree-top level and fly towards the wire at near-stall speed. The grapple would snag the wire, and the agent would be snatched from the ground and wound into the aircraft by the winch.

THE LIGHTS OF VLADIVOSTOK

"I drove with Bob Snoddy and Norman Schwarz to a place called the menagerie. It was a secluded tarmac for all types of planes for special projects. I dropped them near a camouflaged C-47. I saw flame arresters over its engine exhaust stacks. They usurp fuel, and I knew that they were used only on unarmed planes that penetrated enemy airspace.

After a long silence, Snoddy said quietly in a matter-of-fact way, 'I've seen the lights of Vladivostok.'

I asked, 'How about my going with you sometime?'

'Jeez, don't volunteer. Once you get on these, you never get off. The customer figures, the fewer that go, the tighter the security.'

It wasn't their last flight, it was a test hop, but it was the last time I saw them."

- Smith, p217-8; Schwarz and Snoddy were killed when their C-47 was shot down over Manchuria in November 1952.

THE CIA'S FAILED COVERT POLICY

Downey and Fecteau's capture was one of the most glaring examples of the CIA's failed covert policy against China in the early 1950s. Shortly after the two CIA officers were lost in Manchuria, those of us working clandestinely in Asia recognized that covert missions were not revealing much about the closed-off Middle Kingdom. Contrary to CIA predictions. Our missions were unable to locate or exploit the kind of discontent amongst the Chinese population that could be used to establish intelligence bases in China. The Chinese were not willing to side with outside forces. The missions were also costing a lot of money. - *Lilley, p81*

As the C-47 attempted the pickup it was ambushed by gunfire and shot down. The agent and his team had been captured and 'turned' by communist Chinese forces. The request for exfiltration was a trap. CAT pilots Bob Snoddy and Norman Schwarz died in the wreckage of the C-47, but two CIA agents acting as PDOs in the rear of the aircraft survived. John Downey and Richard Fecteau were captured and imprisoned. Because the U.S. government would not acknowledge that they were covert warriors, the Chicoms held onto Downey and Fecteau until the early 1970s. Their fate caused the Truman Administration to re-evaluate the political risk of sending Americans on covert air missions over mainland China.[17]

Taiwan's Potential

Did any of the U.S.-inspired covert actions against mainland China in 1951-53 have the desired effect of stimulating resistance to the Chicoms, and diverting their military resources from the Korean War? It seems unlikely. The disaster of the C-47 shootdown on Operation Tropic served to confirm what was already apparent to many in U.S. military and intelligence circles. The anti-communist forces on the mainland had been suffocated by a blanket of state security. The teams that were inserted to join up with them instead were rounded up and either killed or 'turned' to lure more agents into a trap. When Downey and Fecteau were put on trial in 1954, the Chicoms claimed that 212 guerillas had been parachuted into the mainland between 1951 and 1953. Half had been killed and the other half captured.[18]

Moreover, larger-scale military actions promoted by the ROC and supported by OPC had also failed. In July 1952, the PLA moved decisively against two former KMT generals who were leading the resistance in Sichuan. Another attempt by Li Mi's 'army' to penetrate Yunnan province from Burma in August 1952 was also smashed by the PLA. The claim by Chiang Kai-shek that two million nationalist guerrillas were active on the mainland was thoroughly discredited.

For the China-watchers in U.S. intelligence, SIGINT (Signals Intelligence) seemed a much better bet than unreliable reports from the Taiwan Intelligence Bureau. After an organisational overhaul of U.S. worldwide SIGINT capabilities, the top-secret National Security Agency (NSA) was established in November 1952. By then, the U.S. had already been operating a radio monitoring facility on Taiwan for about two years. The ROC's intelligence agencies provided manpower to help operate, translate, and analyse the communications from the mainland that this station intercepted.[19]

Taiwan's potential as a listening post helped the Republic of China retain influence on U.S. policy. So did the fact that the KMT government had managed to feed and organise the two million refugees on Taiwan. Pro-communist sympathisers on the island had been suppressed by Chiang's secret police. It now seemed that, provided the U.S. Navy continued to patrol the Taiwan Strait, and the CAF was expanded so that it retained air superiority, the nationalists would survive on Taiwan.

The ROC lobbied effectively for influence and support in Washington, and was boosted by the Republican victory in the 1952 federal elections. In his first State of the Union address on 2 February 1953, President Eisenhower declared that he was lifting his predecessor's ban on the ROC conducting military operations against the mainland. This played well to the McCarthyite and anti-communist lobby in Congress.

Privately, though, State Department officials told the Gimo that they would not sanction a large-scale attack that might drag the U.S. into a war with the PRC. Chiang agreed to consult with the U.S. before launching any offensive military operations. However, smaller-scale actions were not ruled out by Washington – provided that the U.S. was in control.[20]

WEI Raids Unsuccessful
In fact, WEI's American leadership was allowed to plan an attack of significant scale on a Chicom coastal target in 1953. Once devised, the plan was turned over to the ROC's regular military forces for execution. Dongshan island, near the border between Fujian and Guangdong provinces, would be invaded by 600 paratroops carried from Taiwan by the CAF's own regular C-46 transports. Five thousand more troops would be landed by the ROC navy, while WEI would contribute 1,500 of its trained Chinese guerillas to be carried from Jinmen by motorised junks. But the pre-dawn airdrop on 16 July 1953 was poorly executed, and the troop landing was delayed because the navy miscalculated the tides. Communist forces counter-attacked, and the nationalists held the island for less than 36 hours, despite air support from CAF AT-6 Texans based on Jinmen. Both sides claimed a victory.[21]

Ten days later, the protracted negotiations to end the Korean War finally led to an armistice. Much of Washington's rationale for WEI's raids against the mainland China coast evaporated. Moreover, the U.S. security guarantee to Taiwan did not formally extend to the offshore islands (except for Penghu, in the middle of the Taiwan Strait). In any case, the PRC was now strengthening its coastal defences. The U.S. military argued that the offshore islands were not defendable, and that the nationalists should withdraw from all of them, including the largest, Jinmen and Mazu.

WEI's days were numbered. And although CAT would soon embark on new paramilitary adventures in Indo-China, the airline's role in covert air operations over mainland China was at an end. Indeed, by August 1953 U.S. policy formally prohibited the CIA from sending Americans on covert overflights. In the future, the U.S. would entrust all such missions over mainland China to a brave group of flyers from the CAF on Taiwan.[22]

A TRIBUTE TO CAT

As the air arm of the CIA in east Asia during the 1950s, the airline provided safe, secure, deniable transportation for a variety of covert projects. CAT performed with a professional excellence. The airline's civilian pilots made more than 100 perilous overflights of mainland China without the benefit or protection of a uniform, risking capture, long imprisonment and death. Rewards were few for these secret soldiers of the Cold War, but they go the job done. - *Leary, p142-3*

Chapter Two

1953-1956

By June 1953, four Chinese nationalist aircrews had been trained to fly special missions at night. During that month they and two black-painted B-17s were moved from Taoyuan to Hsinchu, a fishing town at the head of the Touqian river, 25 miles further down the west coast of Taiwan. Shortly afterwards they were formally designated as the CAF's Special Mission Group (SMG). The group reported direct to the Operations Division at CAF headquarters.

The airbase at Hsinchu already housed the CAF bomber and transport groups that were equipped with B-24s and C-46s respectively. For extra security, the SMG was located separately on the far side of the runway, close to the coast, and with its own entrance to the base. The base commander at Hsinchu was not informed about the SMG's activities.

Chiang Ching-Kuo

In September 1953 the Gimo's son, Chiang Ching-kuo, paid an official visit to the U.S. He had talks with President Eisenhower, CIA chief Allen Dulles, and his brother, the Secretary of State John Foster Dulles. Ching-kuo was already 'the power behind the throne' on

AN AMERICAN VIEW OF HSINCHU

Mud-covered water buffalo grazed in the shade beneath the wing of the old World War II B-17 Flying Fortress. Low rambling sheds, some of them stables and others supply shelters, were scattered along the perimeter of the field. A full stand of grass and small underbrush had grown up through the mesh of the pierced steel plank that had been laid on the ground to form a parking ramp for a collection of clandestine aircraft. Coils of barbed wire had been spread everywhere in a cleverly concealed random pattern, with wild flowers growing through it in abundance.

Yet for all its appearance of tranquillity, this remote airfield was the center of a most active clandestine air activity. The pastoral scene camouflaged the muted industry of teams of Chinese Nationalist specialists who prepared the B-17s for deep flights over the mainland. Agent information told of trouble deep in China that was being exploited by leaflet drops from the old bombers.

- Prouty, Chapter 4

CHIANG CHING KUO (蔣經國) DESCRIBED

Robert Martin, a *US News And World Report* correspondent who had known Chiang Ching Kuo on the mainland, came to Taipei and had several meetings and two private dinners with him. Martin was impressed that this man, who possessed so much "naked and brutal power" and whom "the politicians" and some generals hated, dared to travel around and go to restaurants without bodyguards, and was "totally unpretentious, frugal, modest and informal."...Martin was struck by Chiang Ching-Kuo's "questing mind; a total disdain for what we call democratic rights balanced by a dedication...that is rarely found out here; an internal and spiritual drive that gets him out of bed at 0630 and keeps him working at top speed until midnight; and an ability to relax and enjoy himself because he is a fairly earthy man."

- Taylor, p224

Taiwan. He controlled the ROC's intelligence and secret police networks. Sometimes ruthless, but always approachable and with a down-to-earth manner, Ching-kuo created a favorable impression in Washington, especially at the CIA. Until now Madam Chiang Kai-shek had been the Gimo's main liaison with WEI and the MAAG on Taiwan. Now, though, Ching-kuo took over that role.[23]

The covert airdropping of small agent teams into the mainland continued. The SMG crews flew 42 missions with the B-17s before the end of 1953. In October, a single C-46 and a B-24 converted for reconnaissance were transferred from regular CAF squadrons to the SMG. By the end of 1953, the unit flew the C-46 into mainland China nine times and the RB-24 six times.[24]

Leaflet Dropping
The U.S. began supplying new equipment to the CAF. The first F-84G Thunderjets arrived in 1953, followed by RT-33A jets for reconnaissance in 1954. The bomber force was augmented with some P4Y2 Privateers, a naval version of the B-24. The U.S. extracted a written promise from the ROC that these aircraft would not be used for offensive military action against the mainland, except in defense of the offshore islands controlled by Taiwan.[25]

The Special Mission Group was also boosted by the receipt of two twin-engine B-26Cs. The USAF had used the Douglas Invader to great effect in the Korean War as a night-flying tactical bomber. CAF crews were sent to Japan for flight training on two B-26s that had been transferred to the CIA.

The SMG began flying the B-26s into the mainland in late October 1953. On the night of 15 February 1954 one of them flew over Shanghai on a leaflet-dropping 'raid.' Millions of pieces of paper from the 15 'leaflet bombs' rained down on the port city. The daring mission was timed to coincide with the PRC's Sino-Soviet Friendship Day. The leaflets denounced communism in general and the Soviet Union in particular. They also reminded the residents of Shanghai that more than a million of their fellow-citizens had been killed in the Korean War. After the B-26 returned safely to Hsinchu the ROC propaganda machine made sure that the raid was publicised. However, it pretended that multiple aircraft had been involved, which the mainland's defences had failed to intercept.[26]

With a maximum speed that was almost 100 knots faster than the B-17, B-24, or B-25, the B-26 was more likely to evade Chicom air defences – which were improving fast. During the Korean War, the Soviet Union supplied or loaned some 1,400 jet fighters to the PRC – Mig-9s, MiG-15s, and Yak-15s. Most of them were deployed in Manchuria, but now, since the war was over, the Chicoms transferred more of them south, to new and improved airfields along the east coast. By mid-1953, moreover, the gaps in coastal radar coverage were being filled. A combination of visual observer posts and radar installations provided almost complete coverage along the coast from Hainan Island to the Soviet frontier, according to the latest U.S. intelligence estimates.[27]

The Chicom air defences opposite Taiwan claimed their first victim on 18 January 1953. A U.S. Navy P-2V-5 Neptune maritime patrol plane was shot down in the Strait by anti-aircraft artillery (AAA) on the mainland coast. Only seven of the 13 crew were rescued, and another four Americans lost their lives when a U.S. Coast Guard PBM-5 Mariner amphibious aircraft sent to rescue them crashed on takeoff in the rough seas.[28]

On 26 May 1954 the SMG lost its first aircraft when one of the B-17s crashed in Fujian province en route to another night airdrop. It seems that the aircraft either flew into high ground or took a lucky shot from anti-aircraft guns, although the PRC did not claim a shootdown. The four aircrew led by Captain Nie Jing Yuan (聶經淵), plus the four agents that were being inserted, were all killed.[29]

The Soviets had not yet supplied radar-equipped fighters to the People's Liberation Army Air Force (PLAAF). This reduced the Chicom's ability to intercept intruding aircraft at nighttime or in bad weather. The first SMG mission to be challenged in the air was a B-24 airdrop to the Nanchang area on 22 June 1954. But the crew managed to evade the intercept by one of the Lavochkin La-11 piston-engine fighters that the Soviet Union had transferred to communist China.[30]

B-26 Crew

Despite the crash of the B-17 in Fujian the overflight missions continued. Evasive tactics were upgraded. The U.S. sent a dual-control TB-26B trainer from Japan, and American instructors taught the CAF pilots how to fly at low-level up and down Taiwan's river valleys. Doing this at night took great skill; practically speaking, it could only be done when the moon was at its brightest. From his position in the transparent nose of the B-26, a navigator or 'nosegator' surveyed the terrain ahead and relayed instructions to the pilot – "turn left! turn right! descend! pull up!"

The B-26 carried only one pilot – he occupied the left seat in the cockpit, with a radio operator in the right seat. Behind them sat a second navigator who operated the LORAN system. After an hour or more of low-level flying the pilot would tire of wrestling with the control yoke. Fortunately, the aircraft had a good radar altimeter that could be set to sound an alarm if it flew below the minimum safety altitude setting.

The B-26 was fast, but it was not an ideal aircraft for agent-dropping or resupply missions. It only had enough range to reach Guangzhou or Shanghai. Although the belly and tail gun turrets of the SMG's aircraft had been removed there wasn't much room for payload. Only one or two agents could be carried. During the flight one could rest on a makeshift seat – a chair strapped into the bomb bay. When the B-26 approached the drop zone the agents strapped on their parachutes and lay down in the bomb bay with their package of supplies. Over the drop zone the pilot opened the bomb bay doors, and the force of gravity ensured that the agents and their package dropped out![31]

So the larger but slower aircraft were still in business, for the longer missions. In 1954, the SMG's B-26s flew 43 times over the mainland, the RB-24 logged 40 overflights, the C-46 did 29 sorties, and the B-17s did 14. On some full moon nights the unit was very busy

---

OVER SHANGHAI IN A B-26

We coasted-in at the Huangpu River. The anti-aircraft guns started firing from all sides. We tried to duck by turning left and right, and flying really low – the safest place to be. Then the searchlights came on from behind us. It was so bright, I could see my face reflected in the plexiglass cover to my navigator's table. The AA guns kept firing…we were under attack for a total of 15 minutes. Then we coasted-out, flying southeast towards the Zhoushan Islands. Now we could relax, everything became calm, we were out of danger. I was so relieved, that I started to sing a song that describes the joy of living: "I love to see the evening sun go down…"

- Sun Yong Qing(孫永慶), B-26 navigator, in film "The Secret of the Taiwanese Skies"

MORE DIVIDED FAMILIES

Many members of the Chinese Air Force who flew special missions over the mainland from 1953 onwards, had experienced the anguish of family separation. There was Wu Zhong Zhen (吳鍾珍), who lost contact with his family in Jinan when it was overrun by the communists in 1948. Wu was taking university entrance exams in Nanjing at the time. He was subsequently admitted to the Air Force Communications School, and relocated with it to Taiwan.

Then there was Dai Shu Qing (戴樹清), who began flying special missions in 1956. His father was a lieutenant general in the KMT Army, so the younger Dai was bound to join the military. He chose the Air Force, and graduated from the Academy in 1945. In 1949, he was flying B-24s and lost contact with his father as the civil war reached its conclusion. Dai flew to Taiwan, leaving his mother, father, two brothers and a sister on the mainland.

Liu Jiao Zhi (劉教之)was a radio officer also flying the B-24s of the 8th Group stationed in Dachang near Shanghai. His squadron was so heavily engaged in the civil war, that he did not have time to arrange for his family in Sichuan to be evacuated, before the communists closed in on the airbase, forcing the entire group to make a hasty retreat to Taiwan.

Li De Yuan (李德元) was born into a poor family in Sichuan, and had 16 brothers and sisters. In 1943 he was admitted to the Junior Academy of the Chinese Air Force. In June 1949, he made a trip home to tell his parents the Academy was being evacuated to Taiwan. They refused to let him go, but his brother smuggled him out of the house at night. Li rose through the CAF, and eventually became chief pilot of China Airlines. It wasn't until 40 years later that he was able to return to Sichuan. Only eight of his siblings were still alive. So were his parents, but they had all suffered great hardship under the communists, because of his defection.

- extracted from MND Vietnam Oral History, various biographical pages

indeed. An aircraft would fly one mission during the evening, return to Hsinchu, and be taken over by a fresh crew for a second overflight.

Because so many of the inserted agents were being captured and/or compromised, security was very tight. Sometimes the SMG's aircrew were taken to CAF headquarters in Taipei for the pre-mission briefing in a car with sealed windows. Upon their return to Hsinchu the car would drop them directly by the aircraft. The agents were already onboard, seated in the fuselage. The aircrews were not encouraged to talk to them.

The aircrew were forbidden from telling their families anything about their missions. Some of the flights were staged out of Korea, and the crews would go missing for two days or more. Wives worried but endured in silence. They came to sense that, between the 13th and the 19th day in the lunar calendar their husbands were at greatest risk. These were the days surrounding the full moon, when most of the covert flights were scheduled.[32]

ROC's Right to Fly

Were these agent and leaflet-dropping missions achieving anything? Ambassador Rankin, the senior U.S. diplomat on Taiwan, thought they were merely "tickling the Communist tiger with a feather duster." Nevertheless, Rankin worried that the covert actions might provoke the PRC into military action against the offshore islands. Knowing his opinions, WEI and the MAAG kept him in the dark about covert operations.[33]

But whatever the U.S. Ambassador thought, the ROC maintained that it was the sole legitimate government of all China. Therefore, its air force had the right to fly in Chinese airspace. So the CAF's fighter-bombers were often sent on patrol along and over the mainland coast, as far as their range would take them. This was obviously a provocation to the PRC, even if the aircraft made no attacks. In 1953-4 the CAF lost a total of nine piston-engine F-47 Thunderbolts on these patrols, shot down by anti-aircraft fire or the PLA's fighters.[34]

Loss of Dachen

In mid-1954, tension increased along China's coastline. The ROC Navy captured a Soviet tanker en route to the mainland. PLAAF fighters shot down a DC-4 airliner belonging to Hong Kong's Cathay Pacific Airlines 20 miles off Hainan Island. To protect the subsequent rescue effort, the U.S. Navy launched fighters from Seventh Fleet aircraft carriers, and they shot down two Chicom fighters. Only nine of the 22 passengers and crew on the DC-4 survived.[35]

In September 1954, the PRC shelled Jinmen heavily from mainland batteries. But Chairman Mao's real target was further north - the nationalist-held islands offshore from Zhejiang province. To forestall him, the ROC requested permission to bomb PLAAF airbases in that area. The U.S. refused to allow it. Chiang Kai Shek ordered the 13,000 troops on Dachen island to fight till the death, but wiser counsels prevailed. The U.S. Seventh Fleet stood guard while the ROC forces were evacuated. The PLA refrained from attacking the U.S. warships.[36]

The loss of Dachen spelled the end of WEI. As in Europe, the idea that covert paramilitary operations sponsored by the CIA could roll back communist control was discredited. The CIA revamped its operation on Taiwan. The emphasis changed to intelligence-gathering about mainland China. A new 'cover' was created – the Naval Auxiliary Communications Center (NACC). But for years to come, local Chinese who were in-the-know continued to talk of "The Western Company" when they referred to the undercover American presence on Taiwan.

The NACC was located in a secure compound on the Xinyi road in downtown Taipei. It was home to about 150 Americans. About 15 of them worked for the Air Section, headed by a former Navy pilot, Charles Gabler. He reported to the station chief, Bill Duggan.

Mutual Defence Treaty

The bombardment of Jinmen helped accelerate talks between the U.S. and the ROC for a Mutual Defence Treaty. Reluctantly, the President and Secretary of State Dulles agreed to it, provided that Chiang Kai-shek "was willing to adopt a defensive posture" in the Strait. The treaty was signed in December 1954. But the U.S. refused to unequivocally guarantee the security of the remaining offshore islands – Jinmen and Mazu. There was also a secret exchange of notes between Washington and Taipei that formalized U.S. control over any offensive operations that the ROC planned against the mainland.[37]

New military hardware was supplied to the CAF. The first four F-86F Sabre jet fighters arrived in November 1954. They were followed by a few RF-86Fs for photo-reconnaissance. With U.S. permission and support, the RF-86Fs began low-level overflights of the mainland opposite Taiwan to monitor the continuing build-up of Chicom forces. These daytime photo flights were vigorously opposed by the PLAAF's Air Defence Command.

The MAAG was critical of the ROC military's organisation, especially the undue influence of the political warfare officers attached to each fighting unit. The CAF was demoralized and manned by poorly-trained pilots, it reported.[38]

Whatever the CAF's shortcomings, though, U.S. intelligence identified another overflight mission that the nationalist airmen could undertake. This was electronic reconnaissance over China to monitor the PRC's introduction of new radar defences. While

USAF and U.S. Navy aircraft could 'ferret' ELINT (electronic intelligence) from their offshore patrols, these were prohibited from overflying the mainland.

ELINT Collection

In August 1953 there had been a debate within the CIA's covert division, which was now coyly known as the Deputy Directorate for Plans – DDP. The debate was prompted by a request from the USAF that the collection of ELINT be undertaken during the Agency's covert overflights of communist countries. But the officials in the DDP were reluctant to take on the additional task. They did agree that new recorders could be installed and operated "as a by-product only of overflights mounted for agent drop, resupply and leaflet missions." However, the DDP also noted that "a limited effort in the pure intelligence [eg ELINT] overflight field is possible using planes and crews of friendly nations whose policies do not forbid overflights."[39]

Of course, the ROC was one of the 'friendly nations' that the DDP had in mind. A plan was hatched to convert for ELINT missions one of the P4Y-2 Privateers that had been transferred to Taiwan. Major Willy Homen, a detailee from the USAF to the CIA's Air Branch, was stationed at Far East Air Force headquarters in Japan as a liaison officer. He travelled to Taiwan to supervise the modification of the aircraft and the training of CAF crews. The new mission was codenamed Operation Fox Hunt.[40]

The ungainly four-engined P4Y-2 bomber had been nicknamed 'The Warthog' by the U.S. Navy, which had used some of them for ELINT flights along the Soviet coast in the early 1950s. The Navy had replaced them with the sleeker, faster Martin P4M Mercator. The Privateer was indeed a slow aircraft by mid-1950s standards. In September 1954 the CAF lost one of its P4Y-2 bombers and all nine crew when it was shot down by mainland anti-aircraft guns during the Xiamen bombardment.

The CAF Privateer that was converted to an 'electronic ferret' configuration carried an APS-15 search radar and an APR-9 radar intercept receiver, along with a pulse analyser, a direction-finding system, and a recorder. Homen and colleagues from the NACC Air Section trained two local airmen as the CAF's first-ever Electronic CounterMeasures (ECM) officers, Captains Li Chong Shan (李崇善) and Luo Pu (羅璞). The rest of the Fox Chase crew comprised two pilots, two navigators, one flight engineer, one radio officer, and five gunners. Led by aircraft commander Major Lu Te Qi(呂德琪), they came from the CAF's 8th Group at Hsinchu, which was operating the P4Y bombers.

PHIL LI CHONG SHAN (李崇善) REMEMBERS

I graduated from Beijing High School in June 1948 and joined the Chinese Air Force. They sent me to the communications school. When the school moved to Taiwan in 1949, I had to leave my parents, four brothers and two sisters behind in their home town in Hubei province.

I became an electronics maintenance officer, and worked on our PB4Ys. So when the Fox Hunt ELINT project started, I was selected as an airborne ECM officer. Then I did the same job on the B-17s. I wasn't worried about the danger – I just wanted to serve my country. I believed that if you worked to the best of your ability, you would succeed.

I was on the B-17 mission in 1958 that was hit in the tail by cannonfire from a MiG. There was lots of smoke: I could hardly breathe. We could see through the holes in the tail. But our pilot flew safely home. In fact, that was the only year that we didn't lose an aircraft over the mainland.

After three years in the squadron, you earned the right to a transfer. I stopped flying in July 1958 and became an ECM instructor. In 1961, I became an ELINT analyst in the new analysis center.

- Phil Li Chong Shan, interview

The first Fox Hunt mission was flown on the night of 17 August 1955 – an eight-hour trip across eastern Guangdong and along the entire length of Jiangxi, returning across northern Fujian.

Two more crews were trained, and over the next eight months the modified P4Y-2 flew a total of 14 sorties over the mainland. It ranged far and wide, passing over the coastal provinces opposite Taiwan, then over Hunan and Jiangxi, as far north as Anhui and Hubei. As well as hoovering up air defense signals and communications, the aircraft dropped bundles of propaganda leaflets, and even bags of rice – with nationalist slogans on them, of course! The leaflets told of a better life on Taiwan, and forecast that it would only be a matter of time before the mainland would once again benefit from government by the KMT.[41]

The Chinese crews who flew the Fox Hunt missions were lucky not to be shot down as they lumbered along at 240 knots. Several of the flights were intercepted by La-11 fighters, and one mission was forced back out to sea after encountering heavy AAA over Zhejiang. The pilot, Major Li Min (李瞥), simply flew along the coast for 20 miles and then penetrated over an area that was less heavily defended.[42]

Chinese Radar Coverage

Amongst the radars now installed on the mainland was the P-20 Periskop, a V-beam microwave system supplied to China by the Soviet Union and nicknamed Token by Western intelligence. With dual azimuth and elevation antennas, the P-20 provided efficient early-warning of approaching aircraft up to 300km away, and was also used for Ground-Controlled Intercept (GCI). It could switch between L- and S-band to counter jamming.

The USSR supplied 23 Tokens to the PRC, and they were supplemented by two other Soviet-supplied early warning radars operating in VHF, the P-3 Biryuza and P-8/10 Dolfin, nicknamed Dumbo and Knife Rest respectively by Western intelligence. The old SCR-270s were still in the Chicom electronic order of battle, too. As the Chicoms realized the extent of the night penetrations from Taiwan they tried to reduce the blind spots in their radar coverage by moving some of the units to the tops of hills and mountains. In 1955, the PRC established an Air Defence Command that was modelled on the Soviet PVO Strany, having equal status with the Army, Air Force, and Navy.[43]

The PLAAF had begun to develop a night flying capability, but only 100 pilots were trained, and they were dispersed in many regiments. In 1955 the PLAAF launched 240 night sorties to try and intercept the overflights from Taiwan. But its pilots only saw a target and opened fire on 20 occasions. No kills were claimed.[44]

LU DE QI REMEMBERS OPERATION FOX HUNT

We entered China's airspace under the cover of the night, searching for signals emitted by ground radars and locations of antiaircraft guns. China's air defense capability was rather weak at the time. Therefore the assignments were not very dangerous. However, the flame produced by the engine of the PB4Y-2 could easily be spotted at night. Once I flew over Shangrao in Jianxi province, the aircraft was fired at by antiaircraft guns. I was lucky to escape unscathed. Due to the dangers that accompanied the operation, I quickly accumulated quite a few combat points. I was therefore elected war hero twice, and summoned by President Chiang Kai Shek. I felt much honoured.

- MND Vietnam Oral History, p220

It therefore seems likely that the loss of one of the CAF's B-26s flying over the mainland on the night of 14 April 1955 was another accident. The aircraft, piloted by the SMG commander Major Liu Guan Xiao (劉貫霄), went missing on an airdrop mission into Fujian province. It may have flown into the Taiwan Strait. As well as Liu, the other three aircrew and two agents were all lost. When the B-26 failed to return to Hsinchu, another B-26 piloted by Lt Col Yu Wen Wei (郁文蔚) made a daring but unsuccessful search and rescue mission along the Fujian coast. It was driven back by heavy anti-aircraft fire.[44]

The SMG was much less active over the mainland in 1955 than the preceding year; it logged only 107 hours of 'combat' time against 691 hours in 1954. There were only five B-17 and ten B-26 sorties. The C-46 was withdrawn from airdrop duties, although it still served as a support aircraft for deployments and was on standby for search and rescue duties. The RB-24 flew just five times over the mainland in 1955 and was withdrawn in 1956. The P4Y-2 of the 8th Group flew its last ELINT mission on 24 April 1956. What could replace it?[45]

The answer was the B-17. Willy Homen arranged for SIGINT gear to be added to two B-17s at Tachikawa airbase, in Japan. This comprised the APR-9 radar intercept system with two direction-finding antennas in radomes under the fuselage, plus a communications receiver and some old wire recorders. The modified aircraft were flown to Taiwan by an American crew led by Major Bob Kleyla, another USAF officer now assigned to the Agency.[46]

Kleyla joined the NACC in Taipei as an air operations officer. The CAF's new ECM officers were transferred from the 8th Group to the SMG, to augment the existing B-17 crews. Each overflight now carried 10 or more aircrew. There were two pilots, augmented by a third on the longest flights. The senior pilots took turns to be designated as the aircraft commander. There were two or three navigators, a radio operator, two ECM operators, one or two flight engineers, and three 'kickers.'

The SMG began flying ELINT missions on 9 May 1956. In recognition of the new role the unit was renamed The Technical Research Group (TRG) on 15 July 1956. The fact that the 'technical research' was being conducted over mainland China was not made public! Headed by a CAF Colonel, the TRG was organised into three sections: Ops/Training, Maintenance, and Administration. There were 32 officers, 20 NCOs and eight soldiers assigned.[47]

BOB KLEYLA REMEMBERS

It was Willy Homen that got me involved with Taiwan. I was working in Far East Air Force headquarters in Japan, doing mission planning for the Westwind project. That was the top secret overflights of the Soviet Union with RB-45s and RB-57s, so I had all the necessary clearances. When Homen was tasked to set up the ELINT overflights from Taiwan, he got me transferred to the Agency as another USAF detailee. I was a B-17 bombardier in the Second World War, and trained to fly the B-17 soon after, but with all the postwar cutbacks, I retrained as an ECM officer to stay in the Air Force. Before I left for Taiwan, I got checked out again to fly the B-17 – and the B-26. I helped Homen to install the 'ferret' boxes in the B-17. We called them "Freddy" and "Geoffrey" – one for communications intercept on the lower frequencies, and one for radar intercepts on the higher frequencies. We did it all ourselves. And there were no safety inspectors in that operation, to question our work!

- interview with author

MIG-17 PILOT LU MIN – A COMPLICATED STORY

Lu Min was the ace MiG-17 pilot who shot down the B-17 in June 1956. His family history serves to illustrate the complicated stories of so many who were caught up in China's civil war, and the aftermath of separation caused by the nationalist retreat. His father remained on the mainland when Lu, his mother, and two half-brothers fled to Taiwan. But Lu did not get along with his half-brothers. He persuaded his mother that they should both return to the mainland.

So Lu ended up on the communist side after all. He became a fighter pilot with the PLAAF, and served with distinction in the Korean War, shooting down five F-86s. He was promoted to become an air regiment commander. Meanwhile, one of his half-brothers on Taiwan joined the CAF and became a C-46 pilot.

When Lu was scrambled to intercept the CAF B-17 in 1956, did he have second thoughts about trying to shoot down the nationalist airmen? We don't know. If he did think twice, Lu evidently banished those thoughts.

Incidentally, Lu's half-brother was never allowed to fly sensitive missions for the CAF because of the family history. The other half-brother became a famous actor on Taiwan television. – *C.P.*

B-17 Shot Down

But the enhanced B-17 operation got off to the worst possible start. On the night of 22 June the TRG commander, Lt Col Ye Zheng Min (葉拯民), and his crew of 10 took off from Hsinchu at 2100. Helped by the light of the full moon, they headed north over the sea at low level for more than an hour before turning west to enter Zhejiang province at 6,500 feet. For nearly two hours all went well, as the crew pressed on into Anhui province before turning south into Jiangxi. But Chinese radar was tracking them.

Shortly after midnight, the Air Defense Command alerted the PLAAF's 12th Air Division/34th Air Regiment in Chizhou. It was equipped with the latest fighter to be received from the USSR – the near-supersonic MiG-17. Unit commander Lu Min (鲁珉) was a Korean War veteran who had shot down five F-86s. Guided by GCI he scrambled. With a full moon and no cloud, he made visual contact with the target at 9 km distance. Using his optical sight to line up the target, the MiG pilot was less than 600 metres behind and closing when he fired his cannons. The firing blinded him temporarily so he pulled up to recover. The target's wing was on fire. Lu manoeuvred for a second firing pass, locked on, and fired again at 270 metres. The B-17 exploded into a huge fireball.[48]

Two months later, the Chicoms demonstrated their aggressive night interception intent again. Shortly after midnight on 22 August, a U.S. Navy Martin P4M-1Q Mercator on a nightime SIGINT flight along the mainland coast was shot down in the Bay of Hangzhou. It was an unprovoked attack 32 miles offshore, according to the U.S. Of the 16 crew onboard one body was recovered by a U.S. destroyer and three more by PLA soldiers on the Zhoushan islands.

The PLAAF claimed that the twin-engined, jet-augmented Mercator violated Chinese airspace, but admitted that it was shot down at sea. The early warning radar at Hangzhou airbase in Zhejiang detected the target. Again, it was a standard MiG-17 day fighter that made the intercept. After one unsuccessful firing pass the MiG made two more, scoring direct hits despite return fire from the P4M.[49]

It was time to reassess mainland China's improving air defences. The PLAAF had more than doubled its total of jets to 1,485. The PRC's naval aviation arm was also being expanded. Licence-production of the MiG-17F had just started at Shenyang. The Soviets were soon expected to supply the radar-equipped version, the MiG-17PF. No one on Taiwan who planned or flew mainland overflights could be under any illusion. This was a difficult and dangerous business.[50]

I Fu En

However, the Chiangs and their KMT government were as still committed as ever to going "Back to the Mainland!" Moreover, a new chief of intelligence was appointed at CAF headquarters in May 1955. This was Major-General I Fu En (衣復恩), and he promoted increased cooperation with the U.S. in technical intelligence gathering. Maj Gen I had been Chiang Kai-shek's personal pilot for 10 years before the nationalists fled the mainland. He spoke fluent English after two tours to the U.S., most recently as air attache in Washington. The Americans warmed to I's engaging personality and social skills.

I Fu En would be the CAF's head of intelligence for the next nine years, even after his promotion to be the CAF's Deputy Chief of Staff in 1961. During that time he facilitated a major expansion in the secret projects that were joint ventures between Taiwan and the U.S. His first task was to invite American assistance to upgrade the CAF's ground-based SIGINT operation. The U.S. helped to fund and construct a new listening base at Daxi, near Taoyuan. Opened in 1958, it monitored communications between Chinese radar stations, anti-aircraft units, and fighter interceptors. (The U.S. also set up its own SIGINT station at Shulinkou, near Taipei, in 1957).[51]

His next task was to approve a major upgrade to the covert group flying the night missions out of Hsinchu. They would soon become a fully-fledged squadron – 'The Black Bats.'

IS TAIWAN PLAYING BY THE AMERICAN RULES?

In general, the GRC (Government of the Republic of China) has had virtually a free hand with respect to artillery action. We keep a tight rein on GRC air action. The Chinese have received and accepted a good deal of US guidance on ground and naval operations. No hard and fast rules to cover every possible contingency have evolved, and the understandings which now exist generally came about after mutual consultation on some specific problem. With only two exceptions, the Chinese have requested and have been responsive to U.S. guidance.

- US Dept of State memo, 18 June 1956, (RG59 – 794A.5, Box 3976)

SPECIAL MISSIONS WITHOUT U.S. APPROVAL?

The CAF's major expertise for SIGINT and airdrop missions resided in the Special Mission Group – and thus was subject to U.S. control. But the ROC apparently did not consult with the U.S. about penetration flights over the mainland flown by other CAF squadrons.

These included six missions flown in 1956 by the 8th Group and its P4Y-2 patrol bombers, that were based on the opposite side of Hsinchu airbase. For instance, on the night of 18 October 1956 one of these aircraft flew across Guangdong to drop a single agent into the mountain region bordering Guangxi.

Moreover, the C-46s of the transport squadrons were flown over the mainland 50 times in 1956 to drop leaflets and food parcels. Their crews carried PLA uniforms and the mainland's currency with them – just in case. On 10 November 1956, a C-46 from the 20th Transport Group flew into Zhejiang on another night airdrop mission. It was intercepted by a MiG-17 and shot down, killing all nine onboard.

- Fu, p44-4; airdrop total from KC Feng via Fu email

Chapter Three

1956-1957

The Air-Maritime Division (AMD) in CIA headquarters managed the fleet of aircraft that were deployed in Europe, Asia, and elsewhere in support of the Agency's covert operations. There were the B-17s and B-26s, such as those deployed in Taiwan. There were various C-47, C-54, and C-118 transports, and much smaller L-20 Beavers for flights into small airstrips or grass fields.

The air section of AMD was staffed mainly by USAF officers 'detailed' to the CIA from the Pentagon for a secret tour of duty. Many of them had previous experience of special operations in their military careers. Within the Pentagon a small, secret office provided logistics and communications support to AMD.

But unlike air operations conducted by the U.S. military, the clandestine air operations mounted by the CIA were supposed to be 'deniable.' If something went wrong – such as an aircraft crashing or being shot down – there should be no U.S. 'fingerprints' on the wreckage. The aircraft were 'sanitised' to remove direct evidence of U.S. ownership. And AMD trained foreign exiles as pilots, navigators, radio operators, and 'kickers' (Parachute Dispatch Operators) to crew the aircraft. In the cold jargon of covert action, they were 'expendable assets.'[52]

As noted already, Frank Wisner's notion that liberation movements in countries under communist control could be fostered by the covert insertion of agents and arms was

CHINESE v AMERICAN THOUGHTS

One morning, just after the sun had burst above the eastern peaks of Formosa, I saw two B-17s drop into the pasture for a safe landing after an all-night mission. As they taxied to a halt on the steel plank the Chinese ground crews swarmed around the planes, thrilled at the return of the crews and the success of the night and eager to hear how everything had gone. Then I noticed a few American technicians systematically removing tape and film canisters and other specialized equipment from in the planes to the laboratory for development and processing.

As I watched these two distinct elements work, I saw at first hand a truth that had not been evident back in the Pentagon. The Chinese were very proud of these flights and of their part in doing something for their own people. To the Americans this was just a job, and it was one in which they could not become identified. If a mission failed, the Chinese Nationalists would honor their gallant men. The Americans would have to ignore it and deny they had played any part in the operation at all. - *Prouty, Chapter 4*

HIGHLY-PAID MERCENARIES – NOT!

The rumours that we were highly paid were not true. We were paid our regular Air Force salary, plus an extra US$40 per month living allowance. Then we got combat pay – NT$100 per hour until 1956, then it was doubled to NT$200 per hour. Maybe the CIA gave our government more than that, but that's all I know.

- *Zhao Qin, B-17 and P2V pilot 1955-61, from MND Black Bat Squadron Oral History, p312*

thoroughly discredited by the mid-1950s. Wisner himself was still in charge of the Deputy Directorate for Plans (DDP), into which his old paramilitary Office of Policy Co-ordination (OPC) had been merged, and of which AMD was a part. But after the U.S. failed to exploit the popular uprisings in Poland and Hungary in 1956 Wisner sank into depression, and was eventually replaced in 1958 by Richard Bissell.

Bissell was a rising star in the Agency, and his emphasis was on technical intelligence gathering. He managed the CIA's development and deployment of the U-2 spy plane in 1955-56. But Bissell knew that high-altitude photography could not reveal everything that the U.S. and its allies wanted to know about military developments behind the Iron Curtain.

In September 1955, Bissell wrote a memo that defined his concept of "a new intelligence gathering technique" involving the insertion of small, self-sustaining teams into remote areas of hostile territory to monitor "strategic air bases, land line communications, micro-wave links, missile ranges, and atomic energy facilities." The teams would install interception devices and photographic equipment, some of which might operate automatically and even relay their information. "Radio communication is now feasible from behind enemy lines which is secure in the sense that both the message cannot be deciphered, and that direction-finding upon the point of transmission is impossible," he further explained.

The big problem, Bissell admitted, was "the means of infiltrating and exfiltrating agent teams so they can put such surveillance devices in place and (hopefully at long intervals) service them." The aircraft that dropped agents and supplies were usually tracked by the enemy's air defences; the 'snatch' technique for recovering agents was unreliable; and actual landings on denied territory were "always hazardous." Still, he believed that covert air operations could be further developed, especially a small radio beacon that could be carried by the inserted agents to help pilots identify the drop zones for their resupply.[53]

Improved Aircraft

Bissell's memo summarised the requirements that had already led AMD to begin development of an improved aircraft for covert air operations. After some years of experience with converted USAF transports and bombers AMD staffers had plenty of 'lessons learnt' that they could apply. Also, the SIGINT mission was growing in importance and complexity, and the latest 'ferret' equipment could not simply be scabbed onto old B-17s.

Bissell's main focus was the Soviet Union. But as it turned out, the new aircraft that AMD developed was used mainly over China, and the primary purpose became the gathering of SIGINT rather than the dropping of agents. Over an eight-year period the

THE 'MYSTERIOUS' I FU EN

I was considered to be a mysterious figure, because I was in charge of the secret squadrons. But I was not a legend. I was just a soldier who did the best for his country. The real legends were those young heroes who risked their lives flying into enemy territory. When they were flying a mission, I could not sleep, worrying about their safety. So I would just gaze at the dark sky and the stars. Those crewmen, they borrowed time from God. Most citizens of Taiwan have no idea what they did – so they are unknown heroes. - *General I Fu En, Director of Intelligence, CAF, from MND Black Bat Squadron Oral History, p335*

new aircraft was flown from Taiwan by CAF crews on hazardous missions deep into the mainland.

This aircraft was a heavily-modified version of the Lockheed P2V Neptune. The P2V was the U.S. Navy's standard maritime patrol aircraft, first introduced in 1947. It was an ungainly-looking machine, with two big piston engines mounted on wings that emerged from the middle of a slender, tapering fuselage. The large vertical tail seemed out of proportion. A long boom protruded from the rear fuselage to house a Magnetic Anomaly Detector (MAD) that helped the crew hunt for enemy submarines. A big bulge beneath the fuselage housed a maritime search radar. An early prototype of the Neptune had been named 'The Truculent Turtle.' It flew all the way across the Pacific from western Australia to Ohio – an incredible 55 hour nonstop flight.

The latest production version of the Neptune was designated P2V-7, and made its first flight in April 1954. Like the Martin Mercator that the Navy used for SIGINT, the P2V-7 carried small underwing jet pods to augment the two piston engines. Their main function was to prevent a disastrous asymmetric condition from developing if one of the big piston engines should fail on takeoff or landing. The auxiliary jets sucked too much fuel to be routinely used during cruise flight.

The P2V-7 appealed to the airmen of the AMD as a covert aircraft because of its good low-level performance, long range, large bomb bay, and substantial payload. And, because the Navy used the Neptune worldwide, and it was also being supplied to friendly nations, the deployment of a few more for covert operations might go unnoticed.

P2V-7U

In 1954, the CIA negotiated with the Navy for five airframes that would be taken from the production line and designated P2V-7U. But the Navy was reluctant to get involved in wholesale support for a covert operation. The USAF had to take a lead role in supporting the aircraft. Willy Homen became the AMD's 'case officer' for the new venture, which was codenamed Project Cherry.[54]

The Neptune production line was at Lockheed's Burbank plant. This was also home to the CIA's top-secret U-2 project inside Lockheed's Advanced Developments Projects (ADP) shop, also known as The Skunk Works. The CIA awarded ADP a contract to modify the five Neptunes. The boss of the Skunk Works, Kelly Johnson, appointed Luther McDonald as chief engineer. McDonald organised a team for the project in Hangar B5, across the runway from the main factory. The first aircraft, with Lockheed construction number 7047, was moved into B5 around August 1955.[55]

According to USAF Colonel Fletcher Prouty, who worked in the Pentagon office that provided military support to AMD, two systemic problems plagued Project Cherry from the outset. First, the CIA loaded too many requirements on the new aircraft, adding weight and complexity. The only solution was to make the mission equipment modular, so that it could be easily added or removed for specific missions. Second, the USAF had to set up a support organisation from scratch, duplicating that of the U.S. Navy, for only five aircraft.[56]

McDonald and his team set to work stripping the brand new aircraft of all the provisions for anti-submarine equipment. Some of the standard Navy radio, radar, and navigation gear was replaced by similar equipment to USAF specifications. This included the P2V's maritime search radar, which was replaced by the APQ-24 unit that was a standard in the USAF and more suited to flying overland.

Next, the crew access hatch under the rear fuselage was enlarged for paradropping agents and equipment. Just forward and above this opening, a plexiglass dome was fitted to the crew escape hatch in the upper fuselage. This created a position for an observer, who had a splendid 360-degree view out of the top of the airplane.

The weapons bay of the Neptune was modified to accept at least two special packages. One was a supply container which could be loaded with anything required for agents to operate in denied territory: food rations, radios, etc. It was made of wood so that it could be easily broken up and destroyed after it was airdropped.

The other was a very large and sophisticated propaganda dispensing device. Tens of thousands of leaflets could be stacked in small compartments with motorized doors that were programmed to open in turn to create the optimum pattern of distribution.[58]

A special camera system provided by the Fairchild company was installed in the centre fuselage. It was a trimetrogen system designated Mark IIIA, with three cameras in a fan pointing left, right, and down to obtain maximum coverage beneath and to each side of the airplane. To provide illumination for nighttime photography, mercury vapor arc lamps were fitted behind a new plexiglass front end to the P2V's standard wingtip fuel tanks. They were each powered by a generator which was turned by a small propellor at the wingtips.[59]

Dedicated systems for electronic reconnaissance were also installed. These comprised the APR-9 radar intercept receiver, the QRC-15 direction-finding system, the APA-69A direction-finding display, the APA-74 pulse analyser, and Ampex tape recorders. Most of this equipment was already in service with the USAF, but there was also System 3, a receiver designed especially for the CIA by Ramo Woolridge to intercept air defense communications. New ECM equipment was also added: an APS-54 radar warning receiver, and a basic noise jammer to foil the radar of intercepting fighters.

To give the crews additional help in low-level navigation, the very first doppler radar navigation (RADAN) system was added. Manufactured by General Precision Laboratories (GPL), it calculated ground speed and drift.[60]

The CIA also wanted to add the APQ-56, a new side-looking reconnaissance radar. It could provide low-resolution imagery of airfields and other prominent targets beneath the aircraft at night without giving away the aircraft's position by operating the camera illumination system. However, Westinghouse had not designed the APQ-56 for a low-flying aircraft like the P2V. A larger antenna was required, 15 feet long and two feet wide, with roll stabilisation. The most feasible location for this was beneath the rear fuselage – but that interfered with the bomb bay door opening. The eventual solution was separate antennas on each side of the rear fuselage.[61]

The first of the five modified P2Vs was rolled out and test-flown from Edwards and Eglin AFBs in 1955-56. It was painted with an overall coat of the same dark sea blue color as the Navy's aircraft, but with USAF markings and serial numbers in white. The other four Neptunes for the CIA (7097, 7099, 7101, and 7105) came off the production line and into the Skunk Works from August-November 1956. The USAF provided a 'cover' designation for the aircraft – the RB-69A. But inside the CIA they were usually referred to as P2V-7s.

A B-17 MISSION DESCRIBED BY COL PROUTY

Skilled crews, who flew low to use the terrain as cover from radar, pinpointed the trouble cities on each flight because they were natives of the area. Upon return, one crew reported the city ringed with searchlights probing for the planes through the murky sky. The pilot had dropped through the clouds and actually flown the B-17 in a tight circle inside the ring of searchlights, right over the heart of the ancient city, spraying leaflets all the time. As soon as his leaflet cargo had been dropped, he brought the plane down into the dark path of the river and flew at tree-top level back to the sea coast.

- Prouty, Chapter 4

New Tactics

Meanwhile, on Taiwan the covert overflights of mainland China with the TRG's three B-17s and three B-26s continued. In 1956 there were 29 missions by the B-17s and 23 by the B-26s.

But there were new tactics. Mission planners at the NACC concluded that it was no longer safe to fly by the light of the full moon. From early 1957 the flights were either scheduled for the darkest nights of the lunar cycle, or for before moonrise or after moonset. Of course, this made it more difficult for the PLAAF's fighter pilots to spot the intruding aircraft, but it also made low flying and navigation even more difficult for the CAF's aircrews.

By now, the overflights were usually planned to enter denied territory at 1,500 feet, at a point where previous ELINT had identified a weakness in Chicom radar coverage. Then they would descend to between 900 and 1,200 feet, depending on the terrain. If they were under threat the pilot would descend again to 600 feet. As long as the crews kept to the designated track they would have a safety margin of 10 miles on either side, clear of high ground.

Often there would be cloud cover for at least a portion of the flight. This helped mask the intruders from enemy interceptors, or from searchlights on the ground, but it also buffeted the crews with turbulence. Moreover, the anti-icing system on the B-17 was not very good.

Three ECM officers were now routinely carried, boosting the B-17 crew to 14. In cramped and uncomfortable conditions, the CAF crews put their lives on the line on flights that usually lasted 10 hours, and sometimes stretched to 15 hours.

LEAFLET DROPS AND RADIO PLAYS

Some of the leaflets that were scattered over the mainland from the aircraft of the 34th Squadron, had simple messages. Some had a more sophisticated purpose. They were designed to make the communists believe that resistance movements were growing in certain areas. Even if this wasn't true, it didn't matter, as long as the communists believed it – and diverted security resources to the potential trouble spots. CIA officer Herbert Weisshart was assigned to Taiwan in 1952, and became a specialist in psychological warfare over the next decade. The message of the leaflets was backed up by radio broadcasts, beamed from Taiwan but purporting to come from resistance groups on the mainland. In 1963, Weisshart and his team was sent to Saigon, to devise a similar psy-war program to spook the North Vietnamese. – *C.P.*

(information from "Spies and Commandos" by Conboy and Andrade, p77-78)

Going Further North

Some missions were now being planned to go much further north, to 'ferret' the air defences in Henan and Hebei provinces, including around Beijing. They would usually land at K-8 (Kunsan) airbase in Korea. The crew would rest there for 24 hours before the long ferry flight back to Taiwan.

Lt Col Zhao Qin (趙欽) and his crew successfully completed the first of these overflights of northern China on the night of 2 January 1957. This was a 12-hour epic, during which the aircraft dodged searchlights and AAA fire twice and encountered severe icing conditions. The route took the B-17 directly over Fuzhou and Tianjin and close to Changsha and Wuhan, as well as Beijing. While the ECM operators gathered ELINT, the 'kickers' were busy dispatching propaganda leaflets onto these populated areas.[62]

The ROC government could not resist publicising the flight. It was headline news on 4 January when Taiwan papers reported that "our strong Air Force penetrated the Iron Curtain and flew over nine provinces and as far as the suburbs of Beijing, and airdropped hundred of thousands of paper bombs, bringing new hope to our suffering countrymen in mainland China. The mission returned safely to base yesterday morning."

Two days later, President Chiang Kai-shek summoned the 25 aircrew who had gone on the last three mainland overflights and thanked them for their bravery. The Generalissimo was now 70 years old and increasingly detached from the routine affairs of the party and government. His son, Chiang Ching-kuo, was the power behind the Gimo's throne, and especially in the ROC's dealings with the U.S.[63]

Dark Moon Phase

The new tactics of flying only during the dark moon phase were successful. In 1957 the TRG flew 106 missions: 61 in the B-17 and 45 in the B-26. But the mainland air defences detected only 53 of these overflights and failed to shoot down a single one. A U.S. intelligence estimate in March 1957 assessed Chinese radar detection capabilities in the coastal areas and around major cities as "fair to good," but noted "a shortage of adequate GCI (Ground Controlled Intercept) radars." The PLAAF now had 1,475 jet fighters, and the expanding naval air arm another 30. But the pilots had "inadequate experience in night and all-weather flying." The assessment was undoubtedly based on ELINT obtained in the last year by the CAF's nighttime B-17 incursions, as well as the SIGINT flights along the coast by the U.S. and the CAF.[64]

DAI SHU QING REMEMBERS

The TRG was recruiting new members. Qualified candidates needed to have flown more than 2,000 hours. By that time, I had accumulated over 400 combat points and more than 2,000 hours. I applied.

The pilots were handsomely paid. In addition, there was a monthly flight allowance. Though this was attractive, willing to serve the country out of patriotism was the most powerful incentive.

While serving in the 34th Squadron, I carried out a total of 78 reconnaissance assignments over China...I am filled with grief every time I think of those colleagues of mine who died carrying out assignments there. I remember the old saying: "the wind is blustery and the river water is cold. Once gone, the warriors will never return".

The wife of every member was afraid that her husband might not return, every time they went on a mission...Out of fear of my wife being left widowed and my children orphaned, I persuaded her into not having children. I told her not to keep thinking about me if I died in the line of duty. - *MND Vietnam War Oral History, p175-6, p188, p200*

B-26 LEAFLET DROP SYSTEM

We made a cylinder framework that was six foot long and three foot wide, and covered in hessian. The leaflets would be added, and then the cylinder was hung from the bomb shackles of the B-26. More leaflets were loose-loaded into the bomb bay from the top hatch. They would be dispensed first, by opening the bomb bay doors. Then the crew could fly to a second location, where the navigator would release the cylinder.

On one windy night at Hsinchu, someone opened the bomb bay doors of a B-26 that had been prepared for a mission, while it was still on the ground. The leaflets blew all over the town!

- Bob Kleyla interview

Shanghai enjoyed the biggest concentration of air defenses: over 200 anti-aircraft guns, 140 searchlights, and three fighter intercept divisions. But on the night of 21 January 1957, one of the TRG's B-26s flown by LtCol Zhang Wen Yi (張聞驛) on a leaflet 'raid' managed to evade them all, flying right over the city's airport and suburbs before heading to the coast. A MiG-17F from the 6th Regiment of the PLAAF's 2nd Division did spot the B-26 briefly as it flew out to sea, but could not adjust speed to intercept. The MiG pilot forgot how much fuel his jet consumed during low-level manoeuvres, and couldn't make it back to Hongqiao airbase. He force-landed a half-mile from the runway threshold, a wing broke off, and he was seriously injured.[65]

The Kuomintang's paper propaganda continued to rain down on the mainland cities. 'Surrender Certificates' promised that KMT soldiers would soon be returning to the mainland. The leaflet should be kept by the finder and produced on that happy day, to prove loyalty. 'The Free China Weekly Report' provided newspaper-style coverage of speeches by Chiang Kai Shek and featured reports that contrasted the well being of the citizenry on Taiwan, compared with their compatriots on the mainland, who were suffering the yoke of Communist repression.

The B-26 could drop more than 100,000 of these leaflets. On the night of 10 June 1957 it was Guangzhou's turn to receive the word, as one of TRG's aircraft flew directly overhead just after 22:00. It was not properly detected by Chicom radar stations.

Eventually, on the night of 5 November 1957 luck ran out for the brave flyers of the CAF's B-26s. One of them crashed on a leaflet-dropping mission to Luqiao airfield, in Zhejiang province. It took off from Hsinchu at 2000 with an extra trainee pilot on board. The radioman, Technical Sergeant Chen Ting Bin (陳廷斌), was therefore displaced from his right seat in the cockpit to the nose, where he squeezed in beside the 'nosegator,' Major Zhang Ming Qing (張鳴卿).

There was low cloud at the entry point, which was just north of the Dachen islands. The B-26 approached the coastline at less than 100 feet, doing nearly 250 knots. Major Wang Wei Duo (王為鐸) spotted tracer fire to his left and banked right. As he returned to the straight and level the aircraft was vibrating and the left engine was on fire. Wang tried to boost the right engine to no effect. He had no option but to force-land, and turned back towards the coast. The aircraft hit the ground hard, and the right engine also caught fire. The aircraft slid to a fiery halt. In the nose, Chen and Zhang were trapped, with no chance of escape. As the flames spread the other three crew scrambled clear. Trainee pilot Major Kong Xiang Zhang (孔祥璋) and navigator Captain Li Fu Quan (李復權) were both burnt, but together with Major Wang they fled towards the beach. Within an hour, though, they were captured by the local militia.

THE B-26 CREW RELEASED

The three aircrew that survived the B-26 crash in Zhejiang province in November 1957 flew back to Taiwan from Hong Kong in August 1958. They were met at Sungshan airport by General I, head of CAF Intelligence.

Their return was kept secret. They were transferred to a US base on Okinawa for medical investigations. There, one of Wang Wei Duo's colleagues from the CAF recognised him in the Base Exchange, and thought he had seen a ghost!

Upon their return to Taiwan, they were housed in the guest house at Hualien, where they took lie-detector tests administered by US experts. A subsequent 100-page report verified that they were not brainwashed by mainland China.

Gen I sent the report to Chiang Ching Kuo, who allowed them to resume their flying careers. But evidently, they could not be risked on secret missions any more. Instead, they were transferred to China Airlines. (Unfortunately, Kong was killed in 1970 when the YS-11 airliner he was flying crashed on approach to Taipei Airport).

In September 1990 Wang went to visit his relatives in Beijing. He arranged to meet one of his prison guards from 1957. His big question: why were they released in 1958 at the height of the Taiwan Straits Crisis? Wang still did not get an answer.

- Fu, p 60

The three nationalist airmen were imprisoned at Nanjing, where they endured constant interrogations and indoctrination for nine months. Then Kong, Li, and Wang became pawns in the propaganda war between the PRC and the ROC. They were offered freedom on the mainland but refused. But instead of letting them rot in prison, Communist party officials gave them a tour of some of the PRC's flagship construction projects, and then released them to Macau in August 1958. Now Taiwan had to assess whether they had been 'turned' by their captors, and whether they had revealed critical information about the special missions from Hsinchu. The crew were eventually cleared, but they were not allowed to fly any more special missions.[66]

Did the Chicoms have spies within the top-secret operation at Hsinchu? This was a constant concern for both the U.S. and ROC side of the project. A propaganda war of words filled the airwaves over the Taiwan Straits. Chinese radio broadcasts beamed at Taiwan sometimes specified the names and personal affairs of CAF aircrew. The names might have come from interrogations of their relatives who had stayed behind on the mainland in 1949, or it could have been from penetrations of the CAF squadrons on Taiwan.

Project Circus - Tibet

The U.S. retained ownership and ultimate control of the B-17s and B-26s flown by the TRG. It could re-allocate them to other projects without consulting the ROC. In June 1957, American pilots temporarily withdrew one of the B-17s from Taiwan for use in another covert action over China to which the ROC was not privy. This was Project Circus – CIA support to the independence movement in Tibet. The Khampa tribesmen of eastern Tibet were fiercely anti-Han Chinese. U.S. officials judged – no doubt correctly – that the participation of nationalist Chinese aircrew would not be welcome by these rebels. The Gimo later complained to the U.S. Ambassador in Taipei of being cut out of the action to support the rebels in Tibet.[67]

The B-17 was flown to Clark airbase in the Philippines. A group of Polish airmen who had been flying covert operations for the CIA in Europe arrived. They were trained to fly the old converted bomber by Bob Kleyla. Meanwhile, the first eight Khampas selected for guerilla training were extracted from Tibet to East Pakistan. An unmarked transport provided by Civil Air Transport flew them from Kermitola airbase, near Dacca, to the CIA training bases on Guam and Okinawa. There they were given instruction in parachuting, secret radio communication, and airdrop procedures. The B-17 joined the trainee guerrillas on Guam, and in mid-October it made the long journey back to Kermitola airbase, near Dacca, East Pakistan, from where a mission to drop the first two agents into Tibet was staged. Three more agents were dropped on a second B-17 flight over Tibet the following month. The air operations support to Project Circus was allocated the cryptonym STBARNUM.[68]

The B-17 was not used over Tibet again. When arms drops to the guerrillas began in July 1958 the CIA turned to the trusty American pilots of CAT. They used a C-118 that AMD had 'sanitised,' and which was flown under the cover of USAF's 322nd Air Division (Detachment 1) based on Guam. A second mission followed in February 1959, but the tempo of Project Circus really accelerated after the Dalai Lama fled Tibet in March 1959. The CIA sent over 100 Tibetan nationalists to the U.S. for guerilla training in the Rocky Mountains.

Most of the 44 airdrop missions to the rebels in Tibet were flown between May 1959 and February 1960. From December 1959, the C-118 was replaced by C-130s 'borrowed' from a USAF detachment on Okinawa. Still flown by CAT pilots, the airdrops were flown out of Takhli airbase, Thailand, with USAF markings removed. Over 400 tons of equipment were dropped, but the rebels never posed a serious threat to Peking's control of Tibet. The last airdrop was in February 1965.[69]

Project Cherry
At the Skunk Works, the work on Project Cherry continued. In early 1957 Fred Cavanaugh took over as the Lockheed project manager. In March 1957 the first "RB-69A" (7047) was sent to Eglin AFB, FL, where the USAF conducted Employment and Suitability Testing on behalf of the CIA. A total of 272 hours were flown on 71 flights from Eglin, as the aircraft's performance in aerial delivery and reconnaissance at low level and under "adverse conditions" was explored. USAF Major Frank 'Beanie' Beard was detailed to the CIA for the evaluation and subsequently became the Agency's P2V project pilot. The initial evaluation was completed at Eglin in August 1957.[70]

But the Agency did not wait for the evaluation before deploying its new covert bird. In early April 1957 the second aircraft (7097) was ferried to Wiesbaden airbase. The third (7099) followed a month later. At the German base, 'D Flight' of the USAF's 7405th Support Squadron served as a cover unit. In Europe, the P2Vs were usually flown by the Polish exile aircrews.[71]

Preparations to fly the new P2Vs over mainland China from Taiwan also began. Aircrew from the CAF departed for the U.S. for training. They were led by the TRG's latest commander, Col Yin Yan Shan (殷延珊), appointed in February 1957. He was a tall, strong character – typical for someone who hailed from Shandong province. His training group comprised four pilots, four navigators, and four maintenance sergeants. Most of the specialised instruction was conducted by Lockheed, including flight training at Burbank, Edwards AFB, and Palmdale. The CAF's Electronic Warfare Officers, other rear cabin crew, and maintenance personnel remained in Taiwan for their training on the new aircraft.[72]

The full crew for a P2V mission from Taiwan would be 11 or 12, compared with nine on the aircraft that were flying for the Agency in Europe. The aircraft commander and his co-pilot were augmented by a third pilot who could share the flying during the very long missions. The flight engineer sat behind the two pilots.

There were three navigators. Two sat in the fuselage behind the cockpit, facing right. One operated the search radar and did the dead-reckoning calculations, while the other operated the aircraft's RADAN system. The third navigator sat in the plexiglass-covered nose of the airplane to 'eyeball' the passing terrain, compare it with his maps, and warn the pilot of approaching obstacles – especially during evasive manoeuvres. This 'nosegator' also operated the cameras when carried.

There were two Electronic Warfare Officers, officially known as ECM officers in the CAF, and colloquially as 'Ravens' to both the Americans and the Chinese. They sat next to and in line with the two navigators in the middle of the aircraft, facing right to view their screens, dials, and switches. 'Raven 1' operated the lower-frequency ELINT equipment in the VHF and UHF bands, captured scans from the radarscope and the pulse analyser on film, and warned the pilot if the ground-based searchlight radar was locking on to the aircraft. 'Raven 2' operated the higher-frequency ELINT equipment in the C-, S-, and X- bands. He also operated the noise jammer, which would counter the radars of fighters attempting to intercept.

These crewmen were separated from their colleagues in the rear of the aircraft by the large centre section beam of the P2V. Lying flat on their stomachs, and with parachutes attached to their backs, there was only just enough room between the beam and the top of the fuselage for crewmembers to reach the aft end. Here sat the radio officer at his own station. He helped with the aircraft's defense by monitoring the air defense's ground-air communications via the COMINT system, so that he could warn the rest of the crew when enemy interceptors were taking off, or closing to attack. He was also responsible for transmitting coded messages on the progress of the mission back to the command post on Taiwan via HF radio.

Behind the radio operator sat one or two loadmasters for handling the airdrops. The packages would be stacked around the large circular hatch, or 'Joe Hole,' which would be opened to dispatch the agents, leaflets, or other propaganda equipment. The loadmasters also served as the observers, looking out for trouble through the plexiglass domes on the top and sides of the fuselage.[73]

Improvements at Hsinchu

To prepare for the new aircraft, the CIA paid for improvements and new facilities at Hsinchu airbase to replace the primitive Nissan huts and tents from which the TRG had been operating. These included a resurfaced taxiway leading to a new apron; new buildings for operations, maintenance, and supply; and a ground power shed to house some generators – the local power supply was not to be trusted. A new dormitory was built for Chinese bachelor officers in downtown Hsinchu.[74]

The NACC Air Section organised the U.S. support for the new P2V operation. It was now headed by Colonel Parker, a USAF pilot on classified secondment. The Air Section comprised a mix of USAF officers and airmen detailed to the CIA; maintenance and logistics specialists from the U.S. Navy; civilian technical representatives ('techreps') from companies supplying specialist equipment; and CIA administrative types. None of the military officers wore uniform during their one or two-year assignment to Taiwan,

PARTY TIME!

Most of the Americans who served in the NACC Air Section were on two-three year accompanied tours. For many of them and their families, their time in Taiwan was exotic and memorable, one of life's highlights to be recalled with fond memory in years to come. Even if the wives never really knew what their husbands were doing, because of the secrecy surrounding the project! However, that secrecy did not prevent the Americans and their Chinese counterparts mixing on social occasions. There were many parties, some of them attended by high-ranking officers from the Chinese Air Force, and officials from the nationalist government, including Chiang Ching Kuo.

"Return to the Mainland!" was always the last toast of the night at these parties. The Chinese really believed it. Some of the Americans came to believe in it too...

- C.P.

and the CIA assigned each of them a pseudonym to use throughout their tour. Most of the Americans lived in Taipei and commuted to Hsinchu each week, or as required. But the NACC assigned an administrative officer to reside at Hsinchu. The Chinese side called him 'The Base Commander.'

The Americans from the NACC could fly on test flights and training missions from Hsinchu, including those that flew along the mainland coast to collect SIGINT from offshore. But they were strictly forbidden from joining any of the penetration missions.

The Agency allocated the cryptonym STPOLLY to the operation. ST was the digraph for the CIA's Far East Division. As for POLLY, this name may have been inspired by Polly Rogers, the wife of Buddy Rogers, an electronics specialist assigned to the NACC. Or perhaps it was derived from Polly Wisner, the wife of Frank Wisner, who was still the head of all CIA covert operations as the DDP.

In a briefing document, the CIA defined the main mission of STPOLLY as "to obtain electronic intelligence data over Chicom territory." This would include the location and types of radars; their detection capabilities; and the efficiency of air defense reactions, including anti-aircraft and searchlight capability. The aircraft would carry no defensive armament, relying instead on jamming, chaff dispensing, low altitude flying, and evasive action. The effectiveness of such countermeasures would be tested, the document continued.

ELINT requirements for the project would be consolidated by the U.S. military, specifically the Pacific Command (PACOM). Each proposed mission would be "carefully reviewed in Washington for requirements and tactical feasibility." The final approval would come from the Deputy Director, Plans, i.e the CIA's top covert operations official. The knowledge of Chicom tactics and defensive capability that resulted from the missions would help the bombers of Strategic Air Command penetrate the PRC's territory and deliver

OLD CHINA HANDS

Some employees of the CIA on Taiwan were colourful characters. Some never wanted to go home to America. There was Stan Bardon, a former sea captain in the British Navy, who had helped to organise WEI's raids along the China coast in the early 1950s. He was married to a German lady whose previous husband was a Chinese general. 'Cappy' Bardon spoke good Chinese, and he got a job with the NACC at Hsinchu, as the supervisor of the engineering shop. He was a wonderful story teller.

Then there was Bob Macnamara, the resident manager at Hsinchu from 1959 through 1963. He had lost a leg in the Second World War. He would take off his wooden leg to club the cobras that slid out of the grass and onto the ramp at night. His replacement at Hsinchu went by the unusual name of Dickran Vartanian. He was, in fact, an Armenian. The Chinese called him "Mr. Victor".

– C.P.

their nuclear warheads – if the need ever arose. This briefing said little about Taiwan's role or requirements. From the U.S. perspective, the ROC was clearly the junior partner.[75]

A formal contract was signed between the NACC and the CAF for the expanded covert operation from Hsinchu. According to the contract the project was named after a bird of prey, the Goshawk (蒼鷹, or Cang Ying in Chinese). The one-year renewable agreement specified that "psychological warfare, ELINT or any other combat mission agreed by both the CAF and the NACC" could be performed. The NACC would be responsible for devising the overall policy for the special missions, subject to the CAF's review. The NACC would have to send the plans for each mission to the CAF for approval 48 hours in advance. The NACC would also pass payments to the CAF and compensate the families of any aircrew who might be killed during the operation.[76]

As far as the ROC was concerned, the upgraded operation at Hsinchu was an opportunity to re-assert the right to fly over the mainland; to drop more agents and propaganda materiel; and generally remind the communists that the KMT was still a force to be reckoned with.

U.S. Security Umbrella

The ROC now enjoyed a formidable U.S. security umbrella thanks to the Mutual Defence Treaty. There were over 2,000 American military personnel stationed on the island, and a joint U.S. Taiwan Defense Command. PACAF rotated F-86 fighter squadrons to Taiwan, and the U.S. had also installed nuclear-tipped Matador surface to surface missiles with a range of 600 miles.

Officially, of course, the nationalists still aimed for the "Glorious Return to the Mainland." That slogan was to be seen everywhere on Taiwan. Did the ROC leadership have any concern that the joint operation from Hsinchu was probing for weaknesses in Chicom air defenses that could ultimately help SAC drop nuclear weapons on their homeland? Apparently not. In January 1958 the Gimo even requested his own nuclear weapons and guided missiles from the U.S. The request was refused.[77]

How far could the Gimo be trusted to honor the formal and informal agreements with the U.S.? The NACC made plans to 'bug' him. An all-American crew flew one of the B-26s from Hsinchu on a 'training' flight. It was flown over Chiang Kai Shek's residence to take photographs that could be used to identify the best place to 'tap' the telephone lines.[78]

Col Yin's group completed their P2V flight training in the U.S. Two of the dark-painted aircraft were ferried to Taiwan in their USAF markings. They arrived at Hsinchu in December 1957. Soon, the U.S. Star and Bar insignia was replaced by the 12-pointed sun of the KMT. Intensive local flying training began, by day and by night. [79]

In January 1958, CAF headquarters upgraded the TRG to squadron status. It re-allocated the 34th squadron number from the 8th Group, which was disbanding on the other side of the airfield at Hsinchu. Col Yin reviewed three designs for a new 34th squadron patch. He chose the one submitted by ECM officer Major Li Chong Shan and three colleagues. It featured a black bat in flight against a dark blue sky background containing the seven stars of the 'big dipper' in a three-four pattern. The sky was contained within a thin red circle. The symbolism was apt. The bat represented the squadron's aircraft, flying by night. The red circle represented communist China's airspace.

Chapter Four

1958-1959

On the night of 20 November 1957, China's continuing failure to intercept the night intruders from Taiwan was noticed at the highest levels of the government in Beijing. Premier Chou En Lai (周恩來) was working through the night, as he often did. At 0230, the chief of staff at the Air Defence Command called to inform him that, despite their best efforts, another flight had reached deep into China's airspace, and might now be heading for the capital.

It was a B-17 commanded by Lt Col Zhu Zhi He (朱致龢). The CAF crew had taken off from Hsinchu at 1700 and penetrated Chinese airspace at Huian, in Fujian province. From there it flew all the way across Fujian, Jiangxi, Hubei, and Henan, reaching as far north as Shijiazhuang, in Hebei province. However, Zhu's mission was not planned to include a direct challenge to the air defences around Beijing itself. Instead, the B-17 turned east into Shandong province and left Chinese territory to fly across the Yellow Sea and land in South Korea. But the CAF plane had spent nine hours 13 minutes over China, and despite sending up 18 interceptors the PLAAF had failed to shoot it down.[80]

Premier Chou urged the air defence forces to redouble their efforts. The following month there was a major re-organization to ensure that the unit commanders were held responsible for their actions. The routes of recent incursions were studied and some fighter interceptor units were redeployed. Communications were upgraded, and the Chinese eased some of the rigidities of the air defense control system as taught to them by Soviet instructors. For instance, fighters from one base could extend their interception range by landing at another base, instead of returning to their take-off airfield. Sixty more radars were positioned in the inland provinces along a line from Guangzhou to Beijing. The best GCI controllers were gathered together in an elite unit that would take charge during an interception.[81]

ZHU ZHEN (朱震) REMEMBERS

The interceptors were always after us. They adjusted their speed, and we ended up in a dogfight. I dived to as near the ground as I dared. As we sped along, I could see the tracer fire from the interceptor firing at our shadow on the ground. At a time like that, you can't think about life or death – you must concentrate on trying to escape. After 13 passes, the interceptor must have run out of ammunition. Finally, it was over ! - *P2V pilot, from the film, Secrets of the Taiwanese Skies*

LT COL ZOU LI XU (鄒立徐) REMEMBERS

I flew on over 70 mainland missions as a navigator, and stayed in the 34th Squadron for eight years. I was promoted to chief navigator – because most of my colleagues were shot down and killed.

I married in 1959. We lived in the Hsinchu officers quarters. My wife knew that I flew on special missions. I told her: "Don't worry about me" But I was lucky to survive. We did get extra combat pay, and outsiders thought that made us rich. That's not true. We didn't do it for the money. We had a sense of honour.

We kept on going, for five or six hours over the mainland, despite various attacks that wore us out. If we should panic, we might hit a hillside or fly into the sea. So we kept telling ourselves: "Don't be scared, or we'll be hit!" But after we returned to base, and we heard our onboard conversation replayed during the debrief – then we really were scared!

As well as airdropping food and leaflets from the P2V, we sometimes dropped agents. I remember four of them coming onboard. They told me that they often went to mainland China. Just before we dropped them, they shouted: "See you in Nanjing!"

I was deeply moved. They were the real heroes, not afraid of dying. - *Black Bat Squadron Oral History, p301-2*

Adapting Soviet Hardware

Chinese military technicians were also adapting Soviet hardware as well as tactics. During 1957, the PLAAF's 11th Aviation School and the 14th and 18th Air Divisions worked to improve the performance of the newly-arrived MiG-17PF fighters. The shortcomings of this aircraft's RP-5 intercept radar were already apparent to Western intelligence as well as the Chinese. First, the effective range was only two-and-a-half miles. Second, operating below about 3,000 feet it could not discriminate aircraft targets from ground clutter.

One solution explored by the Chinese to the second problem was to inhibit the radar's -14 degree downward scan in elevation. The upward scan started from two degrees below the horizontal, and might still be adequate for interception, provided that the MiG pilot was well-vectored by GCI to fly towards the target at the same altitude. But the PLAAF soon realised that, in order to intercept a relatively slow-flying target like the B-17, the MiG-17 had to be flown at an Angle-of-Attack (AoA) of 4-5 degrees to keep it from stalling. At this attitude, the -2 degree scan was useless, unless the target was above the interceptor. Since the intruders from Taiwan were now flying at 1,000 feet they were usually below the interceptors. And it would be suicide for the MiG pilots to try and fly lower at night.

The Chinese pilots and technicians thought again. The downward scan of the radar was inhibited by only seven degrees. When the MiG flew at 4-5 degrees AoA the radar scan was effectively 2-3 degrees below horizontal. This could provide a scan of the target without including lots of ground clutter.[82]

Radar-Equipped MiGs

The radar-equipped MiG-17PFs were thrown into the battle to intercept the intruders. On the night of 13 March 1958, one Mig-17PF flown by Wang Guo Shan (王國山) of the 18th Division was the PLAAF's last chance against a B-17 that had flown for six hours over the southern provinces. No fewer than eleven MiG-15s had previously been scrambled further north when Wang took off from Shati airfield, in Guangdong. As the B-17 left the mainland and flew low out to sea Wang pursued it for 50 miles. Running short of fuel, he was directed by GCI to land at Shuixi airfield, on the Leizhou peninsula north of Hainan Island. But fog rolled over the airfield and Wang crashed and was killed as he tried to approach.

It was the second fatal loss of the night for the PLAAF. Earlier a MiG-15bis flown by Yang Yu Jiang (楊玉江) took off from Changsha to act as a radio relay aircraft in the hunt for the B-17. Contact with the pilot was lost soon after takeoff, and the MiG crashed near Datuopu airfield at 2300.[83]

From 20 March 1958 the Chicoms had another type of intruder to contend with, when P2V missions began. On that date, Lt Col Zhao Qin led his crew of 11 on a 13-hour round trip. After takeoff from Hsinchu on a cloudy night they headed southwest, and stayed well off the Chinese coast until they reached Hainan island. From there they headed north and into Guanxi province, passing over Nanning and Wuzhou before turning south to pass over Yangjiang, in Guangdong province, and then heading back out to sea. Their cargo of over 2,000 lbs of leaflets was spread liberally over these cities. The ELINT 'take' from this first P2V mission was rated very good by the analysts.[84]

GCI Procedures

A new U.S. intelligence estimate judged that morale was high in the mainland's air defences, and its personnel were "young and vigorous." But the pilots still lacked experience in night and all-weather flying. GCI procedures were improving, but the radars were still having difficulty in detecting aircraft at low altitude.[85]

In fact, Chinese radars were sometimes detecting the flights from Hsinchu soon after takeoff, and often when they approached the mainland coast. Theoretically, the PRC's early warning radars could cover the whole of Taiwan. The problem for the Chicom air defences was they couldn't yet easily co-ordinate all their assets: early-warning radars, height-finders, GCI communications, and interceptors.

The mission planners at the NACC knew this. In an attempt to sow confusion, they planned a near-simultaneous penetration of the mainland by two B-17s and one P2V on the night of 21 April 1958.

The plan nearly failed disastrously. The P2V and one of the B-17s returned safely, but the other B-17, flown by Lt Col Chen Zhang Xiang (陳章相), was attacked. Chen and his 14-man crew flew into Fujian, near Fuzhou. As AAA batteries opened fire the B-17 climbed to escape. The next hour passed more quietly for the crew as they flew northwest into Jianxi. Then, a MiG-17PF flown by Li Shun Xiang (李順祥) of the 12th Air Division at Nanchang scrambled to intercept. The ECM officer on the B-17 was able to monitor the communications between Li and his ground controllers. They were unable to position the MiG for an intercept, as the B-17 dived for cover. Short of fuel, Li returned to base, while the B-17 flew on into Hubei.

ZHAO TONG SHENG (趙桐生) REMEMBERS

When the P2V landed, the ground crew immediately got on the plane and removed the audio tapes, the photographic film from the pulse analyser, the camera attached to the navigation radar, and the camera from the flight recorder. We handed them all to the US personnel. The flight recorder displayed a clock as well as the navigation course, speed, altitude, and the times when the recording tape and the navigation radar camera were turned on.

The electronic devices on the P2V were able to detect radar signals on all bands, frequency, pulse width, pulse repetition frequency, pulse modulation, signal position and so on.

Since the navigation radar would jam the incoming signals when activated for a long time, it could only be operated briefly to take photographs over vital terrain.

- Zhao was an electronics officer in the 34th Squadron for many years. Interview, extract from MND Vietnam War Oral History, p141-2

After only 24 minutes Li was back in the air. GCI controllers at Jian could not continuously track the low-flying target as it flew towards Wuhan between hills that were as high as 3,600 feet. But they managed to direct the fighter pilot to a stern position. Li descended as low as he dared – to 4,500 feet. On his own radar scope the target showed! It was at 320 degrees, range 5,000 feet. Li closed to 2,600 feet and opened fire with his 23mm cannon. He shot 36 rounds before breaking right. The GCI could not guide him for another attack, having lost the target, so he returned to base.

The B-17 crew realized too late that the MiG was closing. Despite turning sharply left they heard cannon shells ripping into the aircraft. They could smell the gunpowder. The electronics section in the middle fuselage was holed in four places, but none of the equipment was damaged. The canvas rudder had a foot-wide hole in it, affecting the flying control, and the tail was also hit.

Chen and his crew assessed the damage and turned for the coast. The plane was still flying, but they were over 400 miles inland! It was a long, anxious flight over parts of Hubei, Anhui, and Jiangsu provinces, but they did not detect any further attempts at interception. As a precaution they descended even further over the Jiangsu coastal plain before escaping out to sea. Turning south for Taiwan, they were relieved to meet two friendly aircraft east of the Zhoushan islands. The C-46 flown by squadron commander Yin and a B-26 flown by an American instructor pilot had scrambled from Hsinchu to escort them home. The C-46 carried life rafts and rations in case the B-17 was forced to ditch. The formation landed safely back home at midday. The B-17 had been airborne for 17 hours five minutes.[86]

On the mainland, PLAAF commanders ordered all their interceptor units to practice low-level nighttime interceptions against transport aircraft. On Taiwan, the 34th Squadron and its American advisors from NACC realized that the Chicoms were now using radar-equipped MiGs. The B-17's ELINT equipment could not detect the signals, however, and the old bomber had no means to jam them, unlike the new P2Vs.[87]

Leaflet Drop

On the night of 3 July 1958 one of the 34th Squadron's B-26s made a daring leaflet drop over Guangzhou. It was timed to coincide with an international exhibition in the city. The aircraft took off from Hsinchu, but refueled at Tainan further south to stretch the range. It then flew across the South China Sea at 150 feet to evade radar detection. But the four-man crew still encountered heavy anti-aircraft fire over the downtown area. They pressed on and returned safely.[88]

CAF COMINT WITH C-46

From 1956-58, the CAF added communications intelligence (COMINT) receivers to single C-46s of both its Transport Groups and flew them along the mainland coast. The top-secret operation was nicknamed Old Bull, because the aircraft would repeatedly fly in straight lines, north-south, then south-north, just like a bull plowing a field.

Two officers from the ROC's SIGINT unit carried the portable receivers to the airbase, installed them temporarily on the airplane for each mission. The SIGINT specialists then joined the flight crew of three (pilot, co-pilot and flight engineer) for each mission. These lasted 4-5 hours, and were flown two-three times per week, sometimes by day, sometimes by night. The C-46s usually flew at 10,000 ft, to get the best intercepts. The CAF's fighters and bombers flew sorties towards the mainland at the same time, to stimulate the Chicom air defences into action. - *Fu, p42-5*

THE LEAFLET DROPS WORKED!

One minor coup of the Taipei station while I was there, was to participate with the Chinese nationalists in the defection of a pilot complete with MiG-15. We had been dropping leaflets over the mainland for some time, offering substantial rewards in gold for defectors who came out with military equipment or information. One day a young man who had been only a child when Mao's regime took power slipped away from his squadron when it flew through a cloud bank, and headed east for Taiwan. His stories of the status of morale and training in the air force were good intelligence material and, despite its antiquity, the MiG-15 supplied some useful technical data.

- Cline, p202

Mission planners debated whether bad weather provided better cover for the overflight missions. But on the clear, moonless night of 21 August 1958 a B-17 survived no fewer than five attempts at air-to-air interception by MiG-17PF fighters as it flew over Fujian and Zhejiang. Led by Li De Feng (李德風), the B-17 crew was able to monitor each attempt and descend to minimum safety altitude as their means of escape.[89]

Ray Cline
In early 1958, Ray Cline arrived in Taipei as the CIA's Chief of Station. He quickly developed a close relationship with Chiang Ching-kuo, his opposite number in the KMT government. Cline would often accompany CCK and CAF intelligence chief Maj Gen I Fu En on their visits to special joint projects, like the 34th Squadron. Sometimes they visited the families of dead and missing aircrew. CCK had learnt Chinese painting, and presented his painting of pine trees to the 34th squadron, which they hung on the wall of the dormitory.

Throughout Cline's four-year stay in Taipei, the CIA was always more disposed to support the ROC's proposals for paramilitary action against the mainland than was either the U.S. State Department or the Pentagon. After all, it was WEI who had trained nationalist troops as special forces in the early to mid-1950s. Now, the NACC continued to sponsor small numbers of nationalist agents for insertion, including by airdrop from the 34th Squadron aircraft. In addition, in 1957 the Gimo successfully pressed the U.S. to train 3,000 more airborne troops. Theoretically, Washington retained a veto on their use.[90]

Although Cline was a strong advocate for the ChiNats, Desmond Fitzgerald was not. He was now the head of the FE Division of DDP, and therefore in charge of CIA covert operations in Asia. Fitzgerald had a low opinion of Chiang.[91]

But the Agency knew that the ROC was willing – even anxious – to provide men and equipment for anti-communist actions elsewhere in Asia, such as Operation Haik, the CIA's support of dissident generals in Indonesia who had rebelled against left-leaning President Sukarno.

This operation started in February 1958 with airdrops to the rebel forces in Sumatra from Clark airbase flown by the C-46s of CAT, the CIA-owned and Taiwan-based airline. After the rebels were defeated in Sumatra the action switched to Sulawesi. The CIA organised a squadron of three P-51s and three B-26s at Manado, in territory that was controlled by the rebels. But after an Indonesian air raid on the rebel airstrip destroyed half of the squadron and an American pilot from CAT was shot down in a B-26, the CIA pulled out.

Taiwan played a supporting role in Operation Haik. The ROC flew arms to Manado and supplied a few aircraft. They included a B-26 that was ferried from Taiwan by Maj Gen

I Fu En himself, accompanied by Captain Zhang Wen Yi of the 34th Squadron. Zhang and another Black Bats pilot stayed on and flew several bombing missions in the aircraft for the rebels. One of the CAF's venerable P4Y-2 patrol bombers made two 18-hour roundtrips from Taiwan to drop more arms and supplies in Sulawesi on 6 July and 6 August 1958.[92]

The Indonesian rebellion ultimately failed, but the CAF subsequently kept two P4Y-2s airworthy in a special unit whose operations were beyond U.S. control. These aircraft flew arms and equipment to the KMT irregulars who were still based in eastern Burma, much to the annoyance of Rangoon, as well as communist China.[93]

Taiwan Straits Crisis
In mid-July 1958, Mao Tse Tung (毛澤東) ordered the PLA to prepare for an intensive artillery barrage against nationalist-held Quemoy island, just off the coast of Fujian. The preparations did not go unnoticed. The PLAAF sent several jet fighter regiments to six of the seven airfields that it had built in 1955-56 in Fujian province. This move was detected by CAF low-level photo-reconnaissance sorties over the airfields with the RF-84F jets that the U.S. had supplied in 1956. The CIA also flew a high-altitude U-2 spyplane over Fujian. On 29 July two CAF F-84Gs were shot down near Swatow while flying close to the mainland coast.

On 23 August 1958 the PLA finally began shelling Jinmen, which was defended by 86,000 nationalist troops. The attack posed a dilemma for the U.S. Washington was still not formally committed to helping in the defense of the remaining nationalist-controlled offshore islands. The MAAG had advised the ROC not to keep one-third of its army on Jinmen and Matsu.

But for both the U.S. and the PRC, this new Taiwan Straits Crisis was a trial of strength. Mao Tse-tung started the action to test the extent of U.S. support for Taiwan, and to rally internal support for his radical new economic strategy, the Great Leap Forward. In reality, Mao had no intention of trying to take Taiwan itself.[94]

In a Special National Intelligence Estimate three days after the shelling began U.S. analysts came to the same conclusion. The photo reconnaissance flights had shown no preparations for a seaborne invasion of Taiwan and no jet bombers deployed to the coastal airfields. But the estimate warned that if the U.S. stood aside from the crisis China would probably invade the offshore islands. President Eisenhower reluctantly agreed to throw U.S. support behind their defense.[95]

The CAF's F-84G and F-86F fighters diced with the PLAAF's newly-deployed MiGs over the islands and the mainland coast. Nationalist pilots claimed 20 MiG kills for only three losses by mid-September. The U.S. rushed AIM-9B Sidewinder air-to-air missiles (AAMs) to Taiwan for the F-86s, which further boosted the CAF's air superiority. On 24 September 1958 CAF F-86 pilots shot down four more MiGs in the world's first AAM engagement.[96]

The USAF deployed F-100 and F-104 fighters on Taiwan. A new airbase with a 12,000 foot runway was built near Taichung for the USAF and named Chin Chuan Kang after a KMT General killed in the Civil War. The U.S. Seventh Fleet escorted ROC vessels as they resupplied the garrison on Jinmen. The CAF's C-46 transports also made a major contribution to the resupply, although one of them was hit by Chicom anti-aircraft guns. On 6 October Mao suspended the shelling. The crisis eased, although there was another air battle over the area on 10 October. In a tacit recognition of the status quo, China eventually settled for shelling Quemoy every other day!

CAF Credit

The CAF emerged from the crisis with much credit. U.S. analysts praised the "high level of training and excellent caliber" of its fighter units in shooting down about 30 MiGs for the loss of only two F-86s. To help monitor Chicom military deployments opposite Taiwan, the CAF's photo-reconnaissance strength was boosted with four low-altitude supersonic RF-100A and two high-altitude RB-57D jets. But in a visit to Taipei in late October, U.S. Secretary of State Dulles sought to further limit the ROC's military freedom of action, including raids by special forces against the mainland.[97]

The special nighttime low-level operations of the 34th Squadron were stood down throughout October and November 1958. They resumed on the night of 15 December when two B-17s and a P2V all headed for the mainland. One of the B-17s had to evade a MiG fighter near Nanchang.[98]

American policy against air-dropping large numbers appears to have prevailed during 1958. Only a few agents were dropped during the 34th Squadron's 64 missions over the mainland that year. 22 of these missions were flown by the B-17s, 21 by the B-26s, and 11 by the new P2Vs. The ROC probably didn't inform the U.S. of the three flights over Guangdong and Shanxi by the CAF's P4Y-2s, which dropped a total of eight agents.[99, 100]

Low-level Penetrations

According to U.S. intelligence analysts, "the Chinese Communists must have been highly displeased with the performance of their fighter pilots" during the Taiwan Straits Crisis. But in early 1959, those mainland pilots were still on the trail of the 34th Squadron's low-level penetrations. On the night of 9 January, Chinese air defences detected two missions almost simultaneously near Hong Kong and Guangzhou. On 5 February another target was identified as it left the mainland. On both occasions, MiG-17PFs from the 18th Air Division acquired the targets on their radars, but the intruders escaped.[101]

But Chicom air defences were still not picking up all the overflights. There were three penetrations on 9 January, not two. On the night of 4 February there were two missions, not one. The mission planners at NACC evidently believed that there was safety in numbers. On the night of 2 April 1959 they sent both P2Vs and one of the B-17s on overflights. Eight days later they repeated the trick. At the next new moon on 4 May it was one P2V and two B-17s.[102]

On the night of 27 February 1959 the Black Bats flew their last operational B-26 missions. Three of the four remaining aircraft were flown into storage at Tainan, where a major aviation maintenance depot had been spawned by CAT. It operated under commercial cover as Air Asia. Tainan became a training and support base for Air America, a new CIA proprietary company that evolved from CAT to become America's air arm in the secret war in Laos during the 1960s. The B-26s were recycled from there to the USAF in Vietnam.

Meanwhile, CAT continued to operate as an airline. It took on Taiwan shareholders but remained under U.S. control. From 1959 it had new competition. China Airlines was created as a fully Taiwanese-owned airline, which was effectively controlled by the CAF. Chiang Ching-kuo and Gen I Fu En conceived China Airlines not only as a passenger airline, but also as the ROC's own covert air operator. It thus acquired one of the 34th's old B-26s and two PBY Catalina amphibians, as well as a C-46 and a C-54 transport.[103]

B-17s Detected

On 29 May 1959, the NACC again planned simultaneous penetrations of the mainland by the 34th Squadron at the time of the new moon. Two B-17s both entered denied territory in Guangdong province before splitting up. Unfortunately they were both detected. Col Li De Feng (李德風) and his crew headed north towards Jianxi. A MiG-17PF was scrambled to intercept, but GCI controllers lost radar contact. Subsequent analysis of the SIGINT tapes revealed 20 high-frequency and eight low-frequency recordings. Li's B-17 completed its mission and left the mainland near Swatow.

But the other B-17, commanded by Lt Col Xu Yin Gui (徐銀桂), was not so fortunate. It was detected flying low along the coast of southern Guangdong, heading west towards the Leizhou peninsula. The Chicoms then lost radar contact, and the aircraft continued westwards into Guangxi. It was over two hours later before a radar of the 18th Air Division re-acquired the aircraft as it flew back into Guangdong. A MiG-17PF piloted by the unit commander Jiang Zhe Lun (蔣哲倫) was scrambled at 2312. Ground controllers vectored Jiang towards the target, and then ordered him to switch frequency in an attempt to prevent the B-17 crew from monitoring the interception. At 2327 Jiang acquired the B-17 on his own radar, just two miles ahead. He locked on and opened fire at a range of 2,500 feet. Temporarily blinded by the cannon fire, Jiang regained his sight and saw that the target's left wing was on fire. Then he flew into cloud, but GCI gave him new vectors and he re-acquired the target visually and fired again. A huge ball of flame erupted ahead of Jiang as he entered more cloud. The MiG pilot was able to fly into clear air for a third firing pass, just as the B-17 exploded and crashed near Yangjiang at 2340. Jiang had fired a total of 177 23mm shells in the successful attack.[104]

None of the 14 crew on the B-17 survived. The wreckage fell just 25 miles from the coast. The crew had broken radio silence to report that they were under attack, but it wasn't until the PRC reported the shoot down on public radio much later that the loss of the aircraft was confirmed. It was the third B-17 to be shot down over mainland China.

New Estimate

Still, a new U.S. intelligence estimate issued in late July 1959 did not rate the mainland's air defences highly. It mentioned "poor pilot techniques, a shortage of adequate GCI radars and airborne intercept equipment, and only fair standards in GCI procedures." Only about 60 of the Chicom's 1,770 jet fighters were radar-equipped. Accurate height-finding radars were few. However, the estimate noted that the Chinese had developed a new, higher-performance radar (nicknamed Cross Slot by the Western reporting system), adding to their line-up of Soviet and old World War II vintage types.[105]

No one in Western intelligence yet knew that the Chinese armed forces would have to rely on their own resources and ingenuity much more from now on. In mid-1959 the Soviet Union unilaterally terminated the defence agreement it had signed with the PRC only two years earlier. The dispute between the two giants of the communist world over doctrine and influence would last for decades. From now on, the Chinese would have to copy the Soviet military hardware that they had already been given or develop their own.

In fact, those officers responsible for the air defence of the PRC were already striving to develop their own unique methods of intercepting the Black Bats from Taiwan. In 1958, the PLAAF decided to convert three of its vintage Tupolev Tu-2 light bombers into all-weather interceptors by fitting them with the RP-5 radar from the MiG-17PF. The Tu-2 was a Second World War design, a mid-wing, twin-piston engine machine that was fast for its day – the maximum speed was 280 knots. The Soviet Union had given at least 240 of them to the PRC.

With a range of over 1,200 miles, the PLAAF reasoned that the Tu-2 could loiter in the areas overflown by the P2Vs and B-17s for much longer than the MiG-17PF. Typically, the MiGs could only make a couple of attacking passes before running low on fuel and returning to base. Moreover, the speed of the Tu-2 was closer to that of the intruders. The MiG pilots who were scrambled to intercept the slower-flying B-17s and P2Vs were finding that they only had 10 seconds to acquire and fire on the target. This was because the RP-5 had an air-to-air range of only four kilometres. More often than not the MiG pilots were overshooting their targets. They would try to reposition for a second attack from the rear, but after 20 minutes they would be short of fuel. GCI controllers would recall them to base and clear the AAA guns to try their luck, until another pair of MiGs could be scrambled.

By adding the MiG's RP-5 air intercept radar to the nose of the Tu-2, and with two 23mm cannons installed at the wing roots, the PLAAF hoped for greater success. The navigator's station behind the pilot was modified for a second pilot, who viewed the radarscope and flew the aircraft during interceptions. The radio operator's position was retained while a new position was found for the navigator, farthest aft, replacing the second gunner's position on the original Tu-2. Nine crews from the 25th Bomber Division at Lintong airbase, in Shaanxi province, completed their training on the modified Tu-2PFs in mid-1959.[106]

Changes at the CIA

In Washington, there were significant changes at the top of the CIA. Richard Bissell was promoted to become Deputy Director for Plans (DDP) in January 1959, replacing Frank Wisner. The Air Maritime Division was broken up, and its Air Branch was transferred to the newly-created Development Projects Division (DPD). This was an expansion of Bissell's U-2 organization, which was now growing fast as it explored successors to the high-flying spyplane, including Mach 3 aircraft and satellites. Paul Gottke was head of the Air Branch, reporting to USAF Colonel Bill Burke, who ran DPD.

In March 1959 Bissell asked the DPD requirements chief, Jim Reber, to review the value of the STPOLLY program. He wanted to know whether the current standing

AT THE SKUNK WORKS

So that he could concentrate on the U-2, Fred Cavanaugh made me the project manager for the P2V. There were five of us engineers working it. The rest of the Skunk Works didn't know what we were doing. When I started, we thought that our work on the program would only last another nine months. It didn't work out that way!

I loved the P2V – unlike most of our projects, we could fly in it. It wasn't easy, though, crawling over that big box beam in the fuselage, especially since we always wore parachutes. But we had some great fun, especially later on, when we test-flew the terrain-following radar low over the Mojave Desert. The chicken farmers up there raised hell because this big black airplane was scaring their birds to death.

- Bill Giles, interview

approval for up to ten flights per month was still valid. As usual, Reber brought his rigorous analytical style to bear on the task. He told Bissell that the missions from Taiwan were not meeting any of the highest-priority objectives for ELINT collection that were set by the U.S. Intelligence Board (USIB). However, the National Security Agency (NSA) and the 5th Air Force in the Pacific region both valued the intel on Chicom air defences that was obtained during the flights. But Reber concluded that this could be obtained from far less frequent flights, if the collection of ELINT was the only objective.[107]

Bissell wanted to centralize the mission planning in Headquarters, just like the U-2. He queried Desmond Fitzgerald, the Chief of the DDP's Far East Division, on Reber's conclusions. Bissell suspected that the agent and leaflet-dropping requirements were being used to justify the ELINT requirements – and vice-versa.[108]

As part of an overall review of Air Branch activities throughout the world, Bissell sent Colonel Burke to the Far East. There, Burke learned that the nationalist side of the joint operation was pushing for the maximum possible activity, despite the recent shootdown of the B-17. But in Burke's judgement, that incident suggested that all missions over the mainland should be suspended until new countermeasures could be introduced.[109]

Survived

The STPOLLY program survived Bissell's review. However, the overflights were suspended throughout August and September. Their frequency had, in any case, been reduced by halting penetrations by the B-17 after the shootdown on 29 May. Until then, the Black Bats had indeed been flying into the mainland ten times per month. In the first five months of 1959 the squadron logged a total of over 480 P2V and B-17 hours on these 'Eagle' overflight missions – and that was without counting the 'Robin' missions that did not penetrate, but flew up and down the China Coast.[110]

When overflights resumed their frequency was reduced, so that only nine were flown in the last quarter of 1959, all of them by the P2Vs. But operational control of STPOLLY remained in the field. Missions were still planned in Taipei, but they were forwarded to Agency HQ for approval. Colonel James Coates, USAF, arrived in Taipei as the new head of the NACC Air Section.

Bissell's review of Air Branch programs did result in a big reduction of covert air operations in Europe in mid-1959. Most of the CIA-assigned aircraft there were relocated to the U.S., including the two P2V-7s that had been based at Wiesbaden, Germany, since 1957. These aircraft found a new home at Eglin AFB, FL. The black P2Vs were already a familiar sight at the base. The USAF contract to conduct operational evaluations of the "RB-69" had been extended. The Air Proving Ground Command (APGC) performed two more phases of this work at Eglin during 1957 and 1958. The CIA also conducted flying training on the P2V at the Florida base.[111]

P2V Upgrade

In May 1959 a sixth-phase upgrade to the P2V mission equipment was approved. The Air Branch's ECM specialist, Major Willy Homen, again played a key role in the process. The key contractors were two small and innovative electronics companies who worked directly for the CIA – Applied Technology Inc (ATI) and Granger Associates. The integration work was again done by Lockheed Skunk Works at Burbank, where Bill Giles took over as the RB-69 project manager from Fred Cavanaugh, who transferred to the U-2 program.

The new countermeasures to which Burke referred in his report from the Far East comprised a sophisticated air-to-air radar jammer designed by Dr Bill Ayres of ATI. It was a 'smart' system that employed the inverse-gain technique to process the incoming signal from the radar of an intercepting fighter and then repeat it back towards the interceptor, 180 degrees out of phase. This presented a false target on the interceptor's radarscope. Ayres also designed a version of the new radar jammer for the CIA's U-2s. On the P2V it was known as the ATIR (the R standing for Repeater). The transmit/receive antennas were fitted at the tip of the aircraft's rear tail boom. [112]

To operate the ATIR jammer, a new ECM position was added to the P2V crew. This was for a 'Bomber Defense Officer' (BDO), who was squeezed into the nose, behind the 'nosegator.' His cramped station comprised an X-band signal monitor to detect the fighter's radar, a direction finding monitor, and control panels for operating the ATIR jammer and for dispensing chaff. The BDO's console was provided by Granger Associates. [113]

The Phase VI upgrade to the P2V also replaced the APR-9/13 ELINT system with a new-technology 'ferret' system developed for the U.S. Navy by Loral. It was designated ALQ-28, and covered the entire frequency spectrum from 50MHz to 10.75GHz in nine tunable channels. It was a superheterodyne receiver with much greater sensitivy that used the latest Travelling Wave Tube (TWT) technology. The ALQ-28 provided an automatic raster scan of received signals on a 5-inch cathode ray tube. This relieved the ECM officer operators on the P2V from the time-consuming task of searching for the exact frequency of a given signal. 'Raven 2' was also relieved of his responsibility for tuning and operating the old noise jammer, now replaced by the ATIR.

The ALQ-28 was operated alongside a broadband ELINT system (QRC-15) provided by Granger. It also employed TWTs, but scanned more slowly through the frequency bands. It could therefore pick up lower-power signals that might be missed by the faster scanning ALQ-28. The 'Ravens' could gain valuable cues from the QRC-15 that enabled them to tune the ALQ-28 to the exact frequency.

Two 14-channel standard recorders and one seven-channel high-speed recorder captured the signals from these two ELINT systems, and a third was also added. This

DROPPING CHAFF

When the 34th Squadron first employed chaff against the mainland's air defences, it was manually dispensed by the airdrop sergeants through a small window on the right side of the P2V fuselage, upon command from the BDO.

After he joined the squadron in 1959, BDO Richard Gao asked the US side to provide chaff dispensers that were directly controlled by the BDO. But the Americans told him that the current US equipment was too large and heavy to install on the P2V.

So Gao planned his own installation, with help from chief engineering officer Major Wang Ju Ren (王 居仁). A large rectangular metal box was fabricated, into which the belt drive motor from a machine gun removed from an old B-25 was fitted. When the motor turned, it pushed out the chaff bundles. NACC's electronics specialist Jim Whittaker designed an electronic timer which controlled the number of bundles dropped at each command.

After successful tests, the dispenser switch was installed in the BDO's panel, and the box itself in the rear fuselage, and. The airdrop sergeant now only had to replace the chaff that had been dispensed. The design was later adopted for the squadron's C-54 and C-123s.

– C.P.

was a prototype K-band receiver, the first one that was sensitive enough to analyze such high frequency signals: it operated in two bands covering 10-40 GHz. This exotic new technology was also designed by Granger. Unfortunately, no one in the 34th Squadron or the NACC ever heard it pick up a signal over China![114]

The Phase VI modifications to the P2V were also supposed to include a new computer for navigation, the ASN-7. But this idea was dropped when DPD reluctantly decided to remove the P2V's Doppler radar navigation (RADAN) system, which provided ground speed and drift to the computer. The RADAN was designed to aid low-level navigation, but was only guaranteed to work when the aircraft was flying at 300 feet or above. To avoid the intercepting fighters the aircraft were now descending at times to 200 feet or less! Also, the RADAN didn't work as well over water as over land – and the Black Bats were flying some long over water transits before coasting in. After repeated attempts by the technical representative from GPL at Hsinchu to make it work under these demanding conditions the RADAN was canned.

But the removal of the Doppler system had a knock-on effect on the P2V's photo capability. It was rendered useless, since the image motion compensation (IMC) system was fed ground speed data that was continually updated by the RADAN. However, the photo system was proving difficult to maintain, and had hardly been used operationally, either in Europe or over China. Those powerful mercury arc lamps in the wingtip pods shone like a beacon when they were turned on to provide illumination for night photography. The aircraft was suddenly very vulnerable to anti-aircraft guns or fighter interception. Moreover, the lights also almost blinded the pilots! In 1958 strobe lights were fitted to 7047 and flight tested as a less obtrusive alternative means of illumination. But in September 1959 DPD faced reality. "Based on past experience, it is doubtful that the crews will consent to flying the airplane with an illuminating system," an official wrote. The strobe light development was scrapped, and the original arc lamp system was removed from the aircraft.[115]

The last major equipment that was tested as part of the 1959 upgrade was the Fulton Skyhook system. This was an improved device for extracting agents from enemy territory by air, invented by Dr. Robert Fulton. The agent strapped himself to a harness that was attached to a 500-foot long nylon line, on the end of which was a balloon. The agent operated a portable helium bottle to fill the balloon, then released it upwards. The pickup aircraft was fitted with two tubular steel forks protruding from its nose, 30 feet long and spread at a 70-degree angle. The aircraft would fly into the nylon line, snag it with the forks, and a spring-loaded trigger mechanism would rotate to secure the line to the aircraft. As the line streamed under the fuselage it was snared by the onboard pickup crew using a J-hook.

COVERT INSERTIONS – 'A TOTAL WASTE OF TIME'

Although ELINT on the Chinese air defences was the main mission of the 34th squadron by the late 1950s, the covert insertion of agents on some of those same missions continued. According to authors Ted Jup and Evan Thomas, some of the CIA's clandestine service staff were troubled by the continued covert assaults on the mainland. One of these was Peter Sichel, the CIA station chief in Hong Kong from 1956 to 1959. The risks taken by both Americans and Chinese nationalists made little sense to him: "it was a total waste of time and a total death mission for anyone who got involved." In 1959, Sichel quit the Agency, disenchanted with what he saw as a 'cowboy mentality' and mounting casualties.

- Jup, p101 and Thomas, p187

CLINE ON THE COVERT INSERTIONS

We sent off brave Chinese volunteers who were willing to be parachuted into remote areas of the mainland or infiltrated by night by rubber boats on uninhabited coastlines in an attempt to hide with old friends or family while they looked for information we wanted.

The survivability of these agents was limited and we gradually turned to other intelligence techniques: the occasional traveler, the foreign diplomat, and above all, the electronic and photographic collection platforms. It was a very stressful experience to sit in a radio shack perched on the high ground above Taipei, listening for clandestine radio signals from teams in Sinkiang; it was heartbreaking when after a time they came through with the prearranged coded signal that indicated the radio operator had been captured.

- Cline, p200

Meanwhile, the agent would be pulled into the air, trailing the aircraft. The onboard crew then attached the line to a powered winch and the agent was pulled on board. It worked much better than the old All American system that had been used in the Korean War.

However, the Skyhook system was never used to pick up agents from mainland China – where most agents found themselves inserted on a one-way trip, into prison or worse. But one of the Agency's P2V fleet equipped with the Fulton system was detached to the CIA air unit on Okinawa for a time in late 1961. This was part of a plan to snatch CIA B-26 pilot Allen Pope from the prison in Indonesia where he languished after being shot down during Operation Haik in 1958. The Indonesians threatened to execute Pope. However, the sentence was commuted and the plan was dropped. Pope was released in 1962.[116]

DPD hoped to complete the operational testing of all the new Phase VI equipment on the P2V by the end of September 1959. Inevitably, though, delays occurred. After initial flight tests by Lockheed in California, test bird 7047 was flown to Eglin in September for trials with the Fulton system. In early November it was returned to the Skunk Works so that the ATIR jammer and the ALQ-28 and K-band ELINT systems could be installed. Then it was back to Eglin, where the APGC was expected to complete its evaluation by the end of the year.[117]

ENGINE FAILURE OVER THE MAINLAND!

The R-3350 engines on the P2V were the most powerful of all propellor engines. Yet they were prone to metal fatigue, and needed to be replaced after 800 to 1,000 flight hours.

On our way back from a mainland mission, one engine suddenly malfunctioned. We were over the Shandong peninsula, and it was almost dawn. Then we heard a Chinese fighter pilot inform the ground station with a strong Shandong accent: "I've already seen the P2V!". My dilemma was that it was impossible to get rid of the chasing enemy aircraft because only one engine was left running. Yet if I started the back-up jet engine, not enough fuel would be left to fly back to Taiwan.

I decided to start it anyway. Luckily, I was able to fly into the fog over the sea to get rid of the enemy aircraft. Then I switched to 121.5 Guard Channel and made an emergency call for permission to land in South Korea. Fortunately, four US F-86s were sent to escort me to land at K9 base there. *- Dai Shu Qin, from MND Vietnam War Oral History Book, p179-180*

Chapter Five

1960-1961

U.S. intelligence was anxious to explore the air defences around the capital of the People's Republic. On 7 October 1959, the Chicoms shot down an RB-57D photo reconnaissance aircraft flown by a nationalist pilot near Beijing. The CAF had been provided with two of these long-winged spyplanes, and they had been flying over the mainland since January 1959. They were capable of flying at over 60,000 feet – an altitude thought by U.S. intelligence to be safe from interception. The Chicoms did not say how they had shot down the high-flying intruder, nor at what altitude. Was Peking now protected by upgraded height-finding radars and fighter interceptors?[118]

Electronic collection requirements in Asia were co-ordinated by the U.S. Pacific Command (PACOM). The PACOM ELINT Center (PEC) at Fuchu air station, in Japan, processed and analysed the ELINT that was collected by various U.S. platforms in Asia. These included peripheral reconnaissance flights along the Soviet and China coast flown by the U.S. Navy and USAF, as well as the 'black' overflights from Taiwan. After each P2V mission a courier from the NACC delivered the ELINT tapes to the PEC by air.

Following Dick Bissell's scepticism about the real intelligence value of STPOLLY, the PACOM ELINT Requirements Committee and the PEC started producing maps of their desired targets and areas of interest. These were "a distinct improvement over the guidance hitherto provided these operations," noted the DPD requirements chief, Jim Reber. Furthermore, Reber looked forward to the deployment of the new ALQ-28 and K-band receivers on the P2V, in the hope that they would acquire "new and unusual signal data."[119]

But new technical collection systems like this were expensive. Bissell queried the DPD's scheme to equip two more P2Vs with the ALQ-28 and K-band receivers. Since only five operational sorties over mainland China per month were now being planned, he noted, perhaps only one more P2V need be modified.[120]

'Ferret' Missions

In late January 1960, the Black Bats were tasked to fly a series of 'ferret' missions into northern China with the new receivers. The first of these was a 13-hour flight on the night of 25 January led by the 34th squadron commander, Col Yin Yan Shan. The P2V took off

---

DON JACKSON'S TRIBUTE

They were very long missions from Hsinchu – 14 hours or more. We were out there on the airfield when they left and we were out there when they returned. Not because it was required, but because we loved the ROC crews...their professionalism, bravery and dedication. It was a real, close-knit team effort.

- interview

QUALITY MAINTENANCE

I could not have had a better crew of top-caliber technicians – both Chinese and Americans. In my two years in Taiwan, we did not have to scrub a single mission because our equipment was inoperable. Nor did we have a single inflight failure that caused the pilot to abort an overflight.

Fourteen-hour missions were the norm. We Americans would frequently fly on training missions to flight-test the equipment, but we were strictly prohibited from flying operational missions.

- Don Jackson, interview

from Hsinchu and flew all the way to the Liaodong Peninsula before penetrating mainland airspace to fly a wide circuit around Shenyang. It captured 123 signals as searchlight and gun-laying radars tried to illuminate and track the aircraft. Yin and his crew landed at Kunsan airbase in Korea.

The next night, another P2V flight led by Lt Col Zhao Qin from Hsinchu entered mainland airspace over Shandong and then headed towards Beijing, passing over the east side of the capital. During this flight the crew detected at least a dozen MiG-17 sorties launched against them. They coasted-out into the Gulf of Bohai, skirted the Liaodong Peninsula, and flew all the way back to Hsinchu – a 14 hour 25 minute flight. One night later Col Yin and his crew were back over the mainland, taking off from Kunsan and flying a wide circuit of Manchuria and venturing right up to China's border with the Soviet Union along the Amur River in Heilongjiang province.

The P2V then turned south and flew along the Sino-Soviet border, coming close to Vladivostok. Air defense controllers at the Soviet port city reacted by scrambling their interceptors. But the intruder remained in Chinese airspace, and we can only speculate whether the Soviets reached a conclusion on the nationality of the target on their radar screens. The P2V turned again, southwest this time, to fly along China's border with North Korea. It eventually landed at Kunsan after 14 hours, having survived 20 interception attempts by fighters and four attacks by AAA guns. The mission produced no fewer than 168 new signals.[121]

Longest Mission

After the shootdown of the B-17 in May 1959, the 34th Squadron had just one remaining example of the World War II-vintage bomber. Although the P2V was clearly superior for SIGINT missions, this last B-17 did fly a few more missions over the mainland in late

FRANK DALY ON FLYING AND INSTRUCTING IN TAIWAN

I arrived in Taiwan in January 1960, and was the first instructor pilot from the Navy to be assigned to that operation. I had flown the P2V at maximum takeoff weight (80,000 lbs) before – which was useful experience.

Most of the Chinese pilots were good. They were certainly very conscientious. But they did everything by the book. Col Zhao was the exception; I thought he was the best.

The tailplane of the P2V had a variable camber, which was operated by a button on the control yoke.

The spoilers on the wing deployed automatically during a tight turn. Apart from that, the aircraft responded to standard, boosted control inputs.

Col Coates was the head of the NACC Air Section. When we ferried P2Vs to and from the US, he would officially be the pilot-in-command – but I did most of the flying. Coates liked to fly our C-47, and so did Charles Reed, an Air Force Major who was assigned to Taipei as an operations officer. Reed also flew our B-26. - *interview*

GOODBYE TO THE B-17

We were preparing to send our last B-17 back to the US. A Chinese crew stripped the airplane of all the ELINT equipment. But after this work, someone forgot to reconnect the airspeed line to the pitot tube. During takeoff on the subsequent test flight, the airspeed indicator failed to register. But instead of flying by instinct, the Chinese pilot pushed the throttles all the way forward – and fire-walled the engines. He flew round the circuit for a emergency landing. If he didn't make it on the first pass, he told the tower that he would ditch at sea. Fortunately, a flight engineer from Lockheed was onboard and realized what the problem was. He pulled the throttles back so that a safe landing speed was achieved. - *Jackson interview. (The B-17 left the 34th Squadron in November 1960. It was sent to the Skunk Works in 1961, where it was fitted with the ATIR jammer for another covert operation. All four engines had to be replaced. The B-17 was subsequently fitted with the Fulton Skyhook and flown in Operation Coldfeet, when it dropped and then extracted two Americans who investigated an ice station that the Soviet Union had abandoned in the Arctic. The same B-17 became a movie star when the Skyhook was used to pick up James Bond and his girlfriend at the end of the film 'Thunderball')*

1959 and early 1960. One of these may have been the longest ever flown by a B-17 - anywhere and anytime. On 26 February 1960 a crew commanded by Col Li De Feng flew the old wartime bomber over Guangdong, Hunan, and Guizhou provinces, then on over the Yunnan plateau before returning on a roughly parallel track. Extra fuel tanks were installed for this flight, which took off from Hsinchu at 1600 on 26 February 1960. It was 1110 the next morning before they returned – 19 hours 10 minutes later![122]

The Chicom air defences were now detecting nearly every mission by the Black Bats before or shortly after 'coast-in.' The intruders flew over the sea towards the mainland at 500 feet or below, trying to avoid or delay radar detection. But the Chicoms had another warning system: fishing trawlers stationed out to sea, that reported surface or air movements to the shore by radio. By these means the belt of AAA guns along the coast might be alerted to the arrival of unwelcome airborne intruders. Beyond the AAA guns the interceptors were ready to scramble.

Still, to date the Chicom success rate against the P2Vs was zero. As long as the coast-in points were carefully chosen the AAA guns could be avoided. Then, if the Chicoms launched interceptors the P2V crew could hear them coming, thanks to the P2V's COMINT system. The radio operator had little difficulty in intercepting the mainland GCI communications, since the Chicoms used only four channels. System 3 offered a total of 24 channels that were crystal-controlled. Some of the channels were preset to the GCI frequencies, leaving others to sweep the frequency bands.[123]

Not only were the MiGs failing to intercept, but the plan to use the three specially-converted Tu-2 light bombers had not yet worked either. In early 1960 one PLAAF commander came up with another scheme. He suggested that they use a larger bomber,

THE LIFERAFT INCIDENT

In summer 1961 there was a near-disaster when Lt Col Zhou Yi Li (周以栗) and crew took off on a local training sortie. At 5,000 feet power was lost and the aircraft stalled. The tail section sergeant reported that the life raft had deployed from its stowage in the upper wing, and was snagged on the horizontal tail.

The captain started the jet engine to blow it away. The aircraft landed safely.

The life rafts were designed to deploy automatically upon contact with salt water. It was concluded that the actuation switch had operated. Maybe the salt from the coastal air at Hsinchu had gradually accumulated. Or maybe the aircraft had been flown so low over the water, that sea spray had entered the switch! - Fu p102, Jackson interview

the Tupolev Tu-4. This was the Soviet copy of the four-engined B-29. In 1952, ten of them were transferred to China as a personal gift from Stalin to Mao. They served with the 4th Regiment at Shijiazhuang, southwest of Beijing in Hebei province. The Tu-4's speed closely matched that of the P2V, and with a duration of more than six hours it could follow the intruder for a long time.

PLAAF commander Liu Ya Lou (劉亞樓) agreed to an experimental conversion. The bomber's main search radar was transformed into an air intercept system by moving the antenna from the belly to a radome that was added to the upper fuselage, where the forward upper gun turret was previously situated. The Tu-4 still had four other defensive positions where 23mm cannons were fitted. An infrared sight with a range of up to two miles was added to these positions, so that the gunners could visually acquire the P2V as their target and open fire. The bomb bay of the Tu-4 was converted to a command post with a radar screen and places for an airborne intercept officer, two navigators, and two chart plotters. After a month of test flights at Wukong airbase in Shaanxi proved the concept, three more Tu-4s were converted to this novel role of airborne bomber-interceptor.[124]

The first attempted interception by a Tu-4 took place on the night of 1 March 1960. A P2V flew into Jiangsu and almost immediately encountered a MiG-17. The Black Bat crew detected another 13 enemy sorties launched against them during this mission. The flight was found by searchlights for a time. A Tu-4 joined the action and followed them for miles across Henan and Anhui provinces without managing to attack. The Black Bats crew dropped over 2,000 lbs of leaflets along their route and recorded no fewer than 216 enemy radar signals.[125]

Surprisingly, the post-mission summary of this flight that was circulated at the regular weekly DPD staff meeting back in Washington casually noted that "normal Chinese reaction was encountered."[126]

Staging via Korea

The staging of P2V missions via Korea continued. On 25 March 1960, squadron commander Col Yin Yan Shan and his P2V crew took off from Hsinchu on a ferry flight across the East China Sea to Kunsan. There, a reception committee from the NACC and CAF headquarters was already waiting, having flown in earlier on a C-54 loaded with support equipment. The NACC had planned another mission around Beijing to be flown the following night.[127]

To avoid tipping off the Chinese air defences the P2V flew in radio silence, even on ferry flights. The silence was only broken for short, essential messages to the command post on HF radio, such as "coast-in," "coast-out," and short, timed reports at various waypoints

---

THE CRASH IN KOREA

It was a tragedy. Col Yin was a tall, good-looking, gregarious fellow. Everybody liked him. He spoke excellent English.

We had prepositioned to Kunsan in a C-54. It was loaded with spares – there was almost no room for us to sit. We heard that the P2V was overdue, and there were reports of an explosion in the hills. Colonel Wang and I were the first to reach the crash site, in a helicopter at first light the next morning. We

were detailed to supervise the recovery of classified equipment. The plane had flown just 20 feet too low to clear the mountain. The tail section was more or less complete. The fuselage had burned. The engines had gone over the top and fallen down the other side.

The ferry flight should have been 'a milk run'. They had the basic search radar and a radar altimeter to warn them of rising ground. Maybe they were just tired…

- Jackson interview

A BLACK BATS WIDOW LAMENTS

My husband was Li Di Chen (李滌塵), a navigator who died when the P2V crashed in Korea. We often talked about the risks. He took me to parties, and some of the usual faces would be missing. Where were they? Tonight we dance and enjoy the night. Tomorrow he will go on a mission, and maybe never come back.

After happiness comes loneliness. I was two months pregnant with twins when he was killed. Suddenly, the man that I would rely upon for my whole life was gone – in smoke. I pretended to still be happy, but I was now the lonely one amongst the noisy gatherings. Outsiders cannot really understand all this.

-*Zheng Shu Yi (鄭淑儀), in film "The Secret of the Taiwan Skies"*

in the flight. Col Yin and his crew reached the coast of Korea safely, but after turning inland the aircraft slammed into the top of an 800-foot high hill. All 14 crewmembers were killed. Reports of an explosion in the hills were passed to the waiting party at Kunsan. They set off for the site to recover the bodies and the classified equipment.

Accident investigators suggested that the crew mistook the homing beacon at Kunsan for another one nearby on higher terrain, since it broadcast on a frequency only 15KHz removed and had a similar three-letter code. What about the radar altimeter? Maybe the crew had turned it off – that was an additional precaution against detection by the air defences during an overflight. But there was also speculation that the crew were simply not fully alert and functioning after the long ferry flight.[128]

After the tragic accident in Korea, the remaining P2V flew a 10-hour mission from Hsinchu on 5 April along the southern coast of China, finally penetrating Chicom airspace over Hainan Island before returning along the coast. On 25 April another flight headed in the same direction, coasting in at the peninsula opposite Hainan Island before heading close to Kunming. Five nights later the P2V was back over Hainan and Guangxi after another long flight down the coast.[129]

Air Section Expanding

Lockheed Skunk Works project manager Bill Giles and DPD project manager Major Willy Homen travelled to Taiwan to help the bed-down of the new P2V equipment capabilities. Also helping to introduce the new equipment was Don Jackson, an electronics expert from the CIA's ELINT Staff Office in Washington who was reassigned to the NACC in late 1959. The Air Section in Taipei was expanding: there were now over 30 Americans assigned. They included Frank Daly, who in January 1960 became the first P2V instructor pilot to be detailed to the project from the U.S. Navy.[130]

In early May 1960, the first P2V to be equipped with the ATIR jammer (7047) was ferried to Taiwan. To provide the Chinese P2V crews with some realistic training in using the new defensive equipment, Don Jackson from the NACC supervised a deployment by the 34th Squadron to Okinawa to fly against USAF F-102 interceptors from Naha airbase. On the instrumented range there, USAF pilots would use the same tactics as the radar-equipped Chicom MiGs, by flying stern attacks (although the radar in the F-102 was more sophisticated, and capable of mounting side-on attacks). The P2V crews would learn how to use their 'smart' repeater jammer to best advantage. Unfortunately, Jackson was unable to persuade the USAF pilots to fly below 9,000 feet – and certainly not down to 300 feet over

PERSONALIZED PROPAGANDA FROM THE MAINLAND

The KMT government frequently warned against infiltrators and potential saboteurs. The "Keep the Secrets" campaign was taken very seriously – especially by serving ROC military personel.

The mainland beamed shortwave radio programs across the Straits, full of personal details about nationalist military and government officials. The Chicoms usually obtained these details by interrogating their relatives who had been unwilling or unable to flee the mainland in 1948-49. The population on Taiwan was officially forbidden from listening to these broadcasts – but many disobeyed the ruling.

During one of these broadcasts, 34th squadron pilot Zhu Zhen was congratulated on becoming a father by his cousin, who was living in Harbin. – *C.P.*

A FATHER CALLS HIS SON INFLIGHT - TO DEFECT!

Like many others, the family of P2V pilot Dai Shu Qing had been split apart by the Chinese Civil War. His father, Dai Ming Zhong (戴銘忠), was a general in the KMT army who surrendered to the communists. "My father and I were separated by the war, serving antagonistic regimes respectively on both sides of the Taiwan Strait and enduring tremendous emotional torture," Dai recalled.

Chinese communist officials found out that the general's son was flying from Taiwan with the low-level intruder squadron. They forced General Dai to record a message, pleading with his son to defect. The message was played repeatedly over the PRC's air defence communications frequencies during a P2V overflight. By coincidence – or maybe not – Dai Shu Qing was the aircraft commander on that very flight! The general's message was picked up by the P2V's COMINT system. The radio operator on the P2V switched the taped message to intercom, so that all the crew could hear, including Dai.

The general said: "Shu Qing, this is your father Dai Ming Zhong. Your mother is well. Your elder brother is a college professor, and your younger brother and sister are college students. I hear that you often come here. How dangerous it is! Don't come back here ever again!"

When Dai heard his father's words, he was overcome with emotion. Then the Chicom GCI controller cut in: "P2V pilot, now fly 270 degrees. The lights along the runway ahead have been lit for you. After you land, we will give you the reward you deserve." The GCI controller repeated this message two or three times, but Dai wasn't persuaded to defect: "it was impossible for me to betray my country and duty," he said later.

Co-pilot Li De Feng took the controls from the devastated Dai for a while. When the Chicoms realized that the P2V was continuing its mission, they scolded Dai: "You are not a loyal person or a filial son. You have been completely surrounded. You can't get away!" But Dai and his crew cold not detect any Chicom interceptors chasing them. The P2V climbed to 10,000 ft and returned safely to Taiwan, but not before running the gauntlet of anti-aircraft fire upon coast-out. – *C.P.*

SO WAS THERE A SPY IN THE 34TH SQUADRON?

It seemed quite possible. There were the Chicom radio broadcasts, containing all those personal details about 34th squadron crew members. And the Chicom air defenses always detected the penetration flights, well before coast-in. Were they on permanent alert – or were they being tipped off?

The Taiwan side of the joint operation reckoned that the biggest security risk was the local labour hired in Taipei and Hsinchu by the Americans – cooks, cleaners and so on. The American side identified other potential compromises. As Don Jackson noted: "every time we prepared for a mission, the POL trucks were lined up on the airfield, the telephone and cable traffic increased, and more people arrived from Taipei. Then we tested the HF transmitter – and not into dummy load, so anyone could pick up the transmissions. It was pretty obvious what was about to happen."

Another American who served in the joint project believes that loose talk, including crew names, on the UHF communications link between Hsinchu airbase and Chinese Air Force headquarters in Taipei was intercepted by the PRC.

Of course, the Chicoms could have simply stationed a spy just outside the base, who could observe the early evening or night takeoffs that were likely overflight missions, and report them to the mainland by covert radio transmission. – *C.P.*

the ocean, even in daylight! However, the deployment to Okinawa did provide calibrated data that proved the effectiveness of the ATIR jammer.[131]

How did the new defensive tactics work? The radio operator on the P2V monitored Chicom GCI frequencies, as before. He would inform the rest of the crew to the possibility of an attack and alert them when it seemed likely. At almost the same time, the BDO in the nose of the P2V would receive an air intercept radar signal, weak at first. He began reporting its direction and intensity to the aircraft captain. Although the pilots might have already heard an aural warning in their headset, supplied by the radar warning receiver, only the BDO could give them an accurate bearing and distance to the threat.

Because the MiG-17PFs were only attacking from the rear, when they reached that position and the signal became stronger the BDO would advise the captain to turn right or left 10-15 degrees. This turn complicated the MiG pilot's task of acquiring the P2V on his radar, and also helped to focus the high-gain jamming signal from the ATIR in the right direction.

If the MiG's air intercept radar locked onto its target, the P2V's air-to-air jammer would operate automatically. The BDO would also deploy radar-spoofing chaff. The P2V captain would activate the spoilers above the wing to make a sharp turn and reduce altitude. He might also slow down or speed up. The radarscope on the MiG-17PF showed a target, but in the wrong place. The MiG pilot would be further confused as the chaff bloomed on his radarscope. The P2V would escape to one side or the other.[132]

On the American side of the joint operation at Hsinchu, there were hopes that the ATIR jammer would work so well that the P2V would not have to change course to evade the interceptors at all. But the Chinese crews were not willing to place that much trust in the electronic wizardry. After all, it was their lives that were at risk. They worried that the Chicom MiG pilots would react to the jamming of their radar by firing blindly towards their target. They might succeed with a lucky shot.[133]

Moreover, there was always the possibility that the new equipment might stop working in flight. Indeed, shortly after it was introduced the ATIR jammer failed twice within a month over the mainland while the P2V was under attack by MiGs. Both missions were led by Lt Col Dai Shu Qing. On 26 June a MiG fired at the P2V but missed. On 21 July the P2V dived very low to escape. The two missions collected over 70 radar signals and dropped almost five million leaflets.[134]

Propaganda Material

As far as the U.S. side was concerned, SIGINT remained the primary mission of the P2V flights over mainland China. But every flight also carried over 2,000 lbs of propaganda material. The Intelligence Bureau of the ROC Ministry of Defence (IBMND) specified the approximate area for the leaflet drops to the NACC. Then, mission planners in the Air Section – which was a secure, U.S.-eyes only operation located in a windowless room within the NACC compound – specified the exact location along the flight path.

On only a handful of occasions were agents dropped from the P2Vs. On 2 February 1960, six agents and their equipment were inserted into the dry bottom of a reservoir in the mountains of Anhui province. It was hardly a covert insertion, however. En route to and from the drop zone the P2V crew encountered multiple attempts at interception by MiG-17s. A further four agents were dropped into the same location on 29 April 1960.[135]

WHO WAS THE BRAVER?

Black Bats pilot Dai Shu Qing flew the two P2V airdrop missions to Anhui in February and April 1960. During one of them, he talked with the leader of the group being inserted. The agent was wearing the typically drab clothes of a mainland peasant, and had a scar on his face. Dai asked him why. The agent said that communists had chased him and he was injured. Dai asked him how many times he had been to the mainland. "Six or seven times," he replied. Dai told him that the 34th Squadron often flew into mainland China and were regarded as very brave. But the pilot realised that these agents were even braver.

- Fu, p94-.

The guerrillas did not board the planes at the 34th Squadron's ramp. Instead, they were brought separately to the airfield by the Intelligence Bureau and hidden in a trench next to the runway. As the aircraft taxied out they would emerge from the trench and climb into the aircraft through the same hatch under the belly that they would use in flight to exit the aircraft.

Sadly, the two insertions to Anhui province were no more successful than similar previous operations. The first group was all captured, and the radio operator was forced to send messages back to Taiwan, calling for reinforcements. The Intelligence Bureau suspected a plot, but nevertheless heeded the request for a second insertion. On the night of 29 April those agents were ambushed and shot even as they descended by parachute.[136]

The Gimo was not discouraged, however. Every time Chiang or his son met U.S. officials they pushed for approval to mount a larger paramilitary effort against the mainland, to exploit the spreading dissatisfaction. By early 1960 it was obvious that economic conditions on the mainland had worsened. Mao's Great Leap Forward had been a disaster. Refugees began pouring over the border from Guangzhou into British-run Hong Kong.

To keep the Gimo happy, the MAAG in Taipei was authorised to train 3,000 ROC troops as special forces. But an internal State Department memo spelled out the underlying U.S. policy:

"The US does not object in principle to strictly non-military (i.e political, psychological, intelligence and underground resistance) activities by the [ROC] on the mainland. However, there appears to be a difference between us and President Chiang in interpretation of non-military. Air-dropping of large numbers of troops... is quite different from infiltrating agents or dropping them individually or in small numbers...We do not believe that any [ROC] actions on the mainland can stimulate large-scale mainland revolt."[137]

Airdrop Plan

The issue would not go away, however. In February 1960, Chiang Ching-Kuo informed CIA station chief Ray Cline that the ROC had a plan to airdrop 200-300 guerillas into Sichuan, and would proceed unilaterally if necessary. Such a move would have broken the mutual understanding between Washington and Taipei that the ROC would not launch raids against the mainland that were larger than company size.[138]

The airdrops of small teams by the 34th Squadron could not take place without U.S. permission. But across the runway at Hsinchu, the CAF had formed a covert unit that was beyond U.S. control. This was the so-called 3831 Force, which was formed on 1 March 1959. The move followed the Gimo's decision to step up support to the KMT irregulars in Burma. The 3831 Force operated the CAF's two remaining airworthy P4Y2 long-range patrol bombers – the same ones that were used to airdrop supplies to the rebels in Indonesia in 1958.[139]

In the new operation, the P4Y2s took off from Hsinchu in the morning and refuelled at Pingtung airbase, in southern Taiwan. From there they set course for Indo-China, flying all the way across the South China Sea at 500 feet to avoid alerting the mainland's radars. Over South Vietnam the aircraft climbed and turned northwest towards the drop zone close to the Thai-Burma border. It would be dark now, and lumbering planes met no opposition as they offloaded personnel and supplies. Then they turned south to land and refuel in Bangkok under cover of darkness before starting the long return journey to Taiwan (Thailand turned a blind eye to the operation).[140]

The P4Y2s were joined by a few C-46s from the CAF's 6th Transport Wing. They were equipped with extra fuel tanks. In early 1960 the transports of the 3831 Force inserted about 1,000 ROC special forces troops that were sent to re-organise the irregulars in Burma. The Gimo's plan was for this rejuvenated army to enter PRC territory in Yunnan province to help foster an anti-communist revolt throughout the discontented southern provinces.

By early 1961, the 3831 force had even built an airstrip near Wan Kawkaw, next to the Mekong River, which divided Laos from Burma. This was the final straw for the Burmese, who had already seen the irregulars team up with Karen and Shan tribes who opposed rule from Rangoon. On 15 February 1961 one of the P4Y2s was intercepted by three vintage Sea Furies of the Burmese Air Force as it approached the airstrip at dusk. They shot down the P4Y2, and only two of the seven crew managed to bail out. (One of the Sea Furies also crashed during the engagement.)

Burma allowed Chinese troops onto its territory to help counterattack the KMT force. The nationalists were routed and fled into Laos. The Burmese captured weapons and ammunition with U.S. markings, and complained to the United Nations. Politically embarrassed, the U.S. privately pressed the Gimo to evacuate the irregulars. He agreed. The CAF flew more than 4,000 of them to Taiwan, including dependents. But many more refused to go. They settled into a life of opium growing and trading in the remote border area, which became known as the Golden Triangle.[141]

Incidentally, the ROC was also supporting the anti-communist faction in Laos at this time. Weapons were supplied, and the young China Airlines exercised its covert role by forming an offshoot in Vientiane with a C-46 and some C-47s. Two pilots from Taiwan were killed when one of the C-47s was shot down in February 1961 by the communist faction, the Pathet Lao. The ROC named this effort The North Star Team. It was the forerunner of a much larger involvement in neighbouring Vietnam by China Airlines, and then the 34th Squadron, which began a year later.[142]

Overflights Continued

Meanwhile, the overflights of mainland China with the P2Vs that were jointly agreed on by the U.S. and the ROC continued. During a mission on the night of 21 October 1960 led by Lt Col Ye Lin (葉霖), the PLAAF launched no fewer than 13 MiG-17PF sorties to intercept. The P2V crew used the new defensive tactics and equipment to defeat the opposition, and stayed over the mainland for nearly seven hours. One of the interceptors (from the 9th Air Division at Xingning airbase, in Guangdong) made two passes. On the first pass, pilot Zhang Han Min (張漢民) opened fire blindly, after his radar was jammed. On the second pass Zhang maintained his firing run much longer – about 30 seconds. But as he finally broke left, he just failed to clear high ground at 1,300 feet and crashed.[143]

On the night of 19 November 1960 an epic air battle unfolded over the mainland. A P2V commanded by Lt Col Dai Shu Qing entered denied territory over Wenzhou. Several MiG-15s and MiG-17PFs tried and failed for two hours to intercept as the P2V headed northwest, dropping 'surrender' leaflets along the way. One of the newly-converted Tu-4 medium bombers also tried to follow the intruder. The ECM officers on the P2V recorded 30 separate radar signals as the aircraft flew low over Anhui province. Lt Col Dai manoeuvred to evade the interceptors.

Then the special Tu-2PF interceptors were thrown into the fray. Two of them were launched from Zhengzhou, in Henan province. But although GCI successively vectored each of them into position behind the intruder, neither could acquire the target because of radar jamming by the P2V's ATIR system operated by the BDO, Gao Yin Song (高蔭松).

The second Tu-2PF followed the P2V for 27 minutes across Henan at 3,000 feet or lower, making three attempts to attack. The Black Bat crew had no idea they were being stalked by a converted World War II light bomber – the radar signals that they intercepted told them that this was a MiG-17PF, as on so many previous occasions! The workload on the P2V became intense as the crew strived to shake off their pursuer. They even tried a tight 360-degree turn, hoping that the 'MiG' would overshoot.

As the P2V crew continued their defensive co-ordination, the aircraft was heading straight for the famous Mount Song, which rose over 4,000 feet near Dengfeng! Dai increased power and opened the spoilers as he prepared to make a sharp avoiding turn. As the mountain loomed less than two miles ahead the Black Bats pilot followed the directions from nosegator by racking the aircraft into a 60-degree right bank and flying into a narrow valley. At the same time BDO Gao deployed more chaff.

Flying behind and slightly below the P2V, the front pilot in the Tu-2, group leader Shang De Zan (尚德贊), failed to spot his quarry's sharp turn. Meanwhile the second pilot, behind him at the radarscope station, locked onto the chaff. The Tu-2 crew fired at a nonexistent target. And because their radar was switched from 'search' to 'lock-on' mode it did not warn them of the rising terrain ahead. Suddenly the mountain loomed into view, and Shang struggled to climb over it. He failed by 1,000 feet, as the Tu-2 slammed into the peak. As the P2V escaped down the valley its rear observer saw the fireball erupt. The 34th crew flew on, with the radio officer listening to the vain calls from Chicom ground controllers trying to make contact with the crashed interceptor.

The air defence controllers re-acquired the P2V on their ground radars, ordered the other Tu-2 that was still airborne to follow it, and scrambled a third Tu-2. By now the intruder had spent more than four hours over the mainland, and was near Xian, in Shaanxi province. Another firing pass was ordered. One of the Tu-2s closed to within less than a mile. Again, though, its radar was jammed by the P2V. The GCI controller told the crew to fire anyway, but nothing more was heard from Zhao Yong Shou (趙永壽) and his three crewmates in the Tu-2. They, too, had flown into rising ground at about 1,000 feet, southwest of Yexian.

The remaining Tu-2 was recalled to base. At the debriefing, the Chicoms concluded that both losses were caused by the pilots being temporarily blinded by tracer fire from the cannons located in the wing roots.

AN UNFORTUNATE MISUNDERSTANDING

After our great escape on the night of 19 November 1960, the US personnel were very pleased with the outcome. They instructed two clerks to buy a bouquet of flowers in Dongmen market and take them to my home as a gesture of gratitude. My wife opened the door and saw two Americans at the door with a bunch of flowers. They didn't speak a common language. So they tried to communicate using body language. All of a sudden, my wife burst into tears. She thought they had come to deliver bad news. The two Americans, knowing that my wife misunderstood, shook their heads saying "No! No! No!" She called Hsinchu airbase to find out what happened. On hearing that I returned safely, she stopped crying and accepted the flowers happily. - *Dai Shu Qing, from MND Oral History Book, p182-3*

By now the P2V was heading along its return course, but more danger lay ahead as the aircraft passed over Henan again. AAA guns opened up, firing at least 150 rounds. The P2V manoeuvred to escape them. But the aircraft's engines had been operated at maximum power for a long time evading the pursuers, and one of them now began to backfire. Dai retarded the throttles and requested a course direct for Taiwan from the navigator. The rest of the mission was aborted. The P2V limped back to Hsinchu and landed safely after a truly eventful mission that had lasted 10 hours and 30 minutes.[144]

News of this epic escape travelled up the command chain. Chiang Ching Kuo himself came to Hsinchu for a celebration party.

MiG-17PFs Scrambled

No further overflights were launched until the next dark phase of the moon. On the evening of 17 December 1960, Lt Col Zhao Qin was in charge as the P2V flew into northern China after takeoff from Kunsan airbase. One of the five MiG-17PFs that were scrambled from Dandong airbase managed to acquire the target as it penetrated Chinese airspace east of the Liaodong peninsula. Again, though, the P2V's repeater-jammer foiled the intercept. Then, while flying deep over Manchuria along the border with North Korea, the P2V's heating system failed. It was 30 degrees below zero outside, and the crew wrapped themselves in blankets to keep warm. As the electronics and the tape recorders began to freeze up Lt Col Zhao aborted the mission and headed southwest.

As the aircraft coasted-out from the Liaodong peninsula, still at low level, it was again pursued by Zhang Fu Zhen (張福禎) – the same MiG pilot who had come closest to intercepting the P2V four hours earlier. Zhao's crew descended even lower – from 300 to 200 feet. Zhang apparently flew into the sea during the renewed chase. The P2V returned safely to Kunsan.[145]

FREEZING IN KOREA

We ferried a P2V from Hsinchu to Kunsan one evening in December 1960. Then we were supposed to rest before flying into the mainland next evening. But because our presence at this US airbase in Korea was Top Secret, we were assigned to old barracks left over from the Korean War, instead of the BOQ. It was midwinter and extremely cold. After midnight, the kerosene stove ran out of fuel. We all woke up freezing. Also, the water system froze, including the toilets. It was not a good way to prepare for a 14-hour combat mission.

-Gao interview

Generalissimo and Madam Chiang Kai Shek, seen here in 1958. 'The Gimo' led the Kuomintang government in enforced exile on Taiwan from 1949 until his death in 1975. She was very active in support of the nationalist cause.

Despite being owned by the CIA, Civil Air Transport (CAT) was Taiwan's national airline throughout the 1950s. This C-54 was acquired in 1952 and flew secret airdrop missions into China, as well as routine passenger schedules.

Bob Rousselot, chief pilot of CAT, selected and led the aircrews that flew secretly over China during the Korean War.

CAT pilots Erik Shilling (left) and Bob Snoddy (right) with Rousselot next to one of the airline's C-46s. Snoddy was one of two CAT pilots killed in Manchuria in 1952 when their C-47 was shot down by Chinese gunners during a covert mission.

In 1952, nationalist airmen flew their first night reconnaissance missions over mainland China with U.S. support using a couple of converted B-25C bombers.

The CAF's Special Mission Group (SMG) was created at Hsinchu airbase in 1953, where this B-17 is parked, with a B-26 in the background.

These daring CAF airmen flew B-26s on low-level leaflet dropping missions from Taiwan to mainland Chinese cities.

In 1953-54, the SMG flew this C-46 over the mainland to drop agents and supplies. After that, it was used for search-and-rescue and support missions.

After the end of the Korean War, the Chinese communists began deploying MiG-15 jet fighters further south to defend against aerial incursions from Taiwan.

By 1955 mainland China had extended and improved its radar coverage, although there were still gaps in the early warning system.

One of the CAF's P4Y-2 patrol bombers was converted to the ELINT role and flown 14 times over the mainland in 1955-56.

The SMG began using B-17s supplied and converted by the U.S. for ELINT overflights in 1956. The augmented crews numbered as many as 14 on some long missions.

Bob Kleyla served two tours in Taiwan at the NACC Air Section, and also supervised U.S.-sponsored missions over mainland China from CIA headquarters.

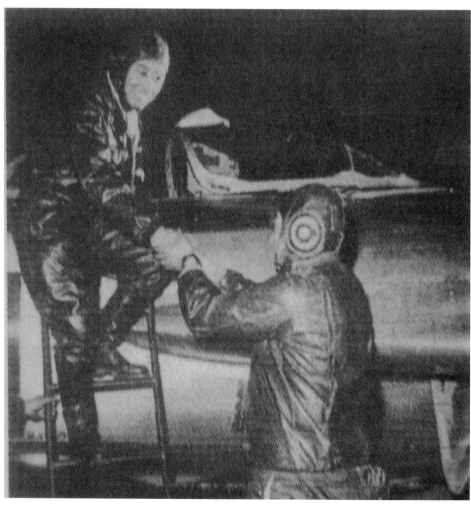

Above: PLAAF pilot Lu Min returns to Chizhou airbase and is congratulated by his groundcrew after shooting down the B-17. Lu Min was a Korean War fighter ace on the communist side, but his half-brothers were on the other side of the Chinese political divide – in Taiwan. Below: More powerful MiG-17 interceptors reached Chicom air regiments in 1955-56. One of them shot down a B-17 from the SMG on the night of 22 June 1956.

In this 1956 photo, Gen I Fu En (seated) is shown with the senior pilots of the SMG. Gen I was appointed chief of intelligence by the CAF in 1955. From left to right: Lt Col Dai Shu Qing, Maj Chen Zhung Fu, Maj Victor Wang Wei Duo, Col Yu Wen Wei, Col Zhao Qin, Col Ye Lin, and Col Zhang Wen Yi. Wang flew the B-26 that crashed on the mainland in 1957 and was lucky to survive. So were Dai and Zhao, who commanded some of the most intense P2V missions over the mainland when their crews fought off multiple attacks by Chicom interceptors and anti-aircraft guns. Ye was killed when his P2V was shot down by anti-aircraft guns over northern China in November 1961. Zhang was killed in Laos in 1961 and Chen in Vietnam three years later; both were flying under contract in support of anti-communist governments.

The U.S. Air Force provided 'cover' for the CIA's choice of the P2V Neptune as a covert aircraft. The aircraft were officially designated RB-69A and flown with military insignia. Seen here at Eglin AFB during operational trials, this is the first of the five P2V-7s (44037) that were converted by the Lockheed Skunk Works in 1955-56.

The cockpit of a P2V-7 Neptune. Unusually, the throttles on this final version of the Lockheed maritime patrol aircraft were mounted above the pilots in the cabin roof (out of picture).

Behind the pilots in the P2V-7, four officers manned positions in the cramped main cabin, facing to starboard. In the CIA's version there were two navigators and two 'Ravens' operating the ELINT equipment. Note the centre wing box behind these positions, over which crewmembers had to crawl to gain access to the rear of the aircraft.

Chiang Kai Shek took a personal interest in the aircrews that performed special missions over the mainland. This B-17 crew was summoned to meet him after a successful overflight in November 1956. Standing immediately behind 'the Gimo' is Gen 'Tiger' Wang, commander of the CAF.

In the mid-1950s, the Chicoms suffered from a shortage of adequate GCI radars, such as this P-20 (Token) system, according to Western intelligence estimates.

Anti-aircraft guns were positioned around most Chinese cities and posed a serious threat to the overflying nighttime intruders from Taiwan.

Radar-directed searchlights lit the skies over China in search of the elusive Black Bats.

Many aircrew from the special mission squadron at Hsinchu received the CAF's Hero Award. The B-26 in this photo montage (862) is flying along the Taiwan coast.

Mainland China published this photo of wreckage from the B-26 (842) that crashed in Zhejiang on the night of 5 November 1957 during a leaflet dropping mission. Three of the five crew survived and were taken prisoner. They were released by the Chicoms 10 months later. The headline reads: "Don't Sacrifice Your Life for the Americans and Chiang Kai Shek!"

An aerial view of the 34th Squadron area of Hsinchu airbase shortly after the arrival of the P2Vs and the building of new facilities to accommodate them. The squadron's other aircraft are also visible in line: four B-26s, two B-17s, and the C-46.

American money paid for the new construction at Hsinchu, including new buildings for operations, maintenance, and supply.

The ELINT equipment on the P2V-7U included the APA-69A Direction-Finder (round scope, top) and APA-74 pulse analyser (square screen, bottom).

Above: The greater sophistication of the ELINT equipment on the P2V required that new test facilities be provided at Hsinchu. Below: Three of the CAF's ECM officers pose in front of a P2V at Hsinchu. On the right is Major Phil Li Chong San, the first to train for this role, who flew on mainland missions in the P4Y, B-17, and P2V for seven years before becoming the ECM instructor for the 34th Squadron.

Although most Americans assigned to the joint project on Taiwan stayed in Taipei and commuted to Hsinchu, the CIA assigned one to be a resident manager at the airbase. Bob Macnamara (left) was the first of these from 1959, succeeded by Dick Vartagnian (right) in 1963.

是當年美國西方公司

American estate cars outside the squadron headquarters on the far side of Hsinchu airbase in the early 1960s

The CAF awarded ceremonial honors to all the senior Americans who served in the NACC Air Section. Here, section head Col Parker and his deputy, Lt Col Allen, receive their Chinese wings.

In Operation Old Bull, the CAF added COMINT receivers to C-46 transports like this one and flew them along the mainland coast in 1956-58.

Most of the Americans assigned to the NACC Air Section on Taiwan rated their tour as a highlight in their careers. The living was easy, even if the work was hard, and exotic Asia was on the doorstep.

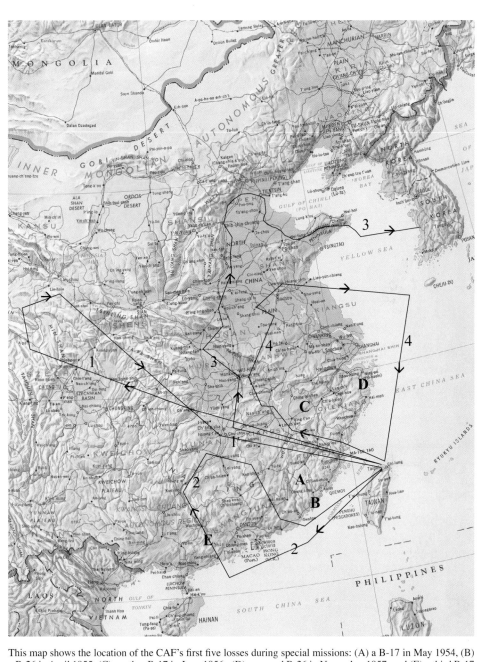

This map shows the location of the CAF's first five losses during special missions: (A) a B-17 in May 1954, (B) a B-26 in April 1955, (C) another B-17 in June 1956, (D) a second B-26 in November 1957, and (E) a third B-17 in May 1959. Also shown are some typical flight paths over mainland China: (1) the long B-17 flights to drop agents in northwest China during 1952-53, (2) an ELINT mission by a P4Y on 14 February 1956, (3) the first B-17 ELINT and leaflet dropping overflight that ventured into northern China on 2 January 1957, and (4) the B-17 mission on 21 April 1958 that survived multiple attacks, including a direct hit by a MiG-17.

Col Yin Yan Shan (center) took command of the TRG in February 1957, and led the cadre that went to the U.S. for initial training by Lockheed on the P2V. He was killed in the P2V crash in Korea in March 1960. Lt Col Zhu Zhi He (left) and Col Yu Wen Wei (right) were senior pilots who flew the B-17 and B-26.

After Chinese air defence troops failed to stop yet another long overflight of the mainland by the nationalist air force in November 1957, Premier Chou En Lai personally urged them to redouble their efforts.

The PLAAF re-organized its air defences to repel the night intruders, modifying some of the rigid operations doctrine taught by the Soviet Union and gathering the best GCI controllers together in an elite unit.

Elite Chinese MiG pilots practised night flying in order to combat the unwelcome overflights from Taiwan. By the late 1950s they were intercepting nearly every incursion.

The Black Bats began flying the newly-supplied P2Vs over the mainland in March 1958. The full crew could number a dozen or more, typically comprising the aircraft commander, two more pilots, three navigators, two ECM officers (three from 1960), a radio officer and one or two loadmasters.

In 1958, Ray Cline (left) became the head of the NACC (eg the CIA station chief in Taiwan). He quickly established a strong rapport with Chiang Ching Kuo (right), in charge of the nationalists' security and intelligence operations, who was the eldest son of President Chiang Kai Shek.

Gen I Fu En inspects B-26 air and ground crew at Hsinchu. The leaflet-dropping missions performed by these aircraft were some of the most dangerous performed by the 34th Squadron, because they flew directly over heavily-defended mainland cities.

Jiang Zhe Lun was the MiG-17 pilot and regiment commander who shot down a B-17 over southern Guangdong in May 1959.

Wreckage of the B-17 shot down by Jiang. All 14 of the Black Bats airmen on board were killed.

The CIA added the Fulton Skyhook to one of the covert P2Vs in 1959. But the system was never used to try and extract any nationalist agents from mainland China – most of them were killed or captured soon after they were inserted.

The Tu-2 was a WWII vintage light bomber that the Soviet Union supplied to China in large numbers. In 1958, the PLAAF converted three of them into radar-equipped interceptors dedicated to countering the overflights from Taiwan.

Above: USAF Col James Coates (second from right) took over as head of the NACC Air Section in 1959. Here he and his wife enjoy a joke with Chiang Ching Kuo (left) and 34th Squadron commander Col Yin. Below: Gen I's wife Lillian (right) talks with Polly Rogers, the wife of NACC communications specialist Bud Rogers at one of the parties that brought the American and Chinese sides together. The CIA used the classified cryptonym STPOLLY to denote the joint project.

Whenever aircraft assigned to the 34th Squadron flew from Taiwan to overseas locations, including ferry flights to the U.S., the CAF insignia was replaced by the Star and Bar. This B-17 (639) was photographed at Kadena airbase, Okinawa.

The Tu-4 was a Soviet copy of the American B-29 bomber from the Second World War. Ten of them were given by Stalin to Mao in 1952 and served in the PLAAF's 4th Regiment.

PLAAF commander Liu Ya Lou (right) meets with Chairman Mao (left) and Vice-Chairman Liu Shao Chi. In early 1960, the PLAAF chief agreed to the unusual conversion of the Tu-4 bomber to an interceptor configuration for use against the Black Bats.

Col Yin (centre) with P2V navigator Lt Col Liu Zhao Chun and his wife at their wedding. She was twice-widowed by airmen assigned to the CAF. Her first husband was killed in the crash of a P4Y. Liu died in the crash of the P2V in Korea, March 1960, in which Col Yin also perished.

Above: More Annual Hero Awards for the brave airmen of the CAF's 34th Squadron. Below: Chiang Ching Kuo meets airmen from the Black Bats, including Richard Gao Yin Song (right). Gao was one of the ECM officers who were assigned to the Bomber Defense Officer (BDO) position in the nose of the P2V after the defensive systems upgrade to the aircraft in 1959-60.

Beneath the damaged wing of their P2V is the crew that survived an interceptor attack over the mainland on 17 January 1961. The aircraft commander was Li De Feng (standing, furthest left), who nursed the holed machine back to Hsinchu and described it as "an interesting flight!" Sadly, no fewer than ten of this crew were killed in action during three subsequent P2V missions over China. Only Li and the loadmaster Lu Yu Sheng (standing, second from right) survived.

Col Coates admires the Chinese wings just awarded to Don Jackson, a fellow member of the NACC Air Section. Jackson was an electronics expert who helped devise and refine the defensive tactics used by the P2V crews when they were attacked over the mainland.

Two nights later Zhao and his crew were again involved in an extraordinary air combat. After takeoff from Kunsan, the P2V flew across the Gulf of Bohai and into the mainland east of Tianjin. It flew around the north side of Beijing on a zig-zag course, but the P2V was intercepted by one of the Tu-4P heavy bomber conversions. The ATIR repeater-jammer did not work against the Tu-4's modified search radar. In the dark, the 34th crew had no idea what was attacking them – they could only deploy chaff and make evasive manoeuvres. (After the flight they would report that their attacker was a Yak-25, a Soviet twinjet interceptor that was never supplied to the PRC.)

For 10 minutes over Zhangjiakou, the P2V and the Tu-4 churned through the sky in a lumbering aerial combat, as low as 100 feet. The waist gun turrets on the Tu-4 swung to fire at the P2V but missed. Because the Tu-4 had a speed advantage - a maximum of 210 knots at low level, versus 160 knots for the P2V - it could recover position after a failed attack and close for a new attempt. The P2V pilots dared not increase their own speed by turning on their auxiliary turbojets, for fear that the glow of the jet exhaust would make them an easier target. At one point the Tu-4 flew underneath the P2V.

The P2V crew managed to shake off the pursuit and continued the mission. Then a MiG made two firing passes. Again the intruder escaped and flew on towards Baotou before turning southeast to begin the long journey home to Taiwan. The P2V was still 90 minutes from coast-out when it was suddenly illuminated by searchlights. About 15 of them focused on the aircraft, and AA guns opened up. But Zhao and his crew led a charmed life that night – they weren't hit. Onwards to the coast! But as they approached it a Tu-4 re-engaged them. It chased the P2V out of the mainland, firing periodically. Fortunately for the P2V crews, the infrared sights on the Tu-4 were not very accurate. Although the bomber's 23mm cannons fired 250 rounds in total they all missed. (Eventually, the Black Bat crews would realize that the Tu-4 had no gun turret in the belly position. It could not therefore fire downwards at the P2V – only from less advantageous positions abeam the target.)

Zhao's P2V turned south and headed for Taiwan. It landed back at Hsinchu after 14 hours and 45 minutes. In addition to the aerial intercepts by MiGs and 'Yak-25s,' the postflight analysis reported that no fewer than 600 anti-aircraft gun rounds and 5,000 heavy machine guns rounds had been fired.[146]

Even Luckier Escape

During the next dark moon phase, on 17 January 1961 a crew led by Col Li De Feng had an even luckier escape. After coasting-in just south of Fuzhou they were attacked by an interceptor that fired at the aircraft. There seemed to be no serious damage, so Li elected to continue the mission. The P2V flew all the way across Jiangsi and Hunan and as far west as Chongqing, in Sichuan province, before turning southeast to cross Guizhou and Guangxi. They flew out to sea and back home. After landing, everyone at Hsinchu was shocked to see a large hole in the left flap and more damage to the engine exhaust fairing and bomb bay doors![147]

This near-disaster was pause for thought. Zhao's crew flew another mainland mission a week later, but then the overflights were halted again while the NACC considered recent events. The Chicoms seemed to have redoubled their efforts, and they were never caught unawares. Of course, they had figured out long ago that the Black Bats would only fly

A 1960 ESTIMATE OF CHICOM AIR DEFENCE CAPABILITY

The early warning system seems to have been designed to meet a threat in daylight at altitudes between 5,000 and 40,000 feet...a further limitation has been the inability of available radar equipment to maintain track continuity at lower altitudes. Morse communications has also continued to limit the traffic-handling capacity of the early-warning system... tracking range for ground controlled interception for most of the system is about 110 nautical miles. Fighters, operating under close control, are thought to be fairly effective in daylight in good weather... despite the fact that the night/all-weather capability is improving, it will remain limited until a substantial number of truly all-weather interceptor aircraft are introduced.

- Air Intelligence Review, UK, December 1960, declassified as AIR40/2726

over during the dark moon periods. But did they actually have foreknowledge of the missions?[148]

There was another awkward consideration. Could it be that the frequency of the overflights was counter to the overall U.S. interest? Every time the Black Bats penetrated the mainland the Chicoms got more practice at intercepting them. If the bombers of Strategic Air Command ever had to attack China, would their chances of survival be increased because of the intelligence obtained by STPOLLY, or decreased because of the full exercising of Chicom air defense capability that the missions prompted?

The DPD Operations Branch at CIA headquarters cabled an urgent enquiry to General Smith, the intelligence chief at SAC headquarters. He was asked if it might be a good idea to reduce the overflights to one each month.[149]

Meanwhile, a new initiative to improve the defensive tactics that the 34th crews employed was launched at Hsinchu. On one of his regular visits to the PACOM ELINT Center in Japan, Don Jackson from the NACC suggested that a more thorough correlation and analysis of all the data collected from recent P2V missions be made. The PEC couldn't spare the manpower, so Jackson got permission from Agency HQ to do this work

CIA AND NSA

The relationship between the CIA and the National Security Agency (NSA) over roles and responsibilities was, at best, strained. The NSA was created in 1952 with a charter to collect and analyze communications intelligence (COMINT). The military services concentrated on electronic intelligence (ELINT) – radar signals and the like. The CIA's ELINT activities also grew as the 1950s progressed. But in 1958, a revision to National Security Council Intelligence Directive No 6 (NSCID-6) assigned management responsibility for ELINT to the NSA. It was an unfortunate decision, that never really worked, and was contested by the leadership in the Pentagon and the CIA.

At the working level, however, secret operations personnel did what they could to co-operate. For instance, when Bob Kleyla returned to Taiwan from CIA headquarters in 1961 for a second tour with the NACC Air Section, he travelled via Japan, Korea and Okinawa to liaise with the NSA interception sites there on what they might learn from monitoring Chicom communications during a mainland penetration by the STPOLLY operation. He subsequently – and unofficially – alerted them by cable when a P2V mission from Taiwan was imminent. Without this tip-off, he feared, they would not assign enough linguists to the nightshift, to monitor all the additional Chicom communications that would be prompted by the mission.

But co-operation could only go so far. When Don Jackson requested that the new Bomber Defence Analysis Center at Hsinchu be allowed to analyze the COMINT of China's air defense reactions, alongside all the ELINT data collected by the P2Vs, the NSA refused. It insisted that the COMINT tapes continued to be sent to 'USA-33', the secret NSA facility on Okinawa, for analysis.

– C.P.

at Hsinchu. Together with one of the squadron's Chinese ECM officers, Major Phil Li, Jackson made a detailed correlation of post-mission data from the P2V's SIGINT, DF, and ECM systems, and readings from the aircraft's navigation system, radar altimeter, and airspeed instruments, together with the intercom recordings of the crew's reactions when they were under attack. The data was consolidated onto a 14-channel Ampex tape recorder and printed out on long reels of eight-inch paper. The result was a close analysis of air defence actions and reactions by the hunters (the Chicoms) and the hunted (the Bats).

This exercise proved the value of doing this post-mission analysis on a routine basis in Taiwan. Reports from two of the recent 'hot' missions were sent to the Office of ELINT at Agency HQ. The OEL liked what they saw and sent them on to Strategic Air Command (SAC).

In 1961, the NACC and the CAF agreed to build a permanent 'Bomber Defence Analysis Center' at Hsinchu. The new facility was commissioned in 1962. The lessons learned from this analysis helped in maintenance and operation of the electronics equipment; in debriefing the P2V crews on defensive tactics for future missions; and in mission planning by SAC, as it devised penetration routes and tactics for nuclear bombers assigned to targets in the PRC.[150]

Suspicion
The suspicion held by the staffers in DPD, that the P2V overflights were actually encouraging the development of greater capability in the Chicom air defences, was well founded. Since September 1960, the air arm of the People's Liberation Navy (the PLAN) had been developing yet another scheme to stop the overflights.

The Chicom interceptor pilots found it very difficult to see the black intruders against the dark night sky, even when GCI vectored them accurately towards their target. Moreover, the mission planners of the NACC tried to ensure that they never routed an overflight directly over a Chinese city, where the aircraft might be silhouetted from above by the lights on the ground. So the naval aviators of the PLAN realized that they should provide their own illumination. A twinjet Il-28 bomber would drop flares just in front and above the enemy aircraft. Then fighter aircraft could see the P2V and attack. The PLAN named their new tactic 'Magic Cannon.' After intensive training, the PLAN formed an Illumination Attack Group within the 4th Division in January 1961.

But because there were no overflights from Taiwan in the following three months, the new Group's first chance did not come until May, when P2V missions over the mainland resumed. The NACC requested no fewer than seven overflights for this month. Two of them were supposed to be short duration penetrations that would be flown concurrently outside the dark moon period, one entering the mainland over Guangdong and one entering much further north. If the air defenses reacted as strongly as usual, against both flights, it would suggest that the Chicoms were indeed being forewarned about the flights.[151]

That was the theory, anyway. In the event, only four missions were approved by headquarters. The concurrent missions were flown on the night of 20 May. Before then, however, the very first penetration since the standdown flew directly into the area where the Illumination Attack Group was waiting.

This flight was commanded by Lt Col Dai Shu Qing and took off from Hsinchu during the evening of 9 May. The P2V made a long overwater journey north as dusk turned into night before entering Shandong province west of Qingdao just after 2000. But the P2V had already been detected, and at the very same time the Naval Air Arm scrambled an Il-28 and a MiG-15UTI two-seat fighter. As the P2V headed north across the Shandong peninsula towards the Gulf of Bohai, Chicom GCI positioned the Il-28 and the MiG-15 for a 'Magic Cannon' attack. Just before the P2V coasted-out the Il-28 released its load of six 165lb flare bombs. Nineteen seconds later the MiG pilots reported visual contact with the P2V about a mile to their right. They lost the target in the turn. By the time they were flying straight and level again the P2V had flown out of the illuminated area.

Dai's crew continued their mission, turning left to cross the mouth of the Yellow River and left again near Tianjin to fly into southern Hebei province. More attempts to intercept them were made, as the P2V turned south and flew a zig-zag course all the way to Nanjing. The ECM officers onboard logged a number of lock-ons from air intercept radars but no shots were fired. The P2V eventually left the mainland over Jiangsu and headed home. It landed safely at Hsinchu after 15 hours 35 minutes - this was one of the longest-ever P2V missions.[152]

On the mainland, the PLAN evaluated their failure to intercept the illuminated target. They concluded that a greater number of photoflash bombs were needed. The six dropped by the Il-28 had lit up a radius of only about two miles. Discouraged, the PLAN disbanded the 'Magic Cannon' unit. But in July 1961 the PLAAF adopted the idea by forming its own illumination-interception group in the Beijing Military Area, which also used Il-28s and MiG-17s. It flew more than 1,000 training sorties over the next two years trying to perfect the technique.[153]

Delicate Balance
The U.S. was still trying to maintain a delicate balance between encouraging and restraining Chiang Kai-shek's 'Return to the Mainland' ambitions. Just before leaving office in January 1961, President Eisenhower agreed to supply a C-130B transport to Taiwan. But the new Kennedy administration reversed the decision; the State Department feared that the aircraft would facilitate the Gimo's paramilitary action plans. A compromise was reached, whereby the U.S. would supply a much older C-54 transport for operation by the 34th Squadron. It could be used to airdrop teams numbering up to 20 for intelligence-gathering purposes – as long as the missions were jointly planned. A CIA estimate in July 1961 noted that the ROC was concealing preparations for mainland raids from U.S. eyes.[154]

The CAF already flew a C-54 as the Gimo's personal air transport. The 34th squadron pilots trained on this aircraft until the CIA transferred one of its specially-adapted C-54G models. It arrived in Taiwan on 28 August 1961. Chiang Ching-kuo and Ray Cline both attended the delivery ceremony. The C-54 offered much more capacity for airdropping agents and supplies than the P2V. It was also equipped with the ATIR jammer, chaff dispensers, and a wideband ELINT system. But nine more months would pass before the newly-delivered C-54 flew its first airdrop mission into mainland China.[155]

On 15 June 1961, the 34th Squadron flew a mission to North Vietnam for the first time. Col Guo Tong De (郭統德) and his crew took off from Hsinchu in a P2V and dropped leaflets in the west part of Guangdong province and the southern part of Kwangsi province. Then they flew along China's border with North Vietnam before turning south, then east, to cross Hanoi and Haiphong. There they dropped another 500 lbs of leaflets before heading

UNDER ATTACK FROM THE TU-4

I had a lot of near-death experiences. Such as the time I was on Zhu Zhen's crew, and we were on our way out over the Shandong peninsula, heading for a landing in Kunsan. The ECM officer identified a Tu-4 on his equipment, coming to attack us. That plane flew to our starboard side and began shooting. I saw the tracer fire flying over our airplane. We were only about 200 feet above the water. The wind was whipping up some huge waves. If we made a sharp turn, the wing could easily hit the water. But what were we to do? The Tu-4 could fly faster than us! So I told the pilot to make a 180-degree turn. We escaped, but after 20 minutes, the Tu-4 appeared again and resumed firing at us. I felt like I was in a movie scene. Even today, I still talk about this drama, when I meet Zhu Zhen. - *Lt Col Zou Li Xu, P2V navigator, from Black Bat Squadron Oral History, p299-300*

When the Tu-4 intercepted us, it was much worse than the MiGs. The attacks lasted for much longer, and we didn't know exactly when to drop chaff or take evasive action. The only electronic indication we got on whether they were getting close, was the strength of their search radar's signal.

I had an opportunity to hear the intercom tape recording of Lt Col Ye's crew, when they were attacked by the Tu-4 over Shandong. You could tell the extreme stress that they endured. They were under repeated attack all the way into the Gulf of Bohai. To this day, I think that they should not have been sent on another mission into Manchuria so quickly. Those in charge should have considered the crew's psychological condition and ordered a postponement – or sent another crew to Korea to fly the mission.

- *Richard Gao email. (Lt Col Ye and his crew escaped the Tu-4 attacks on 4 December 1961. Two nights later, they were shot down by AAA gunfire over the Liaodong Peninsula).*

back to Taiwan along the China coast. The flight recorded signals from 15 radar sites, as North Vietnam had begun to build an air defence system.[156]

Ground-to-Air Fire

From early 1960 until October 1961, the PRC's air defences detected 44 of the 46 incursions by the P2Vs. No fewer than 322 interception sorties were launched, but without success. The PLAAF hierarchy held lots of meetings to review deployments and enhance training. Perhaps there was a better chance of knocking down the intruders with ground-to-air fire in a concerted effort. The PRC now had over 3,100 anti-aircraft guns in service.[157]

In September 1961 the PLAAF adjusted the deployment of mobile anti-aircraft weapons to concentrate them in the areas which were most frequently overflown. Of these, the Liaodong peninsula, which led to the city of Dalian, seemed a good choice. P2V missions out of Kunsan airbase in South Korea habitually passed over here, en route to or from northern China.

Sure enough, two months later the NACC planned new missions to northern China. On 4 November, Lt Col Ye Lin and his crew took off from Hsinchu and flew north along the mainland coast before flying into Jiangsi, Shandong, and Hebei provinces, and directly over Beijing. They came very close to being shot down by one of the Tu-4 bombers-turned-interceptors. The P2V was intercepted over Shandong as it headed out of the mainland, and subject to repeated attacks by the Tu-4 until it reached international waters. Cannon fire from the Tu-4 hit the trailing edge of the P2V's left wing. The P2V managed to escape into the Gulf of Bohai and land at Kunsan.[158]

Ye and his crew were the first to confirm that the large aircraft that had been stalking the Black Bats' overflights for more than a year was a Tu-4. They were seriously spooked by their ordeal. The same crew were due to fly another mainland mission out of the Korean base. The flak damage was repaired by USAF airmen. If the NACC Air Section and the 34th

THAT CREW SHOULD NEVER HAVE BEEN SENT BACK INTO CHINA!

Considering the risks and the state of Col Ye's crew, the fatal mission in November 1969 should never have been flown – period! At the time, I wasn't a participant in mission planning. But after considering this in retrospect a few years later, I was appalled at the lack of judgement of those in charge at the time. I still feel anger that we and the CAF made this happen, and hurt that they were killed.

- *American member of the NACC based in Taiwan, early 1960s, email forwarded to author*

Squadron leadership had any doubts over whether to proceed, they must have suppressed them. Two nights later Ye and his crew were duly rostered to fly another penetration, this time into Manchuria, overflying Shenyang, Changchun, and Harbin.

But they flew into a carefully planned trap. Air defence headquarters at Dalian was wise to the P2V flight half an hour after it took off from Kunsan at 1705. At 1818, the P2V was detected by early warning radar as it flew across the Yellow Sea, range 125 miles, altitude 2,000 feet.

The gun units were alerted. The Chicoms had placed three groups of radar-controlled anti-aircraft guns and searchlights on the Liaodong peninsula in an area that was 20 miles long and up to four miles deep. Between them, the groups deployed 22 companies of 37mm guns; eight of 85mm guns; and three radar units. When the target was 25 miles away the radar unit at the centre of the deployment was ordered to switch from Standby to On.

The P2V's ELINT system detected the radar, and it turned right to avoid the danger. But this only took Ye and his crew towards the left flank of the deployment, where more guns and searchlights were waiting. Here, the radar operators deliberately kept their systems in standby mode until the last possible moment. When the target was only 10 miles away the radars at three searchlight sights were turned on. All three locked on to the P2V and switched on their lights. At the same moment the nearby gun control radar also acquired the target. A barrage of lead from eight separate gun sites peppered the sky. The P2V dived right in a desperate attempt to escape, but it was too late. The aircraft was shot down at 1855, just 30 seconds after the searchlights were switched on. None of the crew survived.[159]

The PLAAF chief of staff rushed to the Liaodong peninsula to congratulate the anti-aircraft troops. He ordered the bodies of the 13 nationalist airmen to be buried. On Taiwan, their families were told that they were 'missing in action.' Within days, however, the CAF commander visited Hsinchu to see them – and arrange the payment of pensions.

All aircrew that were lost in this way received a posthumous one-rank promotion, which increased the compensation payable to relatives. It was only a small consolation. Many aircrew from the 34th Squadron lived in CAF Village Number Three in Hsinchu. So many had now been killed in action that this place became known as 'Widow's Alley.'

Chapter Six

1962-1963

Despite the first loss of a P2V to Chicom air defences, a new U.S. intelligence estimate of China's air defence issued two months later expressed confidence that the country could not counter an attack by multiple intruders – such as that likely to be mounted by Strategic Air Command bombers if war ever erupted. "Chinese radars afford limited protection against electronic countermeasures," it added.

However, the document did note that the Chinese early warning radar system had grown over the past six years from about 200 to 330 sites. The majority of the radars were located in the five air defense districts along the coast. But there were not enough height-finding radars to provide full GCI control to the PLAAF's interceptors, the estimate continued.[160]

Strangely, a British estimate from this time gave a much larger total of early warning radars – 700 of them. But nearly half were obsolete versions of the Western SCR-270 design from the Second World War that the Chinese had modified. The British reckoned that the V-beam, centimetric P-20 (Token) system was mainly used for GCI, along with the P-30 (Big Mesh). The British agreed that communications in the Chinese air defence systems were inadequate. They were still using Morse code over HF radio links between radars and command centres, and simple, four-channel VHF sets in the fighter interceptors, this estimate noted.[161]

Both the U.S. and British estimates noted the increasing number of Soviet radars that had been introduced. But they did not analyse the consequences for the Chinese air defence system of the Sino-Soviet split. Western intelligence still did not comprehend the extent of the fissure between the two great communist powers. In fact, the PRC had now resolved to develop copies of advanced defence equipment supplied from the USSR before the almost-complete withdrawal of Soviet technical assistance in 1960 – such as the SA-2 surface-to-air missile and the MiG-19 fighter. Or they were developing their own systems – such as the air defence radar nicknamed Cross Slot by Western intelligence.

The hundreds of hours of SIGINT and ECM data that had been collected by the Black Bats would have contributed to the estimates. But this was still only a small part of the big picture on China that intelligence analysts sought. New developments in space promised much more. By early 1962 the Corona satellite system developed by the CIA was returning good overhead photography of the mainland. And for higher resolution photography, a major new joint program between the CIA and the ROC promised a windfall. On 13 January 1962, a U-2 flown by a pilot from the CAF's 35th Squadron took off from Taoyuan airbase, climbed to 70,000 feet, and headed deep into the Chinese interior. It was the start

P2V PILOT LI BANG XUN (李邦訓) REMEMBERS

The mainland pilots knew that we weren't armed, so they turned on their landing lights to try and locate us. But because they were not experienced in night-flying, they could not find us, even when we were very close to them. But I could see them very clearly. I thought, if I had a pistol, I could shoot them! - *Black Bat Squadron Oral History, p110-1*

We were often attacked several times during a mission. The bullets would fly just over the top of us – 'almost shaving our head' as one crewmember said. We couldn't actually hear the cannon fire at the time. But after we landed, we would listen to the tapes of the enemy pilots that we had recorded. Then we could certainly hear gunfire! We could have been shot down several times over. It depended whether our plane was hit in a vital area. - *Black Bat Squadron Oral History, p112-3*

Sometimes I was asked – 'Are you afraid?' – especially by new crewmembers when they joined the squadron. 'Of course I'm afraid,' I told them, 'but you must control your fear during a mission.' I used to wonder, why did our squadron mates die? I suppose it was because they panicked under attack, and could not make an evasive maneuvre in the split-seconds before the cannon fire hit them. You had to control the fear, stay calm, and do what was necessary to survive. - *Black Bat Squadron Oral History, p112-3*

After we took off and headed for the mainland, we usually talked quite a lot on the intercom. But I felt very uneasy that day. I asked the crew to be silent – but that made for a scary atmosphere. As soon as we entered China, searchlights lit up ahead of us. I changed direction. More searchlights lit up. I changed direction again. The lights nearly blinded us. Then the flak started – ahead of us. The sky was on fire, and I was sure we could not escape. Suddenly, I felt the plane dive. Fortunately, I recovered and pulled it up. But there was nowhere to go! I wrestled with the yoke, and dived again. Our training in how to fly at low level paid off – it was the only way to save our lives. After landing back home, I went straight to the church, and knocked on the door of an American missionary. I told him that I wanted to be baptised. He said: "Are you crazy? What happened to you?" I said: "I can't tell you what happened. I should be dead. But I am standing here, talking to you. I feel that God protected me." - *Black Bat Squadron Oral History, p114-5*

One time we were hit over the mainland, and a fuel leak developed. I was worried about the engine catching fire, so I couldn't increase speed. We reported the situation to the command post, and they ordered us to divert to (Korea). It was midnight, and snowing. The runway was covered in ice. With the fuel running out, we had to land downwind. I requested the emergency services to be ready. We landed successfully, but there was no fuel left in the tank. Another 30 seconds, and we would not have made it. - *Black Bat Squadron Oral History, p114-5*

P2V NAVIGATOR ZOU LI XU REMEMBERS

We flew a mission to northeast China. I had never been there before. Towards the end of the mission, we heard Russian pilots talking on the radio. I was in the 'nosegator' position, and I saw a MiG pass beneath us – though we were only at 1,000 feet. So we accelerated. Luckily, we shook off that Russian MiG. But the weather was bad, and the LORAN signal was too weak to help us navigate accurately. Suddenly, I saw something very black ahead – it was high ground looming through the cloud. I screamed: "Pull up!"

Everything loose in the airplane was dislodged as we climbed steeply. We almost stalled.

As we left the mainland, we flew close to a small island. It was supposed to be on our right, but it was to our left instead, and we flew within range of their anti-aircraft guns. They fired at us, and I thought that we would all die. But the whole crew worked together to evade them, and we came home safely. - *Black Bat Squadron Oral History, p303-4, supplemented by interview with author*

of Project Tackle. During the next six-and-a half years the Black Cat squadron would make 101 more U-2 overflights of the mainland.

Long Overwater Flight

On the night of 8 January 1962, 34th squadron commander Col Guo Tong De and a crew of 12 took off for a long overwater flight that was intended to collect ELINT and also to drop bundles of water-resistant propaganda leaflets that would wash up along the mainland coast. But contact was lost with the P2V while it was over Korea Bay. It was presumed to have crashed into the sea.[162]

The loss came just two months after the shootdown of Lt Col Ye and his crew over the Liaodong Peninsula. Three of the Agency's original five P2V conversions had now been destroyed. The overflights had to be suspended again, until new crews were trained and replacement aircraft were equipped with the unique ELINT and ECM equipment.

In the meantime, the Black Bats flew only peripheral ELINT missions along the mainland coast using the C-54 that had been delivered in August 1961. With the exception of the BDO, Gao Yin Song, the crew of this aircraft were new to the squadron. The aircraft commander was Lt Col Lu De Qi, a veteran of the Fox Hunt missions in 1955-56! He temporarily assumed command of the 34th Squadron following Col Guo's death.

The bigger picture on China's overall condition was clouded by communist secrecy. However, an important classified document captured from the PLA in Tibet by some of the agents airdropped there by the CIA revealed sharp cutbacks in the defence budget. The document made clear how the Chinese military had not been immune from the low morale and severe food shortages that followed the failure of the Great Leap Forward.[163]

"Back to the Mainland"

For the ageing Chiang Kai-shek this was a new encouragement to go 'Back to the Mainland.' In early 1962 he made a particularly aggressive speech to mark the Chinese New Year. The ROC stepped up pressure on the U.S. to support paramilitary action. Chiang Ching-kuo told U.S. officials that the previous teams of infiltrated agents had been too small. He called for airdrops of at least 200 men, to be delivered by four C-130 transports equipped with ECM, presumably to be operated by the 34th Squadron. Again the U.S. prevaricated – deliberately. It saw no prospect of the ROC fostering a serious rebellion against communist rule, but it didn't want a showdown with the Gimo. The joint intelligence-gathering programs –

A STATE DEPT VIEW OF 'BACK TO THE MAINLAND!'

The GRC (ROC) itself claims less than 300 agents on the mainland. Few report regularly and most are probably not under systematic GRC control. No organized GRC underground exists. Since 1951, the GRC has airdropped small agent teams into the mainland. With the exception of one team in Tibet, none has survived over three months...There is no evidence that the GRC has been able to increase its sabotage, intelligence or underground activities in the last two years.

While there is significant feeling against the (communist) regime...indications are that only a few people want the Kuomintang to return. - *report by Roger Hilsman, Director of Intelligence and Research, 30 March 1962*

Project Goshawk, the U-2s of Project Tackle, and the ground SIGINT stations - were too important for that.[164]

Ray Cline left Taipei for Washington in early 1962, and was replaced as 'Director of the NACC' (eg CIA station chief) by Bill Nelson. Cline was promoted to be the CIA's Deputy Director for Intelligence. He was Taiwan's great advocate within the U.S. government. At his suggestion, the U.S. agreed to supply two C-123 tactical transports equipped with ECM for protection against interception. Not enough for a big paramilitary operation, but sufficient to keep the nationalists happy.

The creation of a "joint planning group" was another part of this strategy to keep the Gimo under control. Officials from the NACC and the ROC MND met formally to consider the feasibility of larger airdrops and other clandestine operations against the mainland. It was known as The 420 Committee after the date of its first meeting – 20 April 1962. Three months later the U.S. agreed to increase the number of C-123s that it would supply from two to five. In September 1962, five experienced crews from the CAF's transport squadrons were sent to Pope AFB in the U.S. to learn to fly the new aircraft. Meanwhile, the U.S. side finally agreed to mount some airdrop missions with the 34th Squadron's C-54G.

As economic refugees poured into Hong Kong, it was obvious that Guangdong was the most restive of the mainland provinces. The IBMND had already stepped up attempts to infiltrate agents along the Guangdong coast by sea. On the night of 5 June 1962 the C-54

SHALL WE USE THE B-26 AGAIN?

Sometime in 1962, the NACC considered sending the B-26 back over the mainland. Perhaps the ROC was pressing for more agents to be airdropped. Whatever the reason, a mission was planned over Southern China. An assessment of the aircraft's survivability was sought from the intelligence experts in CIA headquarters. Their response serves to illustrate the calculations that applied to all mission planning for the low-level overflights by the Black Bats at this time:

Based on past [STPOLLY] missions in this general area of China it can be assumed that the aircraft will be under constant radar surveillance from approximately 40-50 miles prior to Coast in Point to 40-50 miles after Coast out point...past [STPOLLY] missions show that the Chicom do have the ability to track low-altitude penetration with accuracy and continuity...There is one airfield within range of

the mission aircraft that has A.I. equipped fighters (Xingning 2408N-11546E)...it is not anticipated that the fighters [from Xingning] will be launched... the usual Chicom tactic is to hold their fighters until the hostile has to penetrate the AAA "belt" (an area approximately 25-50 miles inland from the coast)... although the mission aircraft route is over no known AAA units, this is the area where least is known concerning location...Because the mission aircraft will have no warning or jamming equipment on board for AAA this produces an additional threat...Searchlights are normally co-located with AAA units. The mission aircraft passes very near to a S/L unit (2257N-11545E) discovered on an [STPOLLY] mission in 1960. If the mission is flown, it is recommended that the Turning Points (TP) be altered to avoid this area.

In view of the above it is estimated that the mission aircraft will have a better than 50% chance of surviving.

AN ELINT ANALYST AT THE PEC REMEMBERS

We had great difficulty understanding the taped comments of the BDO on the P2V, when things got hot during an interception. As the MiGs closed on his tail, the BDO would get real excited and go into his native tongue. We really needed to know what he was saying, to help in our analysis. So I convinced PACOM to establish a Chinese language billet. Many months later, our Chinese language specialist arrived, Tech Sergeant Ho. After he had settled in – with his wife, mother-in-law, and eight children – I brought him into the analysis booth and put a headset on him. He listened for about five minutes, then we stopped the tape and asked the Sergeant what the P2V crew had said. He responded: "I don't know, they talk some kind of technical shit!" Sgt Ho was transferred to our supply unit for the next three years. - *email passed to author from a USAF analyst at the PACOM ELINT Center (PEC), Japan.*

departed Taiwan and flew south along the mainland coast. It stayed well out to sea at low level until passing Guangzhou. Then it turned toward the hills of Yangjiang, aiming to drop a cargo of more than 10,000 lbs of leaflets and food.

The smart white paint scheme of the C-54G was hidden by a temporary coat of water-soluble grey paint, and it was fitted with defensive ECM to help it survive over the mainland. The radio operator monitored Chicom GCI frequencies and warned of attempted interceptions. But the old, four-engine transport was vulnerable. And on this night it was nearly shot down by a MiG-17PF soon after coasting-in. The BDO (Richard Gao) deployed chaff and instructed the pilot to take evasive action, but unlike the P2V, which had spoilers above the wing, the turning radius of the C-54 was very slow. The crew members heard the sound of the MiG's gunfire and the tracers lit up the cabin. Fortunately they were not hit. Plane Captain Wang Ri Yi (王日益) completed his turn and headed out to sea.[165]

New Taiwan Straits Crisis

Within days of this incident the PLA quickly moved an estimated seven army divisions into the coastal provinces opposite Taiwan. Was this a defensive move to deter the ROC from more paramilitary action against the mainland? Or were the Chicoms preparing to invade the offshore islands, perhaps as a diversion from the country's serious domestic problems? U.S. intelligence analysts were unsure.[166]

The U-2s from Taoyuan played an important role in resolving this new Taiwan Straits crisis. Five U-2 missions were flown by the 35th Squadron over the coastal provinces. The CAF's low-level tactical reconnaissance jets were also in action. The 4th Squadron was now equipped with supersonic RF-101s. The photography confirmed that the Chicom deployments were defensive. The Chinese leadership felt vulnerable, and even admitted publicly to disaffection caused by 'economic difficulties.'[167]

The C-54 made another long trip down the mainland coast on 2 August to drop leaflets, radios, rations, and small arms on Hainan Island. It was the Gimo's fond hope that rebellion could be fostered here first. On 5 November the C-54 returned to Guangdong province with a similar load. Planning for this mission may have benefited from a U-2 overflight of Guangdong province by the 35th Squadron on 6 September 1962, which was specifically tasked to collect imagery of seven potential drop zones. The ROC believed that it would be possible to foment rebellion by PLA garrisons in Guangdong if five paramilitary teams could be dropped into the area.[168]

SUPERSTITION IN THE DEPENDENTS HOUSING

We had our own home in the town, and I was busy with our two small children, so I had less time to worry when my husband was away. But most of the families lived in dependent housing around Hsinchu. Many Chinese are superstitious, so if the officer living at house number 5 was killed, and his family moved out, it would be renumbered as 4-1. In the No 1 village, there were many aircrew lost from two P2Vs and a C-123 that went down. So they assigned those quarters to ground crew instead. - *Li Zhen Hua (李振華), wife of Li Chong Shan, ECM officer, 34th Squadron*

The C-54 flew again to Guangdong on the night of 3 December 1962 to insert another four agents and equipment to one of the IBMND's agent groups that had been inserted earlier by sea. As they approached the drop zone in the Yangjiang hills, pilot Lu De Qi was wondering why there was no indication that Chicom interceptors had been launched against them. Lu identified the T-shape sign laid out on the ground and began the countdown for the airdrop. But just as he gave the signal to jump groundfire erupted from below. Lu yelled "don't jump!," but the agents had already left the aircraft.

It was yet another trap. Searchlights lit up and raked the sky. Lu racked the aircraft into a right turn, so steep that his headphones fell off. The C-54 was hit by anti-aircraft flak in the nose and belly. But the damage was light, and the crew were able to fly out to sea and back to Taiwan. But the four agents were captured.[169]

On 29 December, the PRC announced that during the previous three months they had wiped out "172 Chiang Kai Shek agents" – the total strength of nine teams that had infiltrated along the Fujian and Guangdong coast. Eight of the teams had landed by sea, and one had been air-dropped – presumably during the C-54 flight on 3 December. Unusually, the ROC admitted the losses. But it claimed that other teams had been successfully inserted and were continuing to operate.[170]

C-123s Arrive

The five C-123s arrived on Taiwan in February 1963 and formed B Flight of the 34th Squadron (the P2Vs became A Flight). By this time, however, even the CIA was less inclined to support covert action against the mainland. NACC director Bill Nelson judged that, except for the Gimo, Taiwan's enthusiasm for retaking the mainland by force was waning.[171]

The 34th Squadron's C-54 made its eighth and last overflight of Chinese territory on 22 June 1963. Eight agents were airdropped onto Hainan Island.

But their fate was sealed when they couldn't locate the food rations and radio transmitter package that was dropped with them. They had been told to link up with local guerrilla fighters. Instead, they encountered only PLA troops and militias looking for them.

LU DE QI REMEMBERS

My wife never asked what I was doing. Even when there were nights when I didn'ty come home. She knew it was Top Secret.

When I joined the 34th Squadron, I didn't ask her permission. I wanted the assignment because I knew that most of the pilots would subsequently get the opportunity to fly for China Airlines. As it turned out, I didn't get that chance. - *Lu De Qi, in Black Bats Oral History, p82. Lu became the longest-serving commander of The Black Bats, 1964-69. Later, he commanded the Army Aviation Battalion on Taiwan. He retired as a Major General in 1979.*

TRAINING THE AGENTS TO BE AIRDROPPED

When the ROC pressed for the agent drops over the mainland to be stepped up in 1962-63, the US reluctantly agreed. American instructors from the NACC devised a 10-week training program for the agents, who were selected by Taiwan's National Security Bureau (NSB). They were equipped with all the latest gear, including firearms, hand-held radios and a new portable homing beacon. When they were expecting a resupply by air, the group could set up this beacon at the appropriate location. This avoided the need for them to display tell-tale signs or lights to the aircrew flying overhead.

The NSB held a farewell dinner for the group of eight agents that were dropped from the BlackBats C-54 over Hainan Island in June 1963. KMT leaders gave them a pep talk. Their instructions were to try and contact some agents who had previously been sent to the island. If they failed, they should persuade the local people to set up a guerrilla base. Then they should ambush the local militia, and try to collect military intelligence.

This seems like a confused and contradictory set of instructions. The account comes from the communist side – a book published in Jilin in 1968 entitled "In a Special Battle". The account goes on to describe how the group were all rounded up within a few days: "While the National Security Bureau was still dreaming of success, the agents were captured and sent to Guanghzhou."

– C.P.

The group argued amongst themselves over whether to surrender. They split up, but were captured within four days in five different locations. After this latest failure the C-54 flew only coastal patrols to collect SIGINT. These ended the following year.[172]

The newly-supplied C-123s never did fly over the Chinese mainland. Instead, the U.S. and the ROC signed an agreement in March 1963 to use them in Vietnam. There, they replaced an operation codenamed the South Star Team, which Taiwan had established in Saigon in the early months of 1962 in cooperation with the CIA and the government of South Vietnam. This used a C-54 (DC-4) belonging to China Airlines. But no ordinary passengers boarded this plane. The South Star Team trained South Vietnamese paratroopers and airdropped agents into North Vietnam. In effect, the CIA subcontracted its covert air support operations in Vietnam – codenamed Project Haylift - to Taiwan. In July 1963, the China Airlines C-54 was replaced by the C-123s of the 34th Squadron (see Chapter 8).[173]

Another Reorganisation

At Agency HQ there was another reorganisation in 1962, and a new head of technical intelligence-gathering. Herb Scoville led the new Deputy Directorate for Research (DDR) that was created to take over the operation of the CIA's fast-expanding technical collection programs – including the Corona satellite and the new A-12 Blackbird spy plane. The DPD had been running those programs. DPD was moved from the DDP to become part of the new DDR, and was renamed the Office of Special Activities (OSA). But the DDP wanted to retain control of the covert aircraft operations, including the P2Vs. Scoville wanted their control transferred to the DDR because, he noted, "ELINT flights were outnumbering the agent drop flights by 30 to 1." He further believed that the Agency-owned P2Vs were far too valuable as a SIGINT-gathering platform to be risked on agent dropping operations. In July 1962 he noted that they had cost $1.7 million each to build, plus another $1.3 million to add the electronic equipment, which made "these aircraft the most sophisticated of their kind in being." Currently only two of them were equipped for the ELINT mission. One was deployed on Taiwan, and the other was being overhauled in the U.S. They were the Agency's only SIGINT aircraft.

Then there was the investment in training, Scoville continued. Only two crews were on hand, he noted, and it took a year to train the SIGINT operators. "A loss of a P2V aircraft at this time would deny us the SIGINT input for six to eight months," Scoville continued.[174]

CIA Executive Director Lyman Kirkpatrick proposed a compromise. The DDP could retain control of the P2Vs only until the new agent dropping aircraft (eg the C-123s) were delivered to Taiwan.[175]

In fact, the DDP succeeded in retaining permanent control of all the CIA air assets except for the U-2 and the A-12. An Air Section was formed within the DDP's Special Operations Division (SOD). It managed an expanding fleet of aircraft and helicopters employed on covert and not-so-covert operations in southeast Asia, where CIA proprietary company Air America became one of the world's biggest 'airlines' by size of fleet. And the DDP's FE Division retained operational control of the P2Vs on Taiwan.

To augment the dwindling fleet of P2Vs, the Agency acquired and modified one of the last Neptunes to roll off of Lockheed's production line (150283) in September 1962. Jim Winn, a U.S. Navy pilot now assigned to the NACC, collected the new bird from Okinawa and flew it to Taiwan.

At about the same time the Agency switched from USAF to U.S. Navy 'cover' to hide the comings and goings of the P2Vs. When the airplanes needed to be ferried to the U.S. for overhaul or modification the CAF markings were removed and U.S. Navy markings were applied. The usual route was via Okinawa to Wake Island, Barbers Point, and Alameda to Burbank. An all-American crew from the NACC would fly these trips, which totalled 38 hours flying in each direction. The crew were instructed to quote 'Project Cherry' whenever the naval air stations en route queried their request for an armed guard for the aircraft. That always produced the required result![176]

On 9 September 1962 Chinese air defences shot down one of the nationalist-flown U-2s near Nanchang with an SA-2 missile that they had cleverly repositioned under its predicted flight path. The high altitude flights were suspended for three months. They resumed because of the high priority that U.S. intelligence attached to getting tell-tale photography of the known and suspected nuclear weapons facilities in the PRC. The analysts had few clues about China's progress towards the A-bomb.

JIM WINN REMEMBERS

I don't know why I was selected for the project on Taiwan, except that I had lots of experience on the P2V. I had flown the Neptune in the regular Navy for three years, and then as a reservist, so I had more than 2,000 hours. I was back in the regular Navy, as an instructor pilot flying S-2s, when the assignment came up. I reported to the Agency in Washington for a briefing in early 1962. My orders showed I was going to "HQ Support Activity" in Taipei, where I would be met by "my sponsor."

The Air Section was a windowless cave within the NACC building. I was addressed as a naval officer in that building, but whenever we went to Hsinchu, we wore civilian clothes and had to adopt a pseudonym. The only time we ever wore our uniforms on Taiwan was on '10-10" day.

My task was to provide basic flying training to the Chinese crews. But I wanted a taste of how they were flying over the mainland at such low altitude. So I went on one of their overland training missions across southern Taiwan, with the 'nosegator' calling out the Minimum Safe Altitude. - *interview*

Air Sampling Mission

To help them, the 34ᵗʰ Squadron gained a new air sampling mission in October 1962. Large pods containing filter papers were added beneath each wing of the P2V, outboard of the jet engines. Airscoops were added to the lower rear fuselage leading to bottles stowed inside for the collection of gas. A radiation detector was added so that the crew would be alerted to operate these collection systems if they flew through nuclear radiation.

A surprising amount could be learnt about nuclear weapons from analysing these filter papers and gas bottles, which were usually exposed during flights at medium and high altitude. However, it is not clear how much contribution could be made by low-level flights from Taiwan, especially since China had not yet tested a nuclear device. The P2Vs may have made a marginal contribution to the measurement of nuclear weapons development signatures, such as krypton-85, which is emitted from nuclear reactors. There was certainly an operational downside to the pods; they reduced the P2V's speed, making it more vulnerable to interception.[177]

The sampling pods may have first been flown over the mainland during a long P2V excursion across Jiangsu, Anhui, Hubei, Hunan, and Guangdong provinces on the night of 29 November. But the suspected Chinese nuclear sites were far to the northwest of here.

In Washington, the Special Group of the National Security Council renewed its standing approval for the STPOLLY operation on 1 November 1962. Overflights of the mainland could still be scheduled at a rate of two or three during each dark moon phase.[178]

Also, on 1 November Lt Col Sun Yi Chen (孫以晨) arrived at Hsinchu to become the new 34ᵗʰ Squadron commander. He was nicknamed 'Blackie' by the Americans, who rated him highly. Sun motivated the squadron to continue flying over the mainland, despite the obvious combat fatigue. Morale was low at the time. One night at Kunsan airbase, while awaiting a mission, the loadmaster from one aircrew was driven mad by the tension. He rushed out of the barracks and into the snow, crying and completely naked.[179]

The CAF awarded points for each combat mission, which the aircrew could wear as a bar on their sleeve. There was one bar for every 100 points. By now, though, some veterans of the squadron had amassed nearly 2,000 combat points, and the bars extended all the way up their sleeve! The CAF changed the system by introducing thicker bars to represent 500 and 1,000 combat points.[180]

ECM Systems Upgraded

The technical wizards at Agency HQ upgraded the ECM systems on the P2Vs. To counter the anti-aircraft gun-laying radars an S-band jamming system was added, with antennas in the main search radar radome beneath the aircraft. It was operated by 'Raven 2' and nicknamed 'Buster' after its designation, BSTR. More antennas for the ATIR repeater jammer were installed in the P2V's wingtip pods to provide additional coverage that could guard against a side-on attack by a Chicom interceptor.

But there was still no communications jammer on the P2V that could disrupt Chicom GCI. Don Jackson in the NACC Air Section had recommended one, but the idea was vetoed by higher headquarters.[181]

Moreover, the ECM couldn't counter the lumbering but persistent Tu-4 bomber-interceptors. On the night of 26 November 1962, for instance, a Tu-4 chased a P2V out of Jiangsu shortly after it had entered. On 28 January 1963 a Tu-4 fired on a P2V over

Shandong. This mission was trying to drop arms and radios to an agent group, as well as propaganda leaflets. There was no way for the P2V crew to jam the Tu-4's search radar, other than to drop chaff.

On 19 February 1963 another P2V flight had to abandon a penetration over Jiangsu after only 16 minutes. The pilot made repeated 90-degree turns to evade searchlights and heavy AAA fire. The crew thought that they had been hit – fortunately, they were not. The post-mission analysis that was sent to Washington surmised that the P2V was either off course, or "may have inadvertently crossed a temporary unplotted AAA site." Was this an accurate analysis – or were the mission planners at the NACC covering up for their own mistakes? Or were the Chicom defences simply becoming too dense to evade? On 28 March another flight into Jiangsu was aborted due to a combination of bad weather and interception attempts by MiGs and a Tu-4.[182]

On the night of 17 May, the PLAAF's specially-formed and trained 8th group finally got a chance to try out their illuminator/interceptor tactic.

A P2V commanded by Zhu Zhen entered Jiangsu province at 2030 and headed west. The Il-28 illuminator aircraft and MiG-17 interceptor were scrambled from Xuzhou airbase. They were vectored towards the intruder by GCI controllers but made three passes without finding it. On the fourth pass, the Il-28 managed to drop 12 flare bombs just over a mile ahead of the P2V. The target was illuminated, and was spotted by the MiG-17 pilot. The P2V crew saw several red flares light up the night sky and realized that they were under attack. As the MiG positioned to make a firing pass the P2V made a sharp descending left turn to escape. It nearly hit the ground, but the manoeuvre saved Zhu and his crew. The MiG fired 13 times but all in vain. The P2V turned back to the coast and flew safely out of denied territory. With his left engine backfiring Zhu decided to head across the Yellow Sea and land at Kunsan airbase in Korea.[183]

Five nights later, and much further south, another P2V commanded by Lt Col Zhou Yi Li flew a successful mission across the southeastern provinces as far as Changsha. The crew did not see any AAA, although electronic activity was heavy. The mission was considered very successful.[184]

Luck Ran Out

But one month later luck ran out for Captain Zhou and his crew of 14. On the night of 19 June 1963 they were intercepted repeatedly as they flew across Zhejiang, Jiangxi, and Hubei. MiG-17PFs and Tu-4Ps made eight unsuccessful attacking runs against the P2V. A while later, two more MiG-17PFs were scrambled from Xiangtang airbase, flown by the group commander and his deputy. The commander closed with the intruder over Jiujiang.

HOW THE CHICOMS REFINED THEIR INTERCEPTOR TACTICS

We decided that the MiG radar should not be turned on until the target was only 1,200 metres distance. The GCI controller must guide him to that distance, instead of to 2,200 metres, which was the previous practice. The pilot should reduce his airspeed to 350 km/hr by lowering his flaps by 20 degrees. He should follow the GCI instructions precisely. At a distance of 900-800 metres from the target, the pilot should switch his radar to lock-on. He should fire between 600 and 250 metres distance from the target. We should keep training our pilots until they can search, acquire, lock-on and fire at the target, all within 16 seconds. - *Lin, Fight To Protect Motherland's Airspace, p131*

RICHARD GAO REMEMBERS

I joined the CAF in 1948, and left my older brother and sister behind when my training school moved to Taiwan in 1949. I did not contact them for the next 30 years – the KMT forbad it, though I knew some people on Taiwan who sent letters to their relatives on the mainland via intermediaries in Hong Kong.

We all knew in our hearts that we weren't "going back to the mainland" with Chiang Kai Shek. But we could only express such thoughts to our closest friends.

We flew so many missions into the mainland, that we effectively 'trained' the Chicoms in how to intercept us. They became really good at it. I was a Bomber Defence Officer on the P2V and the C-54

for four years, until the 34th Squadron made an ECM instructor in mid-1963. I logged 30 combat missions, and survived multiple attacks on each one. As a professional soldier, you could not openly express the fear, even the desperation. But we did talk quietly amongst ourselves about it, of course. I've had nightmares for many years since.

My brother-in-law Major Feng was the Raven 2 onboard the P2V that was shot down in June 1963. Three days later, I was assigned to fly on another C-54 airdrop mission. I must admit, that I lied to my wife that day. I told her I was no longer flying on the P2V, and that all our C-54 missions were for training only. But when I did not return by midnight, she knew that I hadn't gone on a training flight. She stayed up all night, worrying about me. - *interview*

He tried different tactics – trying to approach the target from the front, instead of the rear. But he was too high to fire. Then he tried a stern attack, only to have his radar foiled by the P2V's jamming. The aircraft continued unharmed in a westerly direction, despite two attempted interceptions by a Tu-4.

An hour later, however, the black intruder returned within range of the fighters from Xiangtang. The deputy group commander, Wang Wen Li (王文禮), took off again. He tried a 90-degree angle attack, but the high closing speeds didn't give him enough time to acquire the target on his radar. He too reverted to a stern attack, achieved what he thought was a lock-on, and fired from about 1,500 feet. He probably fired at chaff, but as the radar lock broke Wang looked out of his cockpit. About 700 feet away and slightly above and to the left he saw a faint blue flame. The P2V's flame suppressors angled downwards, and they could not completely shield the exhausts if they were viewed from below against a dark sky. And the MiG pilot was flying even lower than the P2V![185]

Now Wang could just make out the silhouette of the P2V, but as he tried to manoeuvre into a firing position he overshot. GCI vectored him for a third pass. Again, though, the P2V's jamming system operated and Wang lost radar contact. So he looked out of the cockpit again and spotted the target about 750 feet away. Wang used the optical sight to fire for two seconds at a range of 300 feet. The target burst into flames as Wang climbed steeply to avoid a collision. The P2V fell to the ground near Linchuan, in Jiangxi.[186]

The Chicoms had finally downed a P2V in an air-to-air engagement. Wang, his division commander, and the GCI controller travelled to Beijing, where they received the personal congratulations of Premier Chou En Lai.[187]

The Black Bats had lost a fourth P2V and crew. The penetration missions were suspended yet again.

They were still suspended when Chiang Ching Kuo met President Kennedy in Washington in September 1963. Chiang pressed for larger raids against the mainland. He wanted to use the C-123s, and also asked again for C-130s - five this time, plus more landing craft. But JFK recalled for Chiang his bad experience with the failed Bay of Pigs invasion of Cuba in 1961, "where operations had been based more on hope than a realistic appraisal of the situation." The President asked Chiang how successful the ROC's recent guerilla raids against mainland China had been. Chiang had to admit the casualty rate was 85 percent. JFK was not impressed.[188]

But when Chiang mentioned that "atomic research and development institutions" might be likely targets for airborne raids Kennedy showed interest. The President asked if Chiang thought it possible to send 300 to 500 men by air to such distant locations as Baotou, in Inner Mongolia, the site of a suspected plutonium production facility. Chiang said it was.[189]

Kennedy and his national security advisor, McGeorge Bundy, had already discussed the possibility of sabotaging China's nuclear program, perhaps with help from the Soviet Union. One problem was U.S. intelligence could not yet identify the Chicom nuclear facilities with confidence. Indeed, the PRC's plutonium facility was not at Baotou. It was later discovered to be at Yumen.

However, policymakers in Washington continued to mull the idea of aiding and abetting the ROC to airdrop sabotage teams onto the PRC's nuclear sites. The Air Section of the NACC planned a P2V mission going all the way to Lop Nor. It was a stretch, especially if the sampling pods were also to be carried. But the idea of physical intervention to slow China's development of nuclear weapons never got beyond the exploratory phase in Washington.[190]

Chapter Seven

1964-1969

After the loss of Zhou and his P2V crew in June 1963 there were no more flights into the mainland for nine months. The Agency's fleet of black P2Vs was down to two again. To help train replacement crews, the Agency acquired an older P2V-5 (128355) from the U.S. Navy fleet. This grey-painted aircraft was not fitted with the mission systems. The Black Bats flew only non-penetrating 'Robin' flights along the mainland coast during this period. However, the 34th Squadron was busy elsewhere, supporting the new Southern Star project with the C-123s in Vietnam.

The odds on surviving over mainland China were shortening for the Black Bats. Mission planners were fairly sure that they could route the overflights clear of AAA sites. By now they had good collateral intelligence on the AAA locations, especially from U-2 imagery taken by the other CIA-CAF joint venture, namely the Black Cats' 35th Squadron operating out of Taoyuan airbase. And if a P2V did inadvertently fly within range of a AAA site the BSTR system was proving to be an effective radar countermeasure. On test flights in Taiwan over the ROC Army's own AAA guns the P2V's jammer created havoc, causing the gun barrels to swing wildly in all directions, seemingly out of control.[191]

But since every P2V flight was being detected by Chinese search radars before or soon after coast-in, it was bound to be challenged by airborne interceptors before too long. Desperate measures were floated. In December 1963, the CAF suggested escorting the overflights with its fighters. Although the fighters could not accompany the missions all the way, they could provide protection against air interception during the critical entry and exit phases, according to the CAF. The plan was never pursued.[192]

Then someone suggested that AIM-9 Sidewinder air-air missiles be fitted to the P2Vs. The idea was to launch them at the MiG fighters that would overshoot the P2Vs during their interception run. A trial installation was done at Burbank. AIM-9Bs were hung on each of two launch rails that were fitted under each wing of a P2V, immediately outboard of the jet engines. A live separation firing was then carried out on the China Lake range. Some consideration was given to having the missiles face and fire aft, as the MiGs approached the rear of the P2V. But then the Agency's airmen realized that the infrared seeker head of the AIM-9B was not sophisticated enough to home on the nose of a fighter, no matter how close the MiG was trailing the P2V.[193]

In fact, it is doubtful whether even the forward-facing installation would ever have worked. The cruising speed of the P2V was not fast enough to ensure that the missile did not pitch down upon launch, thus preventing its seeker head from locking-on to the target. Nevertheless, some AIM-9 missiles were transferred to the 34th Squadron from a CAF

F-86 squadron, which was resident on the other side of Hsinchu airbase. But on only one subsequent overflight did a P2V pilot consider using the AIM-9s against fighter opposition. And he reported that the aircraft was not manoeuvrable enough to turn towards the trailing fighter to allow the missiles to be fired with any chance of success.[194]

Terrian-Following Radar (TFR)

In early 1964, a Terrain Following Radar (TFR) designed by Texas Instruments (TI) was fitted to the P2V. TI was the pioneer of these systems, which helped pilots fly at very low altitudes. The radar scanned the terrain ahead of the aircraft vertically, and computed up or down steering commands that were sent to the autopilot. The TFR was added to one of the surviving black aircraft by the Skunk Works at Burbank, where two test flights revealed that it wasn't working properly. A ferry crew arrived to fly it back to Taiwan. The project engineer for Texas Instruments travelled with them.

At Hsinchu there were more test flights, but with only mixed success. TFR technology was still under development – TI had test-flown the system on RF-4C Phantoms, but they were not yet operational. The radar operated in the Ku band, and in the moist, cloudy environment of Taiwan there were propagation problems. Moreover, the P2V could not climb fast enough to safely execute the ascend command from the TFR as the aircraft approached high ground. The P2V pilots and their American instructors eventually resolved to use the system only for Terrain-Avoidance (TA). In this mode the radar also scanned horizontally, and displayed steering cues to the pilot, who remained in full control of the aircraft.[195]

To give the Chinese crews some more realistic training in the threat posed by the ChiCom interceptors, the B-26 that was still allocated to the 34th Squadron was fitted with the radar from an F-86D fighter. American instructor pilots chased the P2V over Taiwan in the twin-engined bomber. The BDOs learned how to jam the B-26 radar with the ATIR and chaff, and the pilots practised evading manoeuvres. The CAF F-86D squadron also flew mock air combat missions against the P2V.[196]

Replacement Aircraft

Back in the U.S., meanwhile, plans were already underway to provide a replacement aircraft that could better perform the STPOLLY mission. It was an ambitious scheme, taking account of multiple requirements from various parts of the Agency. This plane would be a good platform for the latest collection technology, and more survivable over denied territory, it was hoped.

THE CHICOMS EXPLOIT A CAPTURED ECM SYSTEM

According to a semi-official history of the Chinese air defense system, one of the worst fears of US intelligence came to pass, when sensitive electronic warfare technology was recovered from a P2V that was shot down over the mainland, and exploited. In "Chinese SAM Operations Record" (p350), Major Gen Chen Hui Ting (陳輝亭) claims that from March 1963, the PLA Air Defence Command headquarters conducted 27 test flights of an electronic noise jammer. They removed the BSTR equipment from a shot-down P2V. After several months of technical investigation, they understood the technical principles of this equipment. After repair, it was installed in an Il-14 transport aircraft, and tested in conjunction with the gun-laying radar.

– C.P.

In CIA headquarters, the responsibility for covert air operations now rested with the Special Operations Division (SOD). Within SOD, the Air Branch was a relatively small unit with only about 20 billets headed by USAF Colonel Bernie Finan. The Air Branch had remained with the clandestine service (still known as the DDP) when the new technical intelligence directorate, the DDR, was created in 1962. Then, after a complicated bureaucratic power struggle within the U.S. intelligence community, the DDR had been expanded and renamed in mid-1963 as the Directorate of Science and Technology (DS&T), headed by the forceful but effective Bud Wheelon. The DS&T developed and controlled all of the Agency's high-tech intelligence gathering systems, including the U-2 and A-12 spy planes and the satellites.

By May 1963 the new project had been allocated the cryptonym STSPIN. There were plenty of targets in China that required investigation by the project, according to an internal CIA memo. A rocket test facility on the outskirts of Beijing was worthy of urgent investigation by "close-up, low-light photography" and other sensors and collection techniques that were not yet developed. China's nuclear weapons development was, of course, another priority target. Then there were 'targets of opportunity,' such as petroleum refineries (to determine China's production capacity) and seven industrial installations that had been identified by satellite and U-2 photography, the exact purpose of which were unknown.[197]

In theory, the SOD would manage the development and acquisition of the new aircraft. But did this small and operationally focused group have the necessary expertise? Bud Wheelon insisted that the technical specialists within DS&T should have an equal role in the development of STSPIN. He directed Bob Singel from the Office of ELINT (OEL) to work with the Air Branch on the new project.

The U.S. Navy was replacing its P2V maritime patrol aircraft with the new Lockheed P-3 Orion. It was a four-engined turboprop based on the Electra airliner with a much larger cabin, longer range, and greater speed than the ageing Neptune. The P-3 made its first flight in late 1959 and entered service in August 1962. The Agency followed suit and selected the P-3. A budget of $36 million was approved to convert the aircraft for covert operations. The Lockheed Skunk Works was asked to come up with a proposal.

According to Singel, Kelly Johnson responded to the Agency's request for proposals with a two page letter that essentially stated little more than "send money, we will do the P-3 conversion." But the days when black projects automatically fell from the CIA's table into Kelly's lap were over. The Agency needed some estimate of the cost for budgeting purposes. Singel sought an alternative.[198]

In Greenville, Texas, the Aerosystems Division of LTV had developed a good reputation for special electronic modifications to large aircraft, especially for the USAF. The Agency

---

WHY LOCKHEED DIDN'T DO THE P-3 CONVERSIONS FOR CIA

Kelly Johnson assumed that he would get the job of modifying the P-3s. We felt that he had his hands full getting the A-12 working properly, and we did not want to dilute his group's capability. He protested our decision on the grounds that only Lockheed knew the airplane and could modify it. That fell on deaf ears in my office. - *Albert 'Bud' Wheelon, Deputy Director for Science & Technology, CIA, 1963-66, email to author*

asked it to quote for the new P-3 requirement – and Greenville got the business, much to the annoyance of Kelly Johnson and Lockheed. Bob Singel nominated a Navy officer from the Pentagon, Sam Anderson, to be the Agency's representative at the Greenville facility. The general manager of Aerosystems there was Dan Hearn, who reported to the company's president, Fred Buehring. At Greenville, the 'black' P-3 work was named Project Axial.[199]

In June/July 1964 three of the early-production P-3As were taken out of Navy service and transferred to the Agency. LTV Aerosystems embarked on the extensive modifications needed to accommodate the Agency's requirements. There would be new ELINT and COMINT sensors, a new infrared imaging sensor, a side-looking imaging radar, acoustic sensors that could be deployed through the sonobuoy tubes, and air sampling equipment to detect nuclear weapons activity. Then there was a set of requirements connected with covert insertion, such as widening the rear fuselage opening to facilitate airdrops and a motorized dispenser for leaflets and other propaganda. There was also a new defensive ECM suite, flame suppressors for the engine exhausts, and shortened propeller blades to decrease the P-3's noise signature.[200]

Some of the avionics slated to go on the 'black' P-3As would be the same or similar to that already added to the P2Vs, including the terrain following radar and the ALQ-28 ELINT collection system. Other equipment going into the new aircraft was already developed for other CIA programs, such as the Birdwatcher system. This was a covert telemetry system for the U-2 that monitored critical aircraft parameters during an overflight of denied territory and sent the data to the command post via HF SSB radio in burst transmissions.

General I Transferred

In Taiwan, General I Fu En lost his job as head of intelligence for the CAF in February 1964. Chiang Ching Kuo ordered his transfer to the MND as Deputy Chief of Staff for Planning. The order mystified General I, who did not want to leave the special intelligence projects. His replacement as J-2 in CAF headquarters was General Yang Shao Lian (楊紹廉).[201]

On the night of 17 March 1964, after a long suspension, P2V missions into Chinese airspace resumed with a flight over Hainan Island and into Guangxi and Guangdong. But as usual the P2V was detected. In common with units further north, the PLAAF's 9th Air Division was also now equipped and trained for the illumination tactic. It launched two MiG-15s each carrying 75kg flares, plus a two-seat MiG-15UTI trainer to attack the intruder. The P2V crew saw the flares being dropped and avoided the MiGs. They coasted-out west of Macao and returned safely to Hsinchu after nearly 12 hours.[202]

On 9 April, a flight into Zhejiang skirted Hangzhou and returned safely. Four days later a more ambitious sortie into Jiangsu and Zhejiang was mounted, but the flight commander aborted the sortie after four interception attempts. On 7 May a P2V flew around the Gulf of Bohai and the Korea Bay without entering the mainland on a roundtrip from Taiwan that lasted 13 hours. Still, though, a MiG-17 flew out to sea in an attempted interception. On 12 May the Black Bats made their longest penetration of the mainland since the resumption of overflights, passing through Zhejiang, Jiangxi, and Fujian, and flying over several airbases.[203]

More Penetrations

So far, so good. The NACC planned more penetrations for the next dark moon phase. On the night of 11 June 34th Squadron commander Col Sun Yi Chen led a crew of 13 northwards along the mainland coast and past Shanghai before entering the mainland in northern Jiangsu. Then the P2V turned north and flew across Shandong nearly as far as the Yellow River.

But the ChiComs had been tracking the flight since long before coast-in, and the P2V was courting danger over Shandong. Here, the PLAN (naval air arm) had resumed training on the illumination interception technique. The ChiComs fitted 12 more powerful 90kg flares to the Il-28 bomber, which could light up the sky for a radius of seven kilometres. In a six-month period from August 1963 interceptor pilots from the PLAN's 5th Group made over 400 practice attacks, working ever more closely with ground controllers.

As the P2V turned east towards the Shandong peninsula, the PLAN scrambled a MiG-15 flown by squadron commander Chen Gen Fa (陳根發) and an Il-28 flown by Shi Zhen Shan (石振山) from Qingdao airbase on the coast. Guided by GCI controllers, they flew inland towards their target. But the P2V crew must have intercepted the ground-to-air communications, since it took evasive action. GCI guided Chen and Shi back towards their target, but again the P2V altered course to escape. Now the intruder flew into a radar blindspot, and ChiCom ground controllers told the MiG-15 and Il-28 to hold while they tried to re-acquire the target. They succeeded, and now the co-ordinated attack could proceed. The Il-28 was directed to a position about 6,500 feet above and beyond the target, which was flying at 3,000 feet. Shi now dropped his flares. The P2V was caught like a rabbit in the headlights. The crew started a diving turn to the left, but the MiG was well positioned at five o'clock to the target, 5,000 feet away and closing from slightly above. Chen soon spotted his target through the optical sight. He fired from 2,000 feet away and saw tracers hit the left wing root of the P2V. In a desperate attempt to escape the target now banked sharply right, but Chen followed and fired again as both hunter and hunted descended towards the ground. The MiG pilot almost collided with the P2V before managing to pull up just 600 feet from the ground. He watched as the black intruder burst into flames, crashed to the ground, and erupted into a fireball. [204]

It was not long before Beijing Radio was announcing another glorious victory. The wreckage of the P2V was sifted, and the ChiComs recovered three of the four AIM-9 missiles. They were displayed as trophies by the 5th Group.[205]

The awful news was soon apparent at Hsinchu – the popular Black Bats commander and his crew would not be coming home. Lt Col Sun had led from the front. He was the fifth commander of the 34th Squadron to be killed in action. This P2V crew also included the pilot Ge Guang Liao (葛光遼), who was flying his very last mission before reassignment. And another 12 aircrew had also perished as the 34th Squadron lost its fifth P2V, the third to be shot down over the mainland. It was 7047, the very first conversion done at Burbank in 1955-56. All five of the Agency's original fleet of P2Vs had now been destroyed while assigned to Taiwan.

THE COMMUNISTS COUNT THEIR SUCCESSES

In the past several years, we have downed ten US-Chiang spyplanes of different types…including one RB-57A, one RB-57D, one B-17, three P2Vs, one RF-101 and three U-2s. This record shows that US-Chiang Kai Shek spyplanes of whatever type, coming at whatever altitude and resorting to whatever cunning maneuvres, are doomed to destruction.

During the same period, directed by US imperialism, the Chiang Kai Shek gang has continuously sent armed agents to harass the mainland. Since October 1962, the PLA armymen and civilians have put out of action 33 groups of armed US – Chiang Kai Shek agents, totalling 398 men.

- People's Daily editorial, 9 July 1964

Serious Setbacks

The loss of the P2V in June 1964 was followed within weeks by another two serious setbacks in the ROC's operations against the mainland. On 7 July the 35th Squadron lost a third U-2, shot down over Swatow. On the night of 11/12 July four fast landing craft were intercepted and destroyed by the PRC as they attempted to insert some 150 nationalist commandos on the mainland. This was the latest in a series of maritime raids by the nationalists against the southern coastal provinces in 1963-64, as the IBMND attempted to exploit the perceived economic and social discontent against communist rule. But according to a CIA assessment, the raids encountered only the first line of Communist coastal defence, and these forces "displayed no inclination to co-operate with the raiding teams, which were killed, taken prisoner, or driven off in a matter of hours."[206]

The P2V overflights were suspended again. Col Lu De Qi again filled a dead man's shoes, as he became the new commander of the Black Bats. This time his promotion was permanent, and he remained the squadron boss until 1969. Throughout the rest of 1964 the 34th squadron flew only coastal missions. These collected SIGINT and also carried the air sampling equipment. The one surviving P2V was joined by another (135564) transferred by the Navy to the Agency in December 1964. It was modified by Lockheed and flown to Hsinchu in June 1965.

China Joins Nuclear 'Club'

On 16 October 1964, Communist China became the fifth member of the nuclear 'club' by conducting a test shot at Lop Nor, the remote desert site in Xinjiang province. The test came as no surprise to U.S. intelligence thanks to previous overhead coverage of Lop Nor by reconnaissance satellites and photography obtained by the joint U.S./ROC U-2 squadron of the PRC's nuclear weapons related sites that had been identified further to the east. The test itself was detected by the ground network of acoustic and electromagnetic pulse detection stations that was maintained by the U.S. and allies. Then, a variety of aircraft flew air sampling sorties to trap particles from the test for diagnostic analysis. They included some flights along the China coast from Taiwan by the Black Bats, flying at medium altitudes for a change![207]

In a letter to President Johnson five weeks later, Chiang Kai Shek proposed that even if the U.S. considered it impractical to assist the ROC in overthrowing the Chinese communist regime before it could produce nuclear weapons, the next best thing would be for the U.S. to make available the means and assistance to enable ROC forces to destroy the ChiCom nuclear installations. In his reply President Johnson politely ignored the idea.[208]

U.S. policymakers also brushed aside suggestions from Taipei that the ROC be provided with the means to airdrop 5-10,000 soldiers to provoke anticommunist rebellion

GORDON RAYMER REMEMBERS

I had just completed test pilot school at Patuxent River, and was newly-promoted to Cdr, when I was selected for 'a classified assignment'. I became a P2V instructor pilot and mission planner on Taiwan in 1964-65. It was an interesting time. But I don't think it helped my subsequent career in the Navy. The paperwork trail from Taiwan was incomplete, for obvious reasons, and it didn't match the Navy's expectations.

We flew with the Chinese crews on training flights that stayed at least 50 miles off the mainland coast. But I remember one where our ELINT officer warned that mainland fighters were being vectored towards our location. We never saw them, but I dived to 100 feet over the water to present as difficult a target as possible.

I also remember flying back from Okinawa in the squadron C-47. Approaching Taiwan, I got a message from ATC asking us to maintain 270 degrees heading. I heard nothing more for 20 minutes, so I queried the instruction, and got the same response. I believe that it was a Chicom 'lure' towards the mainland. - *interview*

in Yunnan, Guangxi, and Guangdong. The ROC believed that such a move would choke off Chinese military support to North Vietnam. Through a formal military planning and consultation process – the "Blue Lion Committee' – the U.S. sought to convince the ROC that such actions simply were not practical.[209]

Reduced Chances

Under these political circumstances, and given the reduced chances of surviving an interception, the 34th Squadron stayed out of ChiCom airspace throughout nearly the whole of 1965. Instead, 'Robin' missions were scheduled along the mainland coast to collect SIGINT from a safe distance. But what was a safe distance? Sometimes the flights approached to within 20 nautical miles of the mainland. But if the radio operator monitoring the GCI frequencies detected the launch of interceptors on the mainland the P2V retreated to 60 nautical miles offshore.[210]

The coastal flights usually departed Hsinchu in the early evening and returned up to 11 hours later. The P2V crews either flew north from Taiwan as far as the Shandong Peninsula or south as far as Hainan Island. American airmen assigned to the NACC often flew on these peripheral missions.

JOHN McCAULL REMEMBERS

I was a U.S. Navy P-2 instructor pilot, assigned to Taiwan in March 1964. I remember flying a lot of the 'Robin' peripheral missions. Each one was from five to nine hours long, and as IFR as we could make it. We flew a prescribed course, and stayed well offshore, more than 12 miles.

It was on one of my first Robins that I learned that the ChiComs were broadcasting to our aircraft and crews. We were listening on the VOR to the VHF broadcast. I asked my Chinese co-pilot what they were saying. He responded: "they have just offered us $50,000 if we defect and bring you and the airplane to the mainland".

This was a little unnerving at the time, but not really a problem – those ROC flight crews were really dedicated to the mission, and to the nationalist cause.

I ferried a P2V to Da Nang prior to an overflight mission by a Chinese crew. We were about 50 miles south of Hainan Island, in broad daylight at 8,000 feet. The BDO came on the intercom to warn: "AI tracking". About 10 minutes later, he announced "AI locked on!". I thought we were in big trouble, and my Chinese crew went into orbit, all talking in Chinese. We all thought the ChiComs had sent an aircraft out from Hainan to get us!

Suddenly, a Navy F-4 pulled up on our wing, with another beneath us. They were from the CAP on Yankee Station in the Tonkin Gulf. I could see the RIO taking pictures of our aircraft, and our four Sidewinder missiles. Needless to say, I was *very* relieved. I waved to them, but I don't think they knew who or what we were. Neither of the F-4s pulled in front of us. They had seen our Sidewinders... - *interview*

The C-123 transports of the 34th Squadron remained committed to the growing conflict in Vietnam. There was no sign that the U.S. would approve the use of the C-123s further north in any military adventurism to the Chinese mainland by the ROC. Of course, the Chiangs were only too willing to help the U.S. fight communism in southeast Asia, if only as a means to keep Uncle Sam invested in the future of the ROC. Indeed, Taiwan became a logistics and support base for the Vietnam War: KC-135s and C-130s occupied the large parking ramps at Chin Chuan Kang airbase; and Air Asia employed thousands doing overhauls on U.S. military aircraft.

The CIA reduced its manpower on Taiwan as more covert and intelligence gathering resources were diverted to southeast Asia. The last two case officers that were supporting the ROC's seaborne raids along the mainland coast were withdrawn. The cover name of the station was changed from the NACC to the U.S. Army Technical Group (USATG). Harold Ford replaced Bill Nelson as station chief.

Unusually for a station chief, Ford was an analyst from the Directorate of Intelligence rather than a career covert operator in DDP. "The airplanes will be your biggest problem," someone warned him before he left Washington for Taipei. The U-2s were still flying over the mainland from Taoyuan, even though four of them had now been shot down by ChiCom SA-2 missiles. But Ford soon came to the conclusion that the joint operation of the 34th squadron at Hsinchu was "just going through the motions." He believed that it was kept going only for the sake of good relations between the ROC and the U.S.[211]

P-3 Project Survives

Somehow, though, the $36 million project to re-equip the 34th Squadron with a brand new covert airplane survived. Work on the three 'black' P-3 Orions continued at Greenville throughout 1965 and into 1966. It was an extensive modification project, but the CIA defended it on the grounds that it was a useful capability to hold in reserve against the nuclear sites in China, including those in the far northwest. Some Agency staffers even believed that this aircraft could be used to penetrate the Soviet Union's airspace on nighttime reconnaissance missions - if political approval could ever be obtained.[212]

The NSA took a keen interest in the SIGINT systems of Project Axial and sent a large team to Greenville to verify their performance. American Electronics Laboratories (AEL) was supplying some sophisticated new ELINT and DF subsystems that were highly automated. They were optimised for collection at low altitude, and used some ingenious antennas that were flush-mounted on the airframe.[213]

Carl Duckett, the deputy director of DS&T, accompanied Bob Kleyla from the SOD Air Branch to Taiwan, where they briefed top ROC government officials on the P-3A. The CAF was invited to select and send crews to the U.S. for training on the new aircraft. It needed a crew of 10: two pilots, a flight engineer, three navigators, three ECM officers, and one loadmaster. The 34th Squadron sent six pilots and three flight engineers to NAS Patuxent River, MD, where they became the first foreigners to take the P-3 conversion course. The ECM operators were trained at Greenville.[214]

The U.S. Navy assigned three P-3 instructor pilots and three flight engineers to the USATG on Taiwan. The USAF provided navigators and ECM operators for the new aircraft. An all-American crew collected the first P-3 for Taiwan (149673) from Greenville in April

1966. They flew it to Eglin AFB for acceptance tests, including low level night flights to test the terrain-following radar and the aircraft's visibility against searchlights.[215]

In mid-May this crew flew the aircraft to Taiwan. It arrived at Hsinchu on 19 May. On 22 June a ceremony was held at the base to mark the arrival of the P-3. Chiang Ching Kuo (recently confirmed as the ROC's Minister of Defence) flew down from Taipei to inspect the large, shiny black airplane. It was formally presented by CIA station chief Ford.

It looked very impressive, with all the new electronics inside, underwing racks for AIM-9 missiles, airscoops for sampling behind the cockpit, and so on. But despite nearly two years of development there were still technical problems to resolve. Especially if these aircraft were to survive during a new series of overflights into the mainland's defended airspace.

The updated ECM system wasn't working properly against the ground radars. The Terrain-Following Radar (TFR) had problems, according to the newly-trained Chinese pilots. In theory, the TFR made it easier for them to navigate and fly at very low level. The system had two transmitters for redundancy and two selectable settings for a 'hard' ride or a 'soft' ride. But the Chinese pilots believed that the necessary automation of the TFR had the effect of denying them some vital manoeuvring options. For instance, just like Dai and his P2V crew in November 1960, you might want to make a sharp turn into a valley to escape a pursuing fighter, rather than ascending to clear the valley sides.

The criticism didn't stop there. "The TFR on the P-3 called for climbing when not needed. When it called for descent, it could fly you into the ground," recalled one of the Chinese pilots. The American IPs assigned to the USATG disagreed. Navy pilot Paul Herring thought that the TFR on the P-3 was a big improvement over that on the P2V, which he also flew. But even if all the technical problems had been solved to their satisfaction, some of the Chinese aircrew doubted that the P-3 would be any more survivable than the P2V over mainland China. Especially if the ChiComs used the illumination technique again, which had accounted for Lt Col Sun and his crew.[216]

Instead of penetration flights, the P-3s flew peripheral missions along the China coast to collect SIGINT and air samples at altitudes up to 38,000 feet. The ChiComs knew all about the new black birds. They broadcast the offer of a $1 million bounty if an aircrew would defect with one.[217]

Wasting Asset

Across the ramp from the P-3s sat the Agency's last two P2Vs, a wasting asset. They were still flying about ten peripheral missions along the China coast each month at night. The Black Bats maintenance crews kept them in tip-top condition – none of the missions were ever aborted for maintenance reasons. But there had been only two penetrations into the mainland since the shootdown in June 1964. The first of these was on 24 December 1965, when Lt Col Guan Bo Ping (關伯平) and his crew dropped several hundred pounds of leaflets over Guangxi and Guangdong. In poor visibility a MiG-17 tried but failed to intercept. The second was on 15 June 1966, when Guan and his crew flew around Guangdong and territory in the adjacent provinces. They gathered plenty of SIGINT on the ChiCom air defences, but also attracted the attentions of no fewer than six MiG-17 interceptors during the two hours that they spent in denied territory. The intruder was also attacked by an AAA battery, the flak exploding 2,000 feet above the P2V.[218]

Shortly after this latest escape the U.S. Intelligence Board (USIB) reviewed Project Goshawk. The review may have been influenced by a request to the Special Group (now known as the 303 Committee) for approval to fly a daring mission with the new P-3 to northwest China. Mission planners had sketched a route that took off from Korea, entered the mainland south of Beijing at 250 feet, and flew all the way to the Gobi Desert before turning south to cross the Himalayas and land in India.[219]

The USIB voted to terminate the Taiwan program because the risks no longer justified the rewards, and the resources could be better employed elsewhere, particularly in southeast Asia. Board members noted that there had been only two overflights in the past two years because both sides of the joint venture had been fearful of losing another aircraft and crew. Regarding the risk, the Board may not only have been worried about the likelihood of a shootdown. They may also have feared the defection of a Chinese crew with a P-3, which would have compromised the sensitive U.S. collection and countermeasures technology on board. [220]

The decision to scrap the joint project was conveyed to Taiwan by Col Bernie Finan, the chief of the SOD Air Branch. Chiang Ching Kuo was furious – and not only because a relatively low-ranking U.S. officer brought the news. CCK was still upset because the U.S. side remained steadfastly opposed to the KMT's plans for paramilitary action against mainland China, despite the latest upheavals there occasioned by the start of Mao's Cultural Revolution. Now he saw the ending of Project Goshawk as the thin edge of a wedge – one that would eventually force the U.S. to abandon support for the ROC. He began to question the future relationship between the U.S. and the ROC, including the value to Taiwan of the other joint intelligence gathering projects.[221]

This was a delicate situation for U.S. intelligence. Although STPOLLY was no longer judged to be of value, the other projects were providing vital information on China, and especially on its development of nuclear weapons. These were the U-2 flights of the 35th Squadron; the SIGINT co-operation at both the ROC's ground station and the one operated by the USAF; and a newly installed over-the-horizon radar that was designed to track ChiCom ballistic missile tests that took place nearly 1,500 miles away at Shuangchengzi, in Gansu province.

Notice of Termination
The U.S. did not want to lose these projects, but it decided to call Chiang's bluff. In mid-November the CIA served the formal 60-day notice of termination that was required by the Goshawk agreement signed six years earlier. The two P-3s had already been flown out to the U.S. Naval Air Station at Okinawa by the American instructor pilots on the pretext of maintenance. They had never flown a single mission over the mainland. The last P2V

HAL FORD REMEMBERS

For the first year that I was the station chief, I got on well with Chiang Ching Kuo. My wife and his Russian wife Faina also became good friends.

But I was the obvious target for Chiang Ching Kuo's unhappiness, when we closed down the operation out of Hsinchu. From then on, he kept me at arm's length. Although he did relent and throw a great party for me, when I left Taiwan.

I felt that we were open to criticism. One part of the CIA was developing a fancy new covert airplane, the P-3, while another part was developing satellites, which could do the job cheaper. - *interview*

mission was probably flown on 16 November 1966, another flight along the China coast that lasted 10 hours 20 minutes.[222]

When Bill Colby, the head of the CIA's Far East Division, paid a visit to Taipei in mid-December, CCK made clear his displeasure over the Goshawk termination. He told Colby that the ROC had lost some 120 men in the project. With that investment in human lives, Chiang continued, he could not see how to confront his Air Force with the decision to end the program.[223]

It was clearly a serious loss of face for CCK. It is not clear when CAF Headquarters were told that Project Goshawk would definitely be closed, but the Chinese side of the operation at Hsinchu first heard about the termination from their American counterparts. Eventually, officers of the 34th squadron were informed during a visit to Hsinchu by the CAF commander, General Xu Huan Sheng (徐煥昇). He told them that the ROC side had decided to end the joint project.[224]

The two P2Vs were flown out of Hsinchu in late January 1967, and returned to the U.S. Navy at NAS Alameda, CA. The three black P-3s were also flown there for temporary storage. Some of the 34th crews were transferred to the C-123 operation, some to other CAF squadrons, and some to China Airlines – which was still essentially run by the CAF and MND.[225]

Chiang did not act against the other intelligence joint ventures, although he held up some U-2 missions for a while to further demonstrate his displeasure, and insisted on a new written agreement for that project. In reality, both sides knew that Project Goshawk had been living on borrowed time. To vent his frustration CCK cold-shouldered the CIA station chief Hal Ford for the remaining 18 months of his tour.

New Year Message

In a New Year message on 1 January 1967, President Chiang Kai Shek seemed finally to signal an end to the long standing nationalist policy of retaking the mainland by force. Now aged 80 and in failing health, the elder Chiang declared that a counter-attack was now of secondary importance. The real need was to strengthen political preparations for a smooth transition of power on the mainland once the Communist regime had collapsed through its own internal dissensions.

Still, though, the propaganda war was important to the nationalists. To replace the leaflet dropping capability of Project Goshawk, the CIA on Taiwan and the IBMND turned to balloons. Years earlier these had been used in Europe to float anti-communist literature into the Soviet Union and the satellite countries. Now this lighter-than-air method of delivery was revived, apparently with some success. That is, when the winds from Taiwan blew in the right direction! The leaflets, pamphlets, and newspapers were carefully designed to encourage a backlash to Mao's Red Guards. Within weeks refugees began arriving in Hong Kong with examples of the propaganda.[226]

ELINT from Space

And how to replace the SIGINT capability against the Chinese air defense system, on which so much effort had been expended during the Goshawk project? In fact, the U.S. had been 'ferreting' ELINT from space ever since July 1960, when the first covert satellite dedicated to this task was orbited. That first system was tiny, and was targeted against large Soviet radars in the S-band, such as the P-20 (Token), whose signals radiated far into space. But it also detected target acquisition radars associated with surface-to-air missiles. Over the next few years the U.S. launched more capable and larger ELINT satellites – all in secret, of course.

Satellites could obtain signals of interest from deep inside the vast landmass of the Soviet Union and Communist China. However, satellites were not a complete replacement for airborne SIGINT gathering for a variety of reasons.

A new U.S. National Intelligence Survey (NIS) on ChiCom air defences was issued in June 1966. Classified at the secret level, the document contained great detail, including a complete count of early warning and GCI radars by region and a comprehensive survey of the PRC's AAA system. No sources were identified, and the survey was obviously the result of collection and analysis from multiple sources. But few of these could have been HUMINT - spies on the ground. No doubt the high resolution photography produced by the U-2s flying from Taiwan made a major contribution to this NIS. The other most significant contribution may have been the countless hours of collection obtained over mainland China, at great risk, by the Black Bats in their P2Vs.[227]

Major Question

The story would have ended here, were it not for a major question that preoccupied the technical intelligence gatherers of the CIA in the mid-1960s. That question was: what is China's technical path to the development of nuclear weapons and the means to deliver them? It was a most vexing problem. First, because of the effective wall of secrecy that the Chinese had erected. Second, because they had made such rapid progress; in May 1966 they tested a device containing thermonuclear material, just 18 months after their first A-bomb shot. Third, because their next nuclear test shot was a missile. Moreover, no one in the West could be sure whether the nascent Chinese nuclear deterrent would be managed by rational men. The Cultural Revolution was in full swing, and so was a power struggle at the heart of the government in Beijing.

DETAILING CHINA'S AIR DEFENCES

The AAA forces of Communist China consist of an estimated 17 (PLAAF) divisions, six (PLA) divisions, up to an estimated 30 (PLAAF) independent AAA regiments, and 125 AAA battalions organic to PLA line or combat support divisions....It is estimated that Communist China has a total of 3,600 AA weapons, of which 2,000 are light (37- to 75- mm) and 1,600 are medium guns (85- to 100- mm)....The 57-mm and larger calibre AA guns are provided with a fire control radar of the Whiff or Firecan type.

The Chinese Communists have continued to... strengthen and upgrade the capabilities of their radar net...The Chinese-designed radar which has the greatest capability is the Moon Cone, a VHF radar which has been widely deployed. A second Chinese-produced radar which has an extremely important role

in the early-warning and coastal defense system is the Cross Slot, an S-band radar.

As of 1 April 1966, there were 451 early-warning radars in the Chinese air defense system. Included in this total are 224 of the older SCR-270 and Tachi-18 radars, 56 Moon Cones, 105 Cross Slots, 65 Soviet Knife Rest family radars, and one Flat Face.

For height-finder radars, the Chinese are still totally dependent on Soviet equipment. There are 57 Rock Cake /Stone Cake radars active in China. The majority of these are co-located with 62 Token and 22 Big Mesh Soviet radars, which possess a GCI capability because of their V-beam design enabling them to detwermine an approximate target altitude. - *U.S. National Intelligence Survey 39A, "Communist China Air Forces," June 1966*

UNCERTAINTY ABOUT CHINESE

On 27 October 1966 the Chinese announced that they had successfully launched a guided missile which carried a nuclear warhead. We have confirmed that there was a nuclear explosion...detonated in the atmosphere about 100 miles east of the Lop Nor test site. As nearly as we can ascertain, the device was delivered by a ballistic missile, as the Chinese claim. Such a missile, in or near the MRBM class, may have been fired from the Shuangchengzi missile test range over a distance of about 400 nautical miles. At this point, we are not able to judge with confidence what this event implies for China's advanced weapons capability. - *SNIE 13-8-66, 3 November 1966, Top Secret, declassified 2004*

The answer to the question lay in the deserts of remote northwest China. Here was located the PRC's nuclear test site, the ballistic missile range, a plutonium reactor, and other suspected nuclear facilities. These were difficult intelligence targets, almost beyond the reach of the sensors that the West could deploy to monitor (for instance) nuclear emissions, missile telemetry, and local communications.

Shortly before leaving his post as the CIA's Deputy for Science and Technology in 1966, Dr Bud Wheelon approved a program to design sensor pods that could be dropped from a high-flying U-2 into the Takla Makan desert. They would remotely gather and transmit intelligence from the Chinese nuclear sites. Development of the pods was supervised by the CIA's Office of ELINT (OEL). Much of the work was done by the government-funded nuclear weapons development facility in New Mexico, Sandia Laboratories.

Flight tests of the pods started in the U.S. in May 1966, but nearly a year elapsed before the operation was mounted. During that time two CAF pilots from the 35th Squadron were specially trained for the mission. The area in question was beyond the range of a U-2 flying from Taiwan. The mission would be launched instead from Takhli airbase in Thailand – still 1,800 miles from the drop zone just south of Lop Nor. However, the route north from Thailand had the advantage of being at or beyond the range of Chinese radars and interceptors.

On 7 May 1967 the U-2 took off from Takhli with a sensor pod under each wing, successfully released them over Xinjiang, and returned the way it had come. But nothing was subsequently heard from the pods. They were supposed to transmit by HF to the U.S. SIGINT station at Shulinkou, on Taiwan. Meanwhile, on 17 June the ChiComs conducted their third nuclear test, which was the first to contain thermonuclear material. (The first two bombs used Uranium-235, which was a surprise to U.S. intelligence analysts, and another indication of how many gaps in their knowledge still existed.)

In an attempt to stimulate the pods into transmitting a second U-2 mission was flown to Lop Nor along the same route on 31 August 1967. This one carried an interrogator/recorder and deployed a trailing wire antenna over the desert test site. Still nothing was heard from the pods. Moreover, the ChiComs nearly ambushed the U-2 by firing SA-2 missiles from a site that seemed to have been purposely located beneath the flight path.[228]

A new National Intelligence Estimate on Communist China's Strategic Weapons Program pondered whether progress could be affected by "a general breakdown in central authority." It predicted the limited deployment within six months of a medium-range ballistic missile that could threaten U.S. bases and cities all the way from Japan to India. An ICBM capable of threatening the U.S. could follow by the early 1970s. There was still much to learn – and much reason to learn it.[229]

In Taiwan, relations between the U.S. and ROC intelligence remained sour after the Goshawk termination. CIA station chief Harold Ford reported that "while the fact of dependence on the US is accepted by the Gimo and other ROC leaders, the resultant pessimistic and somewhat resentful atmosphere is not an easy one in which to work." The two sides still met formally to review possible strategic targets in communist China. These included the nuclear weapons sites, but the ROC knew by now that unless there was all-out war the U.S. would not attack them. As a result, the ROC now ensured that the CIA station was "effectively closed out of planning for maritime excursions and agent operations against the mainland," Ford reported.[230]

Air Dropping Sensors

The CIA had not given up on the idea of air dropping sensors into northwest China. Starting in early 1968, the CIA and Sandia Labs devised a much larger collection package that could communicate the data that it collected in burst transmissions to a satellite passing overhead.

Bob Kleyla, still an air operations officer in the SOD's Air Branch, suggested that the new sensor package could be air dropped into the remote area by a C-130 Hercules transport. The aircraft would have to be specially equipped to fly low over China, to avoid detection by Chinese radars. Who could fly a large airplane all the way from Thailand into northwest China on a 'deniable' basis to the U.S.? Of course, it was the 34th Squadron of the Chinese Air Force.[231]

Despite the cooling of relations between the U.S. and the ROC, the government in Taipei was still willing to help. Squadron commander Lu De Qi was summoned to a meeting in CAF headquarters with General Yang, the chief of intelligence. General Yang asked him to select two crews: pilots, navigators, flight engineers, radio and electronic warfare operators, and loadmasters. Most of them were from the C-123 operation in Vietnam. The mission would be nicknamed Qi Long (Magic Dragon) by the Chinese side and Heavy Tea by the American side. The group of 24 airmen left for training on the C-130 in the U.S. in late September 1968, led by Col Sun Pei Zhen (孫培震).[232]

The Chinese pilots learned to fly the C-130E version of the Hercules during a short course at Stewart AFB, TN. Then they joined their colleagues who had already moved into Groom Lake, the CIA's top secret airbase in Nevada where the U-2 and A-12 spy planes were test flown. The U-2s were long gone and the A-12s had recently been retired, but the remote base still housed secret projects, notably the MiG fighters that had been covertly obtained by U.S. intelligence. The ROC aircrews were the first foreign nationals to train at Groom Lake. Americans with high-level security clearances working there were amazed to see the Chinese group. However, Sun and his team were prevented from having day-to-day contact with other workers at the base.[233]

Groom Lake

At Groom Lake, Col Sun and his men were introduced to a C-130E that had been specially modified by Lockheed for covert insertions and other classified missions. It had been equipped with a high-speed, low-level aerial delivery system. For navigation, in addition to the standard APN-115 radar, there was a new inertial system that promised only a 2-degree deviation per hour. To aid in low-level night flight there was a Forward-Looking InfraRed

Above: The Bomber Defense Analysis room that was established at Hsinchu in 1962 to analyze the electronic and communications data obtained during the overflights. Below: The operations room of the 34th Squadron at Hsinchu. The four Chinese characters above the board read "Keep The Secrets, Beware of Communist Spies." Security was a constant concern in this closely guarded operation; there were grounds for suspecting that the Chicoms had indeed managed to steal some of the Black Bats' secrets.

In 1960, the Chicom naval air arm developed a new tactic against the overflying intruders. An Il-28 bomber would drop flare bombs so that MiG pilots could see the P2Vs and attack them. The scheme eventually paid off in June 1964, when Col Sun and his crew were shot down over the Shandong peninsula.

When a C-54 was acquired by the 34th Squadron for airdrop missions in 1961 the 'Gimo' paid an inspection visit to Hsinchu.

Chinese air defence commanders strived to develop new methods of shooting down the special missions from Taiwan. In the fall of 1961 they cleverly set an AAA trap for P2Vs entering northern China after takeoff from Korea.

Thumbs-up from this happy group of airmen from the Black Bats. But the mood in the squadron turned sombre when a mission over mainland China failed to return. Col Ye Lin (second from left) led the P2V crew that was ambushed by the Chicom AAA deployment over the Liaotung Peninsula on the night of 4 November 1961.

CAF commander Gen Chen makes presentations to senior aircrew of the 34th Squadron (left to right) Lt Col Liu, Col Dai, Lt Col Zhu and Col Zhao.

Ray Cline and Chiang Ching Kuo were frequent visitors to the 34th Squadron. Here they share a drink and a joke with squadron commander Col Guo Tong De and one of his NCOs. Guo was killed a few months later in the crash of a P2V into the sea just offshore from North Korea.

The C-54 supplied to the Black Bats squadron had the enlarged cargo opening with an inward-sliding door to allow for the speedy airdrop of agents and supplies. It flew eight airdrop missions into the mainland in 1962-63 and was attacked by MiG fighters and AAA on two of them.

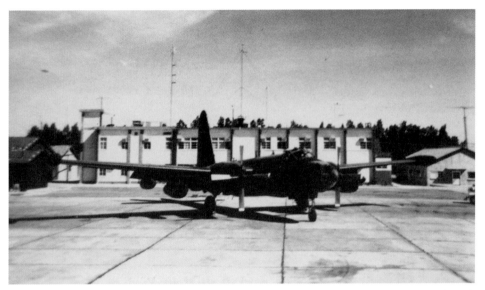

This P2V parked outside the 34th Squadron operations building at Hsinchu is carrying air sampling pods under each wing. They were added in 1962 to help gather intelligence on China's developing nuclear weapons program.

This maintenance crew of four Chinese and one American take a break from working on one of the P2V's auxiliary turbojets.

A P2V faces the maintenance dock at Hsinchu. The wingtip bulge contains additional antennas for the ATIR air-to-air radar jammer.

Col Sun Yi Chen was a popular and effective commander of the Black Bats from late 1962 until he and his crew were shot down over the Shandong Peninsula in June 1964.

P2V pilot Lt Col Li Bang Xun (left) survived many perilous missions over the mainland from 1961-65. Col Guan Bo Ping (right) was aircraft commander for the last two overflights by the Black Bats.

Above: Chinese and American airmen together: Lt Col Zhu Zhen of the Black Bats and P2V instructor pilot Gordon Raymer from the NACC. Below: Bill Nelson (left), who replaced Ray Cline as the CIA station chief, and Col George Rew (right), who was head of the NACC Air Section in 1962-63.

This C-47 (6110) was the second to serve the Black Bats as a communications aircraft. It was acquired in 1962. American pilots from the NACC enjoyed flying it up and down Taiwan as they commuted between Taipei and Hsinchu, and sometimes to the U.S. airbases on Okinawa (where the base exchanges offered superior shopping opportunities!).

The wreckage of P2V (739) shot down over Jiangxi in June 1963 with the loss of all 15 crew.

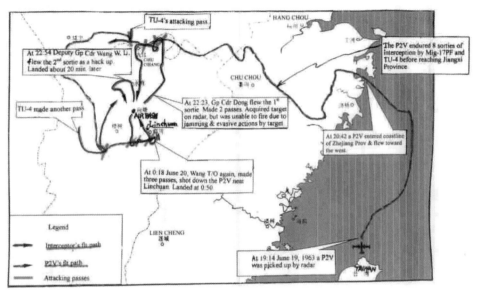

At 22:54 Deputy Gp Cdr Wang W. Li flew the 2nd sortie as a back up. Landed about 20 min. later

TU-4's attacking pass.

HANG CHOU

The P2V endured 8 sorties of interception by Mig-17PF and TU-4 before reaching Jiangxi Province

CHU CHOU

TU-4 made another pass

At 22:23, Gp Cdr Dong flew the 1st sortie. Made 2 passes. Acquired target on radar, but was unable to fire due to jamming & evasive actions by target

At 20:42 a P2V entered coastline of Zhejiang Prov & flew toward the west

Linchuan

At 0:18 June 20, Wang T/O again, made three passes, shot down the P2V near Linchuan. Landed at 0:50

Legend
→ Interceptor's flt path
→ P2V's flt path
~~~ Attacking passes

LIEN CHENG

At 19:14 June 19, 1963 a P2V was picked up by radar

TAIWAN

This is how the Chicom air defences organised the shootdown, after no fewer than eight previous unsuccessful attacking runs by MiG-17 fighters sent up to intercept the P2V that night.

Chinese Premier Chou En Lai congratulates MiG-17 pilot Wang Wen Li and the GCI controller who guided him to intercept the P2V. The eagle-eyed Wang spotted the intruder by the faint glow from its shielded engine exhaust.

This MiG-17PF in a Beijing museum is the one flown by Wang during the successful intercept. Note the radome of the aircraft's RP-5 (Scan Odd) intercept radar in the engine intake.

NACC instructor pilot John McCaull took this inflight photo of a P2V over Taiwan while following in the 34th Squadron's B-26 trainer. Note the underwing racks for AIM-9 Sidewinder air-to-air missiles next to the auxiliary turbojets. Outboard of the missile racks are the air sampling pods.

Following page: This map shows the locations where the Black Bats lost five P2Vs during operations against the Chinese mainland: (A) crashed into high ground, 25 March 1960; (B) shot down by AAA fire in November 1961; (C) crashed into the sea in January 1962; (D) shot down by MiG-17 in June 1963; and (E) shot down by MiG-15 in June 1964. Also shown are four typical missions by the Black Bats: (1) the epic P2V flight on 19 November 1960, which survived multiple attacks and led to the loss of two converted Tu-2 interceptors by the Chicoms; (2) another intense P2V mission on 19 December 1960 that survived multiple attacks from a Tu-4 bomber-interceptor and MiG fighters, as well as sustained fire from anti-aircraft guns; (3) the first airdrop mission by the 34th Squadron's C-54 on 5 June 1962, which was attacked by a MiG-17; and (4) the last overflight of the mainland by a P2V on 11 June 1966.

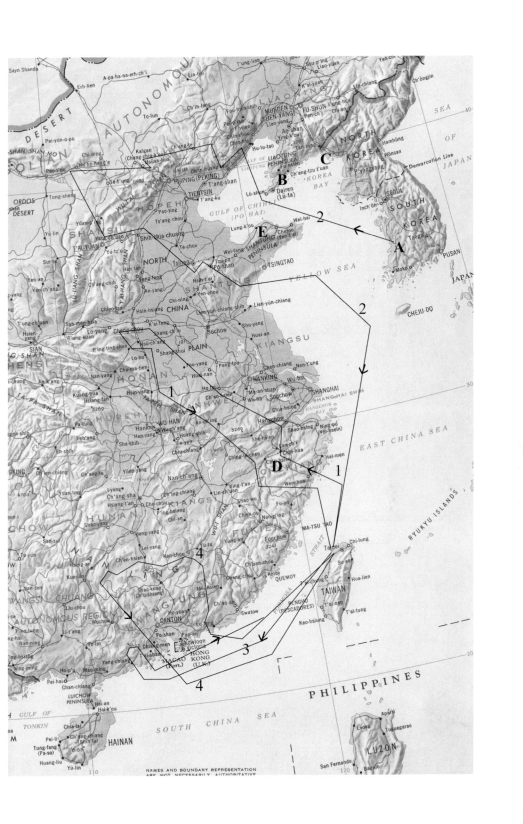

A gray painted P2V-5 aircraft was sent to Taiwan in 1964 to be used as a crew trainer. In this 1966 photo, Chiang Ching Kuo is escorted on an inspection visit to Hsinchu by 34th squadron commander Col Lu De Qi (left), CAF commander Gen Xu Huang Sheng (centre), and Gen Yang Shiao Lian, the CAF's intelligence chief (right).

Black painted P-3A 149673 takes off on a flight test. It was the first of three Navy Orions to be converted for CIA covert operations at Greenville, Texas, by LTV Electrosystems, a forerunner of E-Systems.

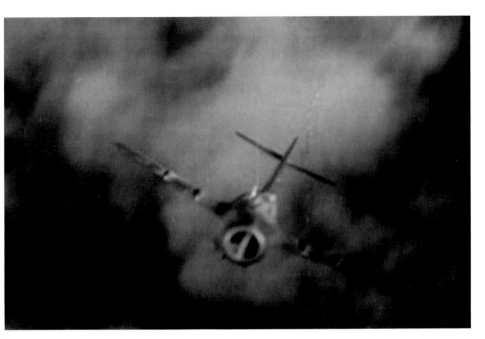

Aircrews on the Black Bats' overflights rarely caught sight of the MiG fighters that intercepted them. They would nearly always attack from the rear quadrant, having been guided to within closing distance by ground controllers.

When Col Sun's P2V was lit up by flares dropped by an Il-28 it was a relatively easy task for MiG-15 pilot Chen Gen Fa to destroy the intruder with his 23mm and 37mm cannons.

The wreckage of the P2V that was shot down over Shandong in 1964 contained the aircraft's AIM-9 missiles. These were recovered by the Chicoms, along with some of the sensitive ECM equipment.

Navy pilot Chen is congratulated by Chinese Premier Chou En Lai after the shootdown.

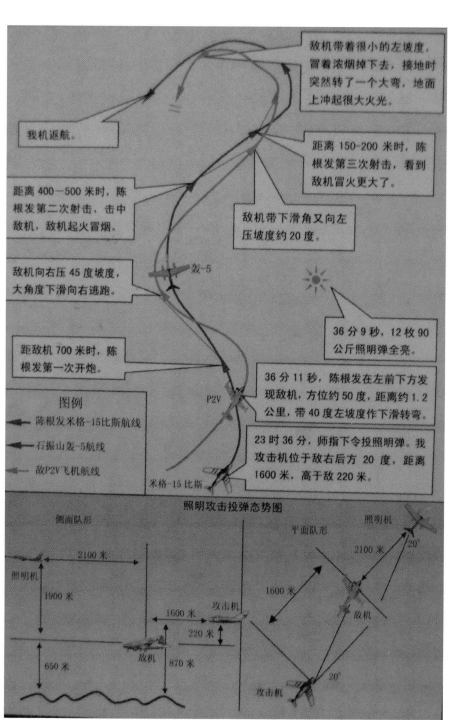

The co-ordinated maneuvering by the Il-28 that dropped the flares and the MiG-15 that pressed the attack on the P2V, are shown in this map drawn by Chinese artists.

Col John Lackey (left) was the head of the Air Section in Taiwan from 1964-66. His opposite number was Col Lu De Qi (right), who took command of the 34th Squadron in August 1964 after Col Sun was shot down.

The large map at the far end of the operations room at Hsinchu shows potential routes and dangers in southern China and North Vietnam. By 1966 this area was the focus of U.S. interest as the Vietnam War escalated.

Don Grigsby was the CIA's manager at Hsinchu during 1965-66 and was succeeded by Jack Grier.

Right: The last two P2Vs at Hsinchu are framed in the window as the CIA's base manager Jack Grier presents 34th Squadron commander Col Lu De Qi with a model of the soon-to-be-received P-3A. Below: American crewmen from the NACC around the modified tail of a P2V at Hsinchu in 1966

P2V instructor pilot John McCaull shares a drink with four Black Bats pilots who were selected for training on the P-3. From left to right: Major Huang Wen Lu; Col Zhu Zhen; Major Lui Hong Yi; and Major Yu Chuan Wen. Yu became the 34th squadron commander in 1970. He was also trained to fly the C-123, C-130, and Twin Otter.

A formal ceremony was held at Hsinchu to mark the arrival of the new P-3s.

Above: CIA station chief Harold Ford and CAF commander Gen Xu cut the ribbon to inaugurate the new aircraft. Note the enlarged and inward-opening door of the converted P-3, suitable for the rapid airborne deployment of agents and supplies. Below: Accompanied by Col Lu and Gen Yang, Chiang Ching Kuo inspects the ECM operator stations inside the P-3. Although designed to replace the P2V on overflights of mainland China, the two P-3s sent to Taiwan never did penetrate denied territory during their short stay.

Head-on view of this black P-3 at Hsinchu shows the intakes for gas sampling on the forward fuselage and twin racks for AIM-9 missiles on the left wing.

Aerial view of the Black Bats area of Hsinchu airbase taken in 1966. Visible are the squadron's gray P2V-5 trainer, a P-3, a P2V, a C-123, and the C-47 transport.

Ramp scene at Hsinchu in 1966. The last two P2Vs have been augmented by the two new P-3s. A C-123B is also visible.

In 1968, the 34th Squadron sent crews to the U.S. for C-130 Hercules conversion training. The rigorous course included five months at the top secret Groom Lake airbase in Nevada, where they learnt to fly a C-130E Hercules that had been upgraded for special missions.

In 1963, the U.S. supplied five ECM-equipped C-123Bs transports to Taiwan for use by the 34th Squadron. Rather than being used to for airdrops over China they were sent to Vietnam, where the nationalist Chinese crews flew covert missions over North Vietnam under contract to the U.S.

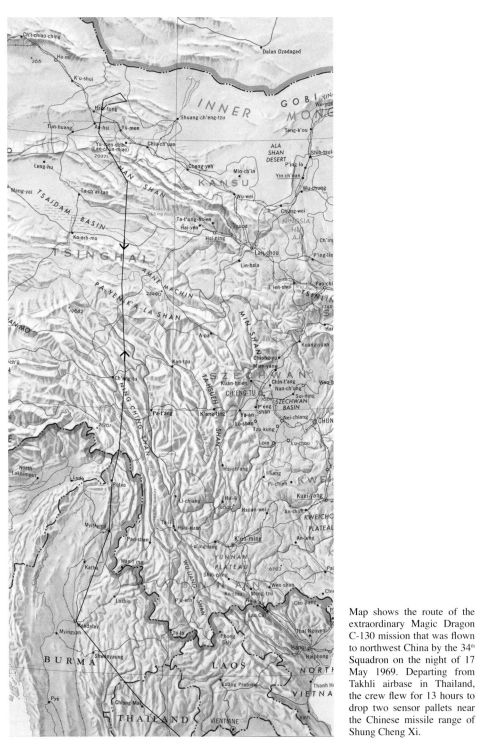

Map shows the route of the extraordinary Magic Dragon C-130 mission that was flown to northwest China by the 34th Squadron on the night of 17 May 1969. Departing from Takhli airbase in Thailand, the crew flew for 13 hours to drop two sensor pallets near the Chinese missile range of Shung Cheng Xi.

Above: Col Sun Pei Zhen (right) commanded the Magic Dragon mission and later became 34th Squadron commander. He is seen here in 1966, greeting Chiang Ching Kuo and Gen Yang on a visit to Hsinchu. Below: The presence of the Chinese C-123 aircrews in Vietnam was kept secret, but the Black Bats were able to incorporate their treasured emblem into the crest of the First Flight Detachment (FFD), which was the official designation of their unit.

The original C-123Bs were replaced with upgraded versions codenamed Duck Hook. The modifications included a terrain-following radar and a coat of 'velvet' radar-absorbent camouflage paint.

In common with most other C-123s, auxiliary turbojets were added to those belonging to the FFD, making them into C-123K Heavy Hook models. After the FFD stopped flying covert missions into North Vietnam in 1968 it switched to airlift missions in support of special forces within South Vietnam. This FFD aircraft is seen at Khe Sanh airstrip.

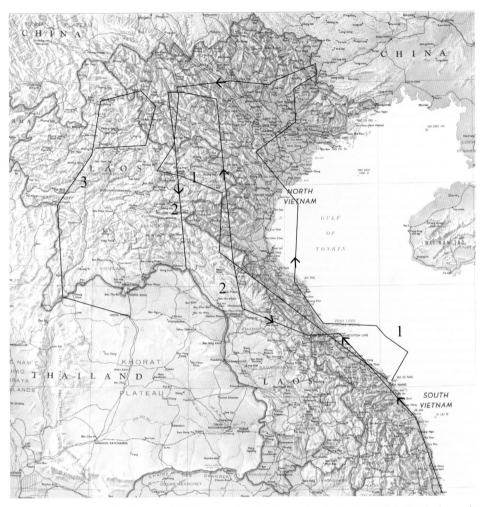

Map shows three covert missions over North Vietnam flown by the Black Bats: (1) a P2V ELINT-gathering sortie out of Da Nang on the night of 20 August 1962; (2) the C-123 overflight on 14 February 1965 to drop agents that was hit by gunfire and made an emergency landing at Nakhon Phanom airbase on the Thai-Laos border; and (3) a typical airdrop mission to the western hills of North Vietnam flown out of Udon airbase in Thailand on the night of 31 July 1966.

In 1971-72, airmen from the 34th Squadron flew this Twin Otter on airdrop missions for the CIA over Laos and North Vietnam.

In pursuit of 'deniability,' the CIA also called on the Black Bats squadron to provide helicopter crews for covert missions from Laos.

The 'Quiet One' outside its special hangar at the PS-44 airstrip in southern Laos. Chinese crews were trained to fly this specially modified Hughes 500 helicopter on a daring phonetap mission into North Vietnam, but the CIA eventually preferred American pilots.

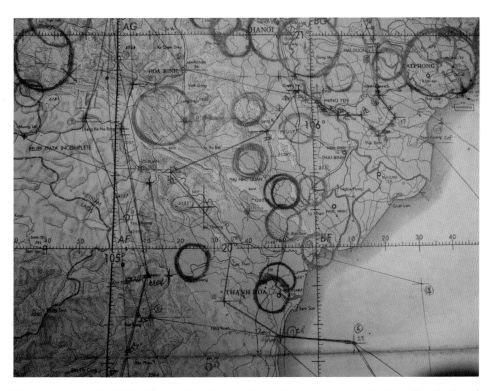

Mission planners at the FFD in Vietnam drew threat circles in blue and red representing the radius of action of radar-directed 85mm and 37mm anti-aircraft guns that were known to be deployed in the Red River delta south of Hanoi. The task was then to devise a route for the C-123 to the required location for an airdrop that would avoid these threats. As can be seen, this wasn't easy!

The CIA's three P-3As were returned to the U.S. Navy in 1967. Two of them were converted to the EP-3B 'Bat Rack' configuration and assigned to VQ-1 squadron as ELINT gathering aircraft.

Left: The Black Bats insignia included the seven stars of the Big Dipper constellation, since its 3 + 4 served to represent the squadron number.

Below and following: A selection of colourful propaganda leaflets that were dropped over mainland China by the aircraft of the Black Bats squadron. Below: "Rise up, all who don't want to be slaves. Follow the example of the Tibetan people!" Opposite Top Left: "We drop rice and foodstuffs to help you." Opposite Top Right: "In 1955, the Communists stole the land from the farmers, and made them work in co-operatives where party cadres give the orders." Bottom: "Uprising in Tibet and the southwestern provinces."

一九五五年
中共實行農業合作化,
把土地收回。

加入合作社,死路一條!

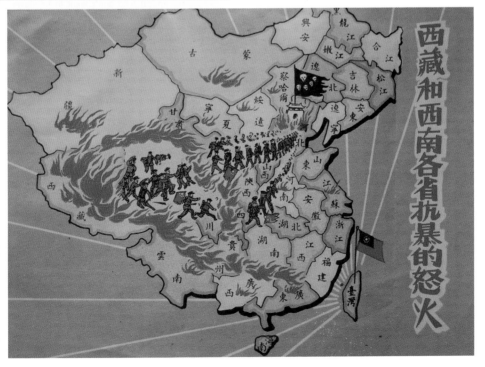

西藏和西南各省抗暴的怒火

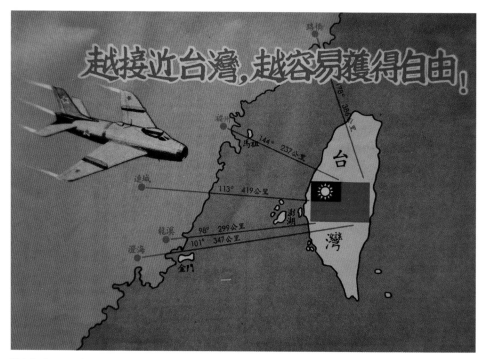

越接近台灣，越容易獲得自由！

This leaflet was dropped over communist airbases opposite Taiwan. It encouraged PLAAF MiG pilots to switch sides by promising them rewards in gold, and specifying the headings and distances that they should fly to reach the nationalist island. The leaflets had some success. A Mig-15 and a MiG-17 that were flown to Taiwan by defecting pilots are seen below. Three more MiG-19s also arrived, plus an Il-28 bomber. All five are still on display at the ROCAF Museum, Kangshan airbase.

An honour guard at the ceremony in 2001 that marked the return from the mainland of the remains of the B-17 aircrew shot down 42 years earlier.

Author Chris Pocock (center) meets veterans of the 34th Squadron in Taipei. They are (left to right) Zhu Zhen, Zhao Qin, Lu De Chi, Liu K Y, Li Bang Xun, and Zou Li Xu.

Zou and Li remember those stirring but sad days when so many of their colleagues perished. Both have contributed their recollections to an oral history of the Black Bats squadron. Some of their frank and powerful comments are reprinted in this book.

Senior commanders serving in today's Republic of China Air Force (ROCAF) join veterans from the 34th Squadron at the opening ceremony of The Black Bat Squadron Memorial Hall in Hsinchu. Phil Li Chong Shan (left) is reading a message of support from his former American colleague in the squadron, Don Jackson. While flying as an ECM officer, Li survived many attacks during missions over the China mainland in the P4Y-2, B-17 and P2V. He helped design the Black Bats emblem, and has been instrumental in preserving the history of this very special squadron.

Three notable Black Bat veterans at the opening ceremony for the memorial hall. Lu De Chi (left); Zhao Qin (centre) and Dai Shu Qing (right) were all pilots who commanded many perilous overflights - and somehow lived to tell the tale!

Charles Yin displays a framed map that illustrates how the mainland air defences shot down his father's P2V over the Liaodong peninsula in 1961. Yin is one of a number of relatives who have travelled from Taiwan to mainland China, to visit the crash sites where their loved ones perished.

(FLIR) system, and a much improved terrain following radar. For self-protection there was a radar warning and jamming system. The Chinese airmen were very impressed with the Herk's avionics; some of them had come straight from the ROC's elderly and basic C-46 and C-119 transports.[234]

The crews began a first phase of operational conversion by flying daylight missions at various altitudes, all the way to the Mexican border in the south and the Canadian border in the north. The USAF launched fighters to intercept them so that they could become familiar with the C-130's defensive systems.

Then came the phase two conversion, which was flying at night and low level, and the airdropping of pallets. The FLIR was a key aid here, although when the training started it could only display still frames of scenery. Later, it was upgraded to provide motion imagery. Over the high ground of Oregon and Washington state, the CAF crews flew over terrain that matched what they would encounter as they flew north across the eastern Himalayas. Around Groom Lake itself the desert terrain matched that of northwest China.

Survival training was also provided. It may have been meant as a morale booster, since it was difficult to imagine how the airmen from Taiwan could have made their escape if their aircraft went down so far from home. In any event, the crews spent two cold and uncomfortable weeks on a mountain in Oregon.

The airmen from the 34th Squadron stayed at Groom Lake for over six months to complete their training. Before they left the U.S. in April 1969, Col Sun selected members for the primary and backup crews. They were flown from San Francisco to Hawaii for a one week holiday, then it was onwards via Midway to Kadena airbase, Okinawa, where they practised some more night flying on the C-130, which had been flown there by an American crew.

Summoned

On Taiwan the Black Bats commander, Lu De Qi, was summoned to meet Chiang Ching Kuo. CCK asked Lu whether the Magic Dragon mission would succeed. He was worried that, if it failed, another large group of Air Force widows would be created. Lu told Chiang that the chances of success were high. But when Lu then flew to Okinawa to meet the C-130 crew he asked each of them to write their wills, in case they did not return.[235]

Then the CAF group was flown from Kadena to Takhli in a USAF C-130. At the Thai airbase they were kept indoors, to maintain maximum security. After three weeks the dark grey C-130E for the mission arrived, and the primary CAF crew flew two more night

MAGIC DRAGON MISSION PLANNING

We relied heavily upon overhead satellite imagery of the Gobi desert. The maps that we had of the area were not very accurate. The imagery was also used to check whether the sensor pallet was correctly camouflaged for the terrain up there. We also used it to check for any air defenses along the route, and to select waypoints.

We could see a lake about 30 minutes from the drop zone, which seemed like a good waypoint. Then someone pointed out that it might be dry at other times of the year. So we requested more satellite imagery of that area according to season. The satellite had to be specially tasked for us. Fortunately, we had time. It took a year-and-a-half to develop the sensor package, train the crews, and run the mission.

We did also have a source in place, who was able to do some reconnaissance on the ground for us. But you just couldn't carry any equipment into mainland China, otherwise we could have deployed the sensors that way. - *Bob Kleyla interview*

training flights. Then came the formal mission briefing. Bob Kleyla and his colleagues from the Air Branch told the Chinese aircrew of their confidence that the C-130 would not be detected by ChiCom air defences during the long flight northwards towards the objective. They needed some convincing. The session included a formal escape and evasion briefing – a charade, really, since no one was going to rescue this aircrew from the eastern Himalayas or the Gobi Desert, and they were hardly going to walk out![236]

The drop zone this time would be on the Shuangchengzi missile test range. The location was 90 nautical miles from the airfield at the missile launch area, but thanks to terrain masking the low-flying C-130 would likely not show up on the radar there. Three SA-2 SAM sites had been identified on the missile range from satellite photography. They posed a serious threat to medium-level bombers or high-flying U-2s. But the ChiComs had no Hawk-type missiles that could shoot down a low-flying aircraft, the mission planners assured the Chinese crew. Under cover of darkness the chances of success were good, they said.[237]

After the briefing the 34th squadron crew studied the maps and the waypoints. There would be few outside references over the desolate, uninhabited terrain that they would be flying over in the dark, for hours on end. They would be in Chinese airspace for seven hours.

Unmarked Aircraft
A few more days passed. Then, on the afternoon of 17 May 1969 Col Sun led his crew of 12 to the unmarked aircraft. He had two co-pilots, three navigators, one radio operator, two electronic warfare officers, a crew chief, and two loadmasters, or 'kickers.'

What looked like two large sandstone rocks were already secured in the rear fuselage, ready to be pushed out of the plane. They were the sensor packages, fixed to pallets and then disguised with Styrofoam to blend with the desert into which they would be dropped. Large parachutes were attached to the 'rocks' to slow their descent. Cordite charges were sewn into the canopies. The charges were set to ignite when the assembly hit the ground, so that no large and tell-tale sections of parachute would remain attached.[238]

In the forward fuselage there were two Benson tanks to provide additional fuel. There was also a gas and particle air sampling system fed by an airscoop. With all this equipment the C-130 exceeded the maximum gross takeoff weight of 173,000 lbs.

At 1700 local time the heavily-laden C-130 taxied for takeoff in radio silence. Eleven minutes later a green light was shone from the control tower. The pilots advanced the throttles and the C-130 lumbered down the runway, slowly picking up speed. It left the ground and climbed away to the northwest.

The aircraft passed over Chiang Mai and crossed into Burma at 16,000 feet. Slowly the C-130 climbed to 19,000 feet as it passed over Mandalay and Myitkina. As it approached the Chinese border the mountains of the Hengduan range were only 800 feet below! The navigators worked the search radar and the FLIR to ensure that they flew the correct course and avoided Indian airspace, not far to the west. It was very dark, and thunderstorms were brewing as the C-130 crossed into China at 2035.

The crew pressed on, flying just 1,000 feet above the high plateau of the eastern Himalayas along the border between Xizang and Sichuan. If they had flown higher, early warning radars at Chengdu, 200 miles to the east, might have picked them up. As the aircraft

THE MAGIC DRAGON MISSION RECALLED

At the secret desert base, our movements were strictly controlled. We were only allowed to go to the bathrooms, the gym, the laundry and the cinema. But we were very comfortable. All meals and drinks were free, and the Americans met our particular needs. The rice and other Chinese food was flown in. They even provided preserved Tofu! The base commander joined some of our leisure activities. An American flight surgeon lived with us full-time. And I remember four other Americans who were always around. I guess that they were sent by CIA to watch over us. - *Lt Col Feng Hai Tao(馮海濤), C-130 navigator, from Black Bat Squadron Oral History, p218*

At first, our English was not very good. And there was no interpreter at the ground school. But we got better. We were specially selected, and realised that we were representing our country. So we studied hard, so as not to lose face. In fact, the training we got in the U.S. was crucial to my future career. I got good grades, and grew in confidence. - *Lt Col Feng Hai Tao, C-130 navigator, from Black Bat Squadron Oral History, p220*

In class one day, I heard a strange-sounding jet taking off. Looking through the window, I saw it was a MiG fighter. The instructor immediately pulled down the blinds and said: "Don't look outside!" He also told us not to talk to other people, when we went to lunch, or to the laundry. The Americans didn't want other people on that base to know we were there. Even the ROC Embassy didn't know exactly where we were. - *Lt Col Feng Hai Tao, C-130 navigator, from Black Bat Squadron Oral History, p222*

As far as I know, the two detection sensors were ...made up of over 30 sophisticated electronic instruments. They had antennae projecting outwards... They were highly sensitive, capable of collecting data including the air's molecular weight and radioactive levels, even capable of detecting a heat source from one kilometre away. - *Wang Zhen Zhong, interpreter, in MND Vietnam Oral History, p163, 165*

When we arrived back at Takhli after the mission, our American instructors hugged us with tears in their eyes. That moved us deeply. They told us that the mission had been attempted several times before, without success. They said that they would be sending a report of our safe return to Washington, and ask the government to reward us properly. We didn't know much about our mission, until we realized that it was to collect information on the mainland's missile tests. No wonder we got such good treatment!

But I do believe that our mission was more difficult than that of the U-2...going in at low-altitude. - *Lt Col Feng Hai Tao, C-130 navigator, from Black Bat Squadron Oral History, p228*

flew further north more early warning radars at Lanzhou posed the threat of detection. But the ECM officers on board the C-130 reported only one fleeting radar contact.[239]

The crew were supposed to make a coded, burst transmission to the command post in Thailand at each waypoint. At the third of these inside China, at the point where the borders of Qinghai, Sichuan, and Xizang (Tibet) meet, the Birdwatcher transmitter failed. The subsequent silence was a discomforting development to the CIA group that were monitoring the flight at Takhli.

Nearly six hours after takeoff the aircraft passed over the Kola lake and entered Gansu province. It descended into the Ochinaho basin of the Gobi Desert and maintained a height of 500 feet above the ground. The last waypoint before the drop zone was abeam the small desert town of Anxi. The kickers sprang into action as the moment of truth approached. Just before midnight the first of the two pallets was released. The second was released a few miles further on. The drop zone was only 90 miles from China's border with Mongolia.

The crew reversed course to head back the way they had come. Had they been spotted by radar at Shuangchengzi airfield, 125 miles to the east?

As the C-130 passed over a large village, near a dam, all the lights suddenly went out. The crew thought it was a reaction to their overflight – a blackout. Mindful that the dam might be defended by anti-aircraft guns they made a sharp detour. But there were no more alarms, and once they were well clear of the missile range the pilot climbed back to 1,000 feet.

Now came the long haul back across the eastern Himalayas. All went well until they approached the Yunnan/Xizang border, where they flew back into the thunderstorms. St Elmo's Fire danced along the aircraft's surfaces and played havoc with the electrical systems. The gyro-navigator failed, and a fuel gauge began to read erratically.

At 0332 the aircraft finally left Chinese airspace and flew back into Burma. Navigating by ADF only, it was another two hours before they reached the border with Thailand. Rather than trying to reach Takhli, Col Sun decided to make a precautionary landing at Chiang Mai. He touched down there at 0610 after a thirteen-hour flight. Another C-130 flew up from Takhli to fetch them. There were emotional scenes as the crew were reunited with their American sponsors.[240]

After resting 24 hours the 34th Squadron crew were flown home to Taiwan. CAF commander Lai Ming Tang (賴明湯) hosted a banquet for them. A few days later Chiang Ching Kuo presented them with medals and a bonus of NT$6,000 in a secret ceremony inside the MND.

The Chinese crew were not told whether the sensors that they dropped had performed as advertised or not. But the USAF Major who served as liaison officer to the Chinese group told interpreter Wang Zhen Zhong (王振中) that the sensors began operating normally. The pallets had a battery life of six months. Retractable antennas were supposed to transmit the collected data, possibly to a 'T' series satellite that the CIA had recently deployed for communication with agents operating in denied territory. It seems that some useful intelligence was returned from the desert of northwest China, but Operation Heavy Tea has never been declassified by the U.S.[241]

Another Flight

Early in 1970 the CIA began planning another flight. In March, the 34th Squadron crews returned again to the U.S. and the Groom Lake base for refresher flying. Since Col Sun was taking over command of the 34th Squadron from Col Lu, deputy squadron commander Col Yu Chuan Wen (庾傳文) led the group. He had been the backup crew commander for the first C-130 mission.

The nickname for the operation was changed to Golden Whip. There were some other changes: the drop zone would be moved 280 miles to the west, close to Lop Nor but further away from the Shuangchengzi range head and its air defences. The FLIR on board the C-130 would be upgraded to provide better image quality.[242]

But for reasons that were never explained to Yu and his crew the operation was called off while they were still in the U.S. Maybe it just wasn't so important anymore, to run the risk of exposure. The PRC's strategic weapons development program had not made the progress envisaged a few years earlier. Maybe it had been slowed by the Cultural Revolution. Maybe the technical challenges were too great for the PRC. From the satellite coverage that was now comprehensive, U.S. intelligence was confident that no operational MRBMs had been deployed. Moreover, statements from the Chinese leadership that they would never be the first to use nuclear weapons were reassuring.

Therefore, the remarkable C-130 mission to northwest China flown by the Black Bats in May 1969 became the 586th and last overflight of the mainland by the 34th Squadron and its predecessors.

Chapter Eight

Southeast Asia
1960-1973

In December 1960 Taiwan sent a C-46 and a C-47 to Laos to help the government's desperate need for air transport. At the time, no one could have foreseen that airmen from the nationalist island would fly many hundreds of airlift and airdrop missions in southeast Asia throughout the coming decade. About half of these missions would be covert, at the behest of the U.S. government. Moreover, 76 Chinese airmen would lose their lives while supporting the anti-communist cause in this troubled region.

The C-46 and C-47 belonged to China Airlines (CAL), which was created by the government in Taipei in 1959. Although China Airlines would provide competition to the CIA-owned Civil Air Transport (CAT), the move was approved by the Taipei station chief, Ray Cline. Indeed, CAL became Taiwan's second 'deniable' airline, supplementing routine commercial services with contract work for the CIA through the nationalist government. The relationship between the Chinese Air Force and CAL was symbiotic. They were "like twins," according to Gen I Fu En, who helped to set up the new airline, even though he was officially serving full time as the intelligence chief in CAF headquarters.[243]

The 26-strong group from CAL that went to Vientiane was named the North Star Team. This provided flight operations and maintenance for Veha Akhat Airlines, a new airline that flew more than conventional air transport routes. In February 1961 the C-47 was airdropping supplies to anti-communist hill tribesmen when it was shot down by the Pathet Lao, killing the crew. CAL sent replacement aircrews and two more C-47s to Laos. But the operation would soon be dwarfed by the growth of Air America, the proprietary airline that helped the CIA fight a 'secret' war against the communists in Laos throughout the 1960s.[244]

The South Star Team
In the spring of 1962 the CIA turned again to China Airlines, this time for help in Vietnam. There, a program to insert native agents into North Vietnam by air had been started. Project Haylift used a small group of Vietnamese aircrews led by Lt Col Nguyen Cao Key who

---

CHINA AIRLINES

When China Airlines was founded, it entered into an agreement with the Chinese Air Force to rent its aircraft and equipment without approval from the US advisers. The MAAG head, Gen Kenneth Sanborn, once protested to me mockingly. He pulled from his pocket a small notebook in which he had recorded the dates when China Airlines 'borrowed' aircraft and equipment, and a list of US-trained personnel employed by the company without his approval. "Frankly, I keep one eye open and one eye closed," he said. To which I replied, "Ken, you'd better keep both eyes closed!"

- Gen I Fu En memoir, p181

UNDER COVER IN VIETNAM

Judging by my easy entry into Vietnam, Nguyen Cao Ky seemed to enjoy a fairly special and venerated status. I obtained a Vietnamese identity almost immediately: Mt Thanh. Col Easy (a pseudonym) of the US Air Force thought my hair was too short to look like a Vietnamese. He urged me to grow it longer so I could work under cover.

We wore plain clothes in Vietnam. Several American airmen working for the CIA interfaced with us. They also used assumed names.

China Airlines rented two four-storey apartment buildings in Saigon for the Project members. CAL was handsomely paid according to the number of assignments completed. - *Dai Shu Qing, MND Vietnam Oral History, p191-2*

were trained by Air America pilots to fly night covert airdrops using a C-47. The operation was given a commercial airline 'cover' story - Vietnamese Air Transport (VIAT). After inserting three teams the C-47 was shot down on a resupply mission. The Agency supplied a C-54 to replace it. But after inserting a fourth team the Vietnamese C-54 crew flew into high ground while approaching the drop zone on a resupply mission.[245]

China Airlines agreed to take over the air operations of VIAT – in return for a large payment by the CIA. CAL created the South Star Team and sent to Saigon 23 air and ground crew and two C-46 transports. The aircraft and most of the crew came from the CAF. The deal also included maintenance of VIAT's remaining C-54 in Taiwan. When Lt Col Key flew it back to Saigon he was joined by some of the South Star Team, including Col Dai Shu Qing, the former Black Bats B-17 and P2V pilot.

The China Air Lines contingent in Saigon masqueraded as Vietnamese. The Chinese C-46 and C-54 crews each comprised two pilots, two navigators, and two flight engineers. They flew sensitive personnel and cargo within South Vietnam, as well as the covert insertions into North Vietnam. The South Star Team flew its first such mission in May 1962, dropping a sabotage team of seven Vietnamese soldiers. Another drop was completed four days later, and a number of resupply missions to teams that had been inserted earlier were flown later in the year.[246]

During 1962 the U.S. agreed to supply the ROC with five C-123Bs that might be used for airdrop missions over mainland China by the 34th Squadron – subject to mutual agreement (see Chapter 6). The C-123 was a medium-size airlifter powered by twin P & W piston engines. The Fairchild company built 300 of them for the USAF during the 1950s. It could take off in less than 1,500 feet and land in 1,000 feet. It carried about 20 paratroops, or a cargo load of 23,000 lbs. The rear loading ramp opened hydraulically in flight so that pallets and other equipment could be airdropped in quick succession. This was a considerable improvement on the side-opening door of the C-54, through which the dropping of loads took more time, meaning that they were more widely spaced when they hit the ground.

VIETNAMESE AGENTS

The U.S.-trained Vietnamese agents were all very bright and resourceful. However, they seemed to need more training in parachuting. Some of them got scared when it was time to jump. When that happened, the 'kickers' would grasp them and kick them out of the plane…The intervals at which they were supposed to parachute were delayed as a result…resulting in them landing off the target zone. Compounded by the obstacles created by the rough terrain, the six agents would have a hard time finding each other… - *Dai Shu Qing, in MND Vietnam Oral History, p196*

Modified C-123Bs

In early 1962 the CIA acquired five C-123Bs from the USAF for use by Air America in Laos and Vietnam.

In mid-1962 the CIA acquired five more C-123Bs for Taiwan, and sent them to the Lockheed Skunk Works for modification as covert insertion aircraft. The 'smart' air-to-air jammer that had proved its worth over mainland China on the P2Vs was to be added. So was the BSTR system to jam the radars of anti-aircraft guns. A defensive operator's station was added to operate the jammers. Other additions to the five C-123Bs included extra fuel in underwing tanks, one on each side.

But ATI ran into manpower problems, since the CIA was also pressing the small company to develop new ECM systems to protect the U-2. There were delays in adding the ATIR and BSTR jammers to the C-123s at the Skunk Works. Meanwhile, the 36-strong Chinese contingent of pilots, navigators, ECM officers, and engineers that had been sent to the U.S. for training completed their conversion course at Pope AFB in late November 1962. The new recruits to the Black Bat squadron returned to Taiwan without their new aircraft.[247]

Meanwhile, there were more difficult negotiations between the U.S. and the ROC over how to use the C-123s. Eventually, a deal was done whereby two of them would be used in the covert airdrops over North Vietnam, flown by the Chinese crews. In March 1963 the U.S. and the ROC signed the South Star II agreement for that purpose. Again, China Airlines was the intermediary for the contract.

The five C-123Bs were flown from the U.S. to Hsinchu that same month. The U.S. government was still stalling on the question of whether the C-123s could also be used over mainland China. Despite Chiang Kai Shek's assurance that an expansion of airdrops would pay dividends, there had been a string of covert insertion failures along the mainland coast since mid-1962. The 34th Squadron's C-54 that was dedicated to airdrops was twice nearly shot down over Guangdong.

The CAF's new C-123 crews had only gone through a basic conversion course in the U.S. They needed more instruction in low-level and nighttime flying. American instructors from the NACC devised a training program, but this had hardly begun when one of the C-123s crashed into the Pingtung Dahu mountain in southern Taiwan on the night of 10 May. All 12 Chinese crew were killed. At least one instructor from the NACC, electronics

---

THE C-123 CRASH IN TAIWAN

In order to prevent a leak, all classified electronic devices onboard the aircraft had to be dismantled and retrieved. One colleague and I was tasked to go along with a US electronics chief and P2V instructor pilot Mr. Hurly (not his real name: US personnel used aliases). Hurly flew us in the C-47 to Pingtung. We hired local aborigines there to guide us to the crash site. The terrain was like a canyon, and we walked along the riverbeds. The way became steeper…there were loose rocks and bushes, but no trail to climb up. We felt the menacing sun over our heads. Hurly looked quite confounded, his usual elegance as a flying instructor disappeared.

Finally we all got to the peak of the mountain, soaked in sweat. We dismantled the classified equipment and asked the aborigines to carry them on their backs down the mountain. The bodies of the crashed pilots had been carried down the day before; it was sad to see their bloodstains left on the control column. - *Zhao Tong Sheng* (趙桐生), *MND Vietnam Oral History, p144*

specialist Fred Severo, might have been on the plane, but his wife insisted that he return to Taipei for a party. Three of the unfortunate Chinese crew were making their last flights before being posted to other squadrons.[248]

The setback could not have come at a worse time. The CIA station in Saigon had an urgent new task for the Vietnamese teams that were being inserted into the North. Hitherto, their purpose had been to gather and report intelligence on the North's military dispositions. But as North Vietnam stepped up its support for the Vietcong and the Pathet Lao, the Agency was trying to sabotage that effort. A number of Vietnamese teams had recently been trained to blow up bridges, railroads, powerplants, and so on. To get these saboteurs into North Vietnam the CIA needed the new C-123s, with their ECM protection and the ability of their crews to fly under dark moon conditions. Instead, they had to make do with the CAL C-54, supplemented by the 34th Squadron's own C-54, which was flown to Saigon in early June by Lu De Qi and his crew. Between 4 and 9 June the two elderly aircraft inserted seven more teams into North Vietnam on five flights.[249]

A team from Air America was sent to Taiwan to beef up the training program for the remaining C-123 crews at Hsinchu. It was led by Captain John Lee, a Chinese-American who had been one of the first Air America pilots to qualify on the C-123 the previous year. In mid-June one of the Chinese crews was declared ready, and flew off to Saigon with their unmarked, gray-painted C-123. When they arrived Vietnamese markings were added to the plane. For the first six months of the operation Air America provided maintenance support at Saigon.

First Operational Mission

On 2 July 1963 the Black Bats flew their first operational mission in the C-123. Taking off from Tan Son Nhut airbase, they climbed to 7,500 feet and headed north. Over Da Nang they turned out to sea and descended to 300 feet to fly up the Gulf of Tonkin. Despite flying at low level, the ECM officer reported that they had been detected by early warning radars on Hainan Island, as well as in North Vietnam. Still, the mission pressed on, turning west to coast-in over Thanh Hoa province. Some propaganda leaflets were dispersed before the C-123 approached the drop zone at midnight. The eight ethnic Vietnamese agents, code named Giant, and their supplies were despatched from 1,800 feet. Two of them didn't want to leave. A few miles further on the 'kickers' despatched a 'dummy' drop of paratroops – to

---

JOHN LEE AND THE C-123

John Lee was a Chinese-American who flew for Air America. He spoke Mandarin and was therefore a good choice as an instructor pilot for the C-123 crews. According to Air America historian William Leary:

The Chinese crews had minimal training at Pope AFB and were not really familiar with the C-123. Lee had to motivate and encourage, building confidence in the airplane. He started from scratch: rank was not important – decisions on aircraft commanders would be based on proficiency. He practised low-level night airdrops: fly 200-300 feet off the water using radar altimeter, simulate penetration of the coast, fly terrain by moonlight, simulate drop. He also demonstrated the capabilities of the airplane: for example, he would come in at 1500 feet over the end of the runway, chop power, dump full flaps, come stright down; flare out, reverse and land within 1000 feet. *- Leary's interview with Lee, from the University of Dallas, Texas, Air America collection (UTD/Leary/I B8F9)*

AIRDROP MISSION PRECAUTIONS – AND DISAGREEMENTS

When an agent (in North Vietnam) needed supplies, he would make a request using a transmitter. If the agent was captured by North Vietnamese forces, such (airdrop) assignments would become excellent opportunities for the enemy to capture us…Therefore when carrying out such assignments, I never indicated the correct arrival time and always approached the target in a different direction from the one instructed by the station. Moreover, I would not hesitate to fly over the target (without dropping supplies) for the safety of the crew.

Before an assignment, Col 'Easy' briefed us on the task and coordinates. After a careful study of the route, I pointed out that the map showed the target had never been surveyed, and its elevation was unknown. There could be serious consequences flying the route. Col Easy wanted me to survey the area first. I flew past the area quickly and found the mountains there were very high. Col Easy sent another C-46 to inspect the area. The aircraft circled looking for the target for half an hour before returning. I predicted that something bad would happen. The enemy could have discovered our route because we spent too much time there. My concern proved to be real. When another crew was sent to carry out a mission along the route, they crashed, killing everyone on board. - *Dai Shu Qing, in MND Vietnam Oral History, p193-5*

keep any observers on the ground guessing as to the exact location of the drop. Then the C-123 set course for Da Nang and Saigon, landing safely after a nine hour flight.[250]

Two days later another two insertion teams were flown north in the China Airlines C-54 on its last Southern Star mission before a second C-123 arrived to take over. But after the first team was successfully dropped the C-54 flew into bad weather and disappeared. No wreckage was ever found.[251]

The second C-123 arrived from Taiwan. On the night of 10 August 1963 both aircraft were sent north. One C-123 successfully made two drops over North Vietnam to insert 10 agents and their supplies. The other was sent to resupply and reinforce a team code named Europa, which had supposedly been operating behind enemy lines ever since being dropped from the VIAT C-54 in November 1962. As the C-123 approached the drop zone in the hills around Hoa Binh the pilots could see the 'T' signal that had been lit on the ground by the waiting team. Suddenly, the ECM operator detected anti-aircraft gun radar. Then tracer fire arced towards the plane and shells exploded all around. The C-123 was flying down a steep valley and could not turn to avoid the gunfire. The pilot dived to the valley floor and the ECM operator started radar jamming. Amazingly the C-123 was not hit, and managed to fly out of trouble. It flew south along the border with Laos and landed at Da Nang, the agents and their supply pallets still on board. The Chinese crew were badly shaken.[252]

A Trap

It was a trap set by the North Vietnamese, and it was only to be expected. Of the 13 teams that the CIA had sent into the North in the past seven months only one was still in radio contact. There were other indications that the entire 'black entry' program going back to 1961 had failed. North Vietnam's rural security force was just as efficient as the people's militias in China in rounding up dissidents and intruders. Of course, no one from the CIA told the Chinese crews about this. William Colby, a veteran of behind-the-lines operations during the Second World War, was station chief in Saigon when the covert insertions began. He remained committed to them after his transfer to Tokyo as deputy head of the FE Division in mid-1962. In fact, all five members of the Europa team had been captured within a day of landing. The radio operator had been 'turned,' in time honored fashion, and was transmitting false reports at Hanoi's bidding.

Ten days later a P2V was sent from Taiwan to make a low-level electronic reconnaissance of the area where the C-123 had been attacked. An American crew from the NACC helped to ferry the aircraft from Hsinchu to Da Nang and back. The operational mission from Da Nang was flown by a 34ᵗʰ Squadron crew led by Zhu Zhen. They recorded numerous AAA radars over North Vietnam and Laos, including over the drop zone of the C-123 mission. In the Dien Bien Phu area anti-aircraft guns opened fire on the P2V but it wasn't hit. The mission also dropped leaflets.[253]

The air defence system in North Vietnam was rapidly expanding thanks to Chinese help, especially along the coast. But policy makers in Washington prevented the airdrop missions from being flown into North Vietnam via Laos. Mission planners preferred this route of entry since radar coverage was weak in that area, and terrain masking could be used to shield the penetrating aircraft. However, the Kennedy administration strangely insisted on sticking to the letter of the 1962 Geneva Agreement on Laotian neutrality, even though the U.S. was sponsoring a growing anti-communist covert action on the ground there. The airdrop missions were obliged to use the same few entry points along the Gulf of Tonkin where gaps in the radar coverage had been identified.[254]

The group of Chinese airmen now assigned to Saigon had other concerns. They complained that the first three airdrops had been too heavily laden with supplies, affecting the aircraft performance, especially when flying through the bad weather that was so often to be expected over southeast Asia. It was now obvious to them that the Southern Star missions would be just as difficult and dangerous as those that their squadron had flown over mainland China for so many years.[255]

But the missions continued. Another 11 were completed by the end of 1963, although five of them were aborted because of bad weather or equipment failures. These included the ECM equipment; both the ATIR and the BSTR jammers failed on one flight. Three of the flights encountered AAA fire. The crews used chaff, manoeuvring, and the jammer to stay alive. When it worked, the BSTR system could quickly break the radar lock of the AA guns.

One improvement was made to the modus operandi by the end of 1963. Instead of making the crews fly all the way from Saigon each time – a roundtrip of up to 14 hours, depending on the location of the drop zone in the North - the missions were flown from Da Nang. The C-123s were ferried to and from Da Nang by the Air America training team led by John Lee, who was still assigned to the operation.[256]

MAINTAINING THE C-123s IN VIETNAM

Since Tan Son Nhut airport lacked maintenance facilities, the electronic equipment was stored in the US Embassy, and installed on the aircraft whenever it was going out for a mission. This made overall operations extremely inconvenient. It rained frequently in Vietnam, so the very modest facilities for the C-123s leaked easily. The electronic equipment was prone to malfunction when it got wet.

Later the C-123s were relocated to Nha Trang, where the US personnel took over the maintenance. - *Zhao Tong Sheng, from MND Vietnam Oral History, p146*

LU DE QI REMEMBERS

The U.S. handsomely rewarded China Airlines for each assignment carried out (by the South Star team). However, China Airlines paid dearly for the income, losing more than ten aircraft and forty outstanding airmen. The developing history of China Airlines was much shed with the blood of the Air Force's servicemen.

During our stay in Vietnam, we were always in plain clothes and wore employee badges issued by China Airlines.

Our US associates were very fond of Chinese food. We frequently got together, establishing a good relationship. Due to the confidentiality of the project, they all used aliases, which made it hard for us to stay in touch after the Project was over. What a pity.

When carrying out the assignments in North Vietnam, the intelligence on the flight routes provided by the US was fairly accurate. Before each missions, we spent a lot of time studying the maps, planning the routes, and memorizing the locations and firepower of North Vietnam's antiaircraft artillery.

We didn't usually fly straight to the North overland. Instead, we went out to sea after takeoff. The captain would choose the coast-in point; we took a different route each time to avoid being ambushed.

Though accompanied by US personnel, (our flights within) South Vietnam were not always free of danger. Sometimes we came across gunfire from Communist guerrillas. - *MND Vietnam Oral History, p224-8*

U.S. Military Takes Control

Meanwhile, the CIA was preparing to hand control of the 'black entry' operations to the U.S. military. The growing strength of the Vietcong had awakened interest in paramilitary operations within the Pentagon. A new Operational Plan (Oplan 34A-64) was drafted. It called for the progressive escalation of pressure on North Vietnam, with the aim of dissuading it from supporting the communist insurgents in the South.[257]

On 1 February 1964 the covert insertions became the responsibility of the newly formed and coyly named Studies and Observations Group (SOG). It was part of the U.S. Military Assistance Command Vietnam (MACV) in Saigon, and was headed by a U.S. Army Colonel from the Special Forces. SOG would become the largest clandestine military unit since the OSS in World War II. The CIA continued to run the secret war in Laos with air support from its proprietary company, Air America. Meanwhile, SOG ran a semi-secret war from its bases in South Vietnam.[258]

But it was a measure of the CIA's failure that of the 36 single or team insertions by air and sea that it had sponsored since 1961, only five were thought worthy of transfer to the SOG in early 1964. The others had now been given up as lost causes – some of them confirmed when North Vietnam went public and put some of the captured agents on trial. By now even Colby was persuaded that the effort was pointless. He now favored the psychological approach – more leaflet drops and 'black' propaganda.[259]

In addition to taking over the black entry operations into North Vietnam, SOG's charter included psychological warfare. The leaflet airdrops were a key part of the strategy. To gain attention, the propaganda message was often attached to a North Vietnam currency note that had been skilfully counterfeited. The aircraft had to fly a specified track and height to ensure that the leaflet bundles were dispersed in the desired direction, according to the wind. That meant flying straight and level for up to 10 minutes as up to 40 bundles were kicked out of the airplane.

SOG also expanded reconnaissance and supported interdiction of the Ho Chi Minh trail. The group recruited Montagnards from the hill tribes of South Vietnam and ethnic Chinese Nungs from the suburbs of Saigon to serve alongside troops from the American Army special forces. South Vietnamese commandos also participated. But as the Vietnam war intensified, SOG's role expanded to various not-so-covert actions beyond the borders of South Vietnam, including the rescue of POWs and downed airmen and the snatching of NVA and Vietcong prisoners for interrogation. The Green Berets of the SOG took heavy casualties and demonstrated countless acts of heroism.

As far as the Chinese C-123 crews were concerned, there was little immediate change when the U.S. military took over and SOG was created. The outfit was formally re-designated as Det 1 of the USAF's 75th Troop Carrier Squadron (TCS), but within SOG it was known as the First Flight Detachment (FFD). John Lee from Air America continued as the liaison officer and instructor pilot to the Chinese crews for a while. Later in 1964 he was replaced by Ben Coleman.

P2V Mission
The covert airdrops into North Vietnam resumed in late April 1964. Before then a P2V and Chinese crew led by Major Li Bang Xun (李 邦 訓), deputy commander of the 34th Squadron, was summoned from Taiwan to fly an electronic reconnaissance mission. Once again American pilots from the NACC helped ferry the aircraft to Vietnam and back. Taking off from Da Nang on the evening of 16 March 1964, the P2V flew up the Gulf of Tonkin before coasting-in west of Haiphong, heading northwest. It then flew all the way down North Vietnam's border with Laos in an attempt to map the air defences in the area where SOG planned to insert or resupply agents. Li's crew managed to stimulate and intercept seven AAA signals and 14 early warning radar signals. Of particular interest they also heard two GCI radar signals.[260]

On 8 June 1964 the Black Bats finally flew a C-123 mission into Chinese airspace, but it was not over the mainland. The aircraft took off from Hsinchu and flew to Hainan Island with an extra fuel tank in the fuselage. It dropped fake travel permissions; fake food coupons; rice; toothpaste; and leaflets. This was the only time that one of the squadron's C-123s ever flew over Chinese territory.[261]

The C-123s of the FFD flew a total of ten airdrops over North Vietnam from Da Nang by late summer, a mix of new insertions and reinforcements. On 29 July one flight was followed by an unknown aircraft, even after the C-123 pilot dived into cloud to escape. But the possibility of being ambushed by AAA fire upon coast-in or over the drop zones was usually of much greater concern to the Chinese crews. According to pilot Major Chen Dian Cong (陳典聰), their CIA liaison officer told them not to believe the mission planners at the SOG when they declared that the chosen route was free of AAA guns. The relationship with SOG worsened when mission planners asked the Chinese crews to fly orbits to collect ELINT on the air defense system, in addition to the airdrops. "Our planes were very vulnerable, and we started getting tracers all the time," Chen complained.[262]

On a more positive note, the restriction on flying into North Vietnam via Laos was lifted in July. This provided safer entry points that were terrain-masked and less well defended by communist radars or AAA.

Project Duck Hook

On 1 May 1964, the Chinese air force sent seven more crews to the U.S. for C-123 training. Led by Colonel Lu De Qi, the 40 Chinese airmen were joined by three crews from the South Vietnamese air force. After language school the ECM operators went to Oxnard AFB for technical training. The pilots moved to the 1ˢᵗ Air Commando Wing at Eglin AFB. Here, they converted onto a new modification of the C-123 that the SOG had commissioned. Under Project Duck Hook, six more C-123Bs were acquired and fitted by Lockheed Air Services at Ontario, CA, with the ATIR and BSTR ECM package. But unlike the previous conversions, these aircraft also received the ASN-25 Doppler navigation system and an APN-153 terrain-following radar. A console for a radio operator, plus new radios including HF, was added. The aircraft were painted in a mottled camouflage of seven green and black shades.

The first of the Duck Hook C-123s arrived in Vietnam in August 1964 for operational trials. That same month the Tonkin Gulf incident led to the first American air strikes on North Vietnam. But even though the air war rapidly escalated from hereon, the U.S. evidently still valued the 'deniability' of the airmen from Taiwan – as well as their expertise. In October, a new agreement for their continued services was signed in Taipei by General Westmoreland, the commander of MACV; Bill Nelson, the CIA station chief in Taiwan; and Gen. Yang Shao Lian, the intelligence chief at CAF headquarters.

The 'South Star III' agreement was a generous deal for the Chinese side. The pilots got NT$14,000 per month, other aircrew slightly less, but all of them also gained NT$260 per hour in flying pay. China Airlines got a fat fee. Covert airdrops would still be the main task, but the crews would also be asked to fly other missions within South Vietnam for MACV. These included airlift of U.S and Vietnamese personnel and supplies, and the parachute training of U.S. and Vietnamese special forces from Long Thanh airbase. Three complete Chinese crews were usually available in Vietnam, serving a three-month TDY from Taiwan. Another crew would be in training or standby status at Hsinchu. A fifth crew would be on leave.[263]

The Duck Hook C-123s were based at Nha Trang, a coastal town just north of Cam Ranh Bay. The First Flight Detachment was commanded by a lieutenant colonel from the USAF and had a couple of American crews for training who could also fly the aircraft on regular airlift missions within South Vietnam, as required. The Black Bats crews carried identification as employees of China Airlines. The aircraft carried South Vietnamese markings, but these were removed for the flights into the North, or for ferry flights to and from Taiwan, where China Airlines was responsible for periodic maintenance.

WANG ZHEN ZHONG (王 振 中)REMEMBERS

I was a liaison officer for the South Star III Team in Nha Trang. I relayed information between the 34ᵗʰ Squadron and the US on issues regarding the flight equipment, ground support and electronic devices. Sometimes the pilots would write in Chinese. Then I would have to translate into English for the US personnel to read.

Team members took turns taking leave and returning to Taiwan after working in Vietnam.

When we got together with the US consultants in free time, we often entertained them with food and sorghum liquor, or Gaoliang. They praised the drink profusely, likening its powerful taste to the thrust generated by JP4 jet fuel. - *MND Vietnam Oral History, p158-161*

The two original C-123Bs and some of the crewmen returned to Taiwan at the end of their contract in November 1964. On 10 December the replacement operation started very badly. One of the new Duck Hook C-123Bs flown by a Vietnamese crew took off from Da Nang on a dark, rainy night and slammed into nearby Monkey Mountain. It was on a practice airdrop, carrying a large sabotage team code named Centaur that was 28-strong, plus two U.S. instructors. There were no survivors.[264]

On 14 February 1965, a C-123 commanded by Captain Li Jin Yue (李金鉞) took off from Nha Trang to drop a seven-man team in Yen Bai province. After a three hour transit across South Vietnam and Laos, the aircraft entered North Vietnam but found the drop zone covered in cloud. The mission was aborted, but as the aircraft turned back it was hit by gunfire. One of the kickers was fatally wounded, and five others on board were injured, including Li. Engine power and hydraulic pressure began to drop. The pilots jettisoned the fuel drop tanks and nursed the aircraft to an emergency landing at Nakhon Phanom airbase in Thailand. It veered off the runway, but there were no further injuries.[265]

The crew counted 31 bullet holes in the aircraft. But they weren't caused by AAA fire, as was believed at the time. Years later, it was learnt that the C-123 had been attacked by a T-28! The piston-engine monoplane had arrived in North Vietnam two years earlier, flown from Laos by a defecting pilot. Hanoi had brought it into service specifically to target the airdrop missions. The two instructor pilots who flew the twin-seat T-28 played badminton and table tennis in the dark to improve their night vision! This was the mystery aircraft that had tried and failed to intercept a C-123 the previous July. This time, the North Vietnamese pilots were directed to the scene of the airdrop because it was a resupply to the team code named Bell. Like so many others, this team had been captured and the North Vietnamese were sending the message for reinforcements to set another trap. They knew when and where the C-123 would fly. The T-28 pilots were able to close on their target when the rear ramp was lowered for the airdrop and they spotted some illumination inside the fuselage.[266]

LIU JIAO ZHI (劉教之) REMEMBERS

I was a radio officer flying on the C-123s in Vietnam. Generally speaking, carrying out assignments within (South) Vietnam was less dangerous than those on the border with North Vietnam. Nevertheless, the Communists were very adept at guerrilla warfare. We had no way of predicting when or where they were going to launch an attack. The most dangerous moment came on landing or takeoff, as that was within their firing range. When an aircraft returned to base for inspection, we often found bullet holes on the airframe.

The spirits of my good friends were in the wreck (of the C-123 that was shot down by the Vietcong on approach to Saigon in June 1965). I was assigned to escort the ashes of our deceased colleagues back to Taiwan. The aircraft circled around Taipei for 20 minutes, as though it was taking them to bid final farewell to the land that they had once defended. Only the CAF commander-in-chief, the honor guard and the crew members were there when we arrived. The families were not there to welcome them. The scene was not unusual for members of special operations. On the day they joined the team, they already prepared their posthumous papers. They were not allowed to tell their families anything about their missions. They lived and died lonely.

We lived in the same barracks as US soldiers, divided only by a basketball court. We often had volleyball contests, barbecued or swam at the beach with them. On majorm festivals including Chinese New Year and Christmas, we invited each other to get together and have a good time. - *MND Vietnam Oral History, p280-287*

Re-tasked

Operation Rolling Thunder, the American bombing campaign over North Vietnam, began in early March 1965. SOG's insertions of sabotage teams were now somewhat irrelevant when USAF fighter-bombers could bomb the targets instead. SOG refocused the covert insertions on intelligence gathering missions. In the meantime, the First Flight Detachment was retasked for more ELINT missions, this time over the Gulf of Tonkin. These flights also dropped propaganda packages that could float inland on an easterly wind, or be picked up by fisherman, or wash up along the coast.

In late June 1965, intelligence indicated that the Vietcong were preparing to attack Nha Trang airbase. The four C-123s were flown out to Saigon on the evening of 27 June. But when approaching Tan Son Nhut, the aircraft captained by Major Yang Cun Hou (楊存厚) was shot down by the Vietcong. They had rigged a 20mm cannon under the approach that they previously removed from a crashed A-1 Skyraider. All 14 onboard were killed: 12 Chinese and two Americans from SOG. The predicted attack on Nha Trang was never launched, and the surviving aircraft and crews returned there a few days later.[267]

Yet another Duck Hook C-123 was lost two months later. On 31 August one of two aircraft being ferried to Taiwan for maintenance disappeared in the South China Sea with the loss of its nine crew.

Serious Threat

In 1965 the Black Bats flew 69 operational C-123 missions, of which 14 were aborted due to weather or equipment failures. That was 23 more than the previous year, despite the ever-increasing capability of North Vietnam's air defences. Bolstered by Chinese manpower and equipment, and now starting to receive SA-2 missiles from the Soviet Union, they were now posing a most serious threat. The large-scale, classified map of the North on the wall of the FFD's operations room displayed ever more 'threat circles' – depicting the locations and range of AAA and SAM sites. Later in 1965, the Chinese crews refused outright to fly a resupply mission to the Eagle team, which was located near to the deadly anti-aircraft defences around Haiphong.[268]

The SOG sought alternatives. It used South Vietnamese H-34 helicopters for some insertions close to the Lao border. USAF CH-3 helicopters based at Nakhon Phanom took small teams into North Vietnam via refuelling stops in Laos. For resupply missions, canisters containing clothes, food, and ammunition were loaded onto A-1 Skyraiders and F-4 Phantoms and dropped at high speed. Finally, the USAF provided four new C-130E

SOG's FAILINGS DESCRIBED

Besides mishandling ties with the [Chinese] plane crews, SOG also showed a disturbing lack of imagination when targeting its airborne teams. Quick to blame better North Vietnamese defences for its initial failures, SOG had made it easier for Hanoi by repeatedly running the same basic missions into the same areas. For example, the Attila team was parachuted during April 1964 into Nghe An Province; the following team to go north, Lotus, landed in the same province. The next team making a blind drop, Scorpion, went to the same general location used by earlier teams Bell and Packer. Buffalo, the next to head north, jumped into almost the exact target area as Ruby. North Vietnamese security forces were no doubt on alert from the previous jumps. Not surprisingly, every one of these SOG teams failed to make radio contact. - *Conboy and Andrade, Spies and Commandos, p97*

(I) Hercules transports that were specially modified for covert operations. They were fitted with the Fulton recovery system, plus infrared and ECM, and APQ-115 terrain following radar. These big black-and-green-painted aircraft reached Nha Trang in October 1966 via Taiwan. They flew their first insertion on 24 December. They were flown by regular American airmen from Det 1, 314th Tactical Airlift Wing, who nicknamed their operation "Stray Goose."[269]

Despite these alternatives, the Black Bats in their FFD C-123s still flew 70 operational missions in 1966, although 26 of them were aborted. Some were ELINT missions up into the Gulf of Tonkin. But there were still regular airdrops – of leaflets as well as intelligence agents. The leaflets urged North Vietnamese soldiers to defect when they were sent south to fight. The main area for the airdrops was the panhandle, where SOG had new hopes of fostering a genuine insurgency movement. These flights usually staged via Nakhon Phanom or Udon airbases in Thailand in both directions. Sometimes the ECM officer heard AAA radar signals, but the air defences were far thinner along the northern border with Laos than they were along the coast and around Hanoi and Haiphong.[270]

During 1966 the Duck Hook C-123s were further improved by adding an RDR-10 weather radar and an ARN-131 homing receiver. The paint scheme was changed to a four-color camouflage design that featured a 'velvet' coating to absorb some of the energy of radar beams that struck the aircraft from the ground.[271]

From 1967 on SOG became heavily involved in the rescue of downed American airmen. The ground reconnaissance missions along the Ho Chi Minh trail increased. In both types of operation helicopters were the preferred means of inserting and withdrawing the brave teams of American and native soldiers. As a consequence of this, and the arrival of the 'Stray Goose' C-130s, there was a big reduction in the workload of the First Flight Detachment. The C-123s inserted no new teams of agents in 1967, and flew only nine resupply missions to existing teams. But there were 22 flights to drop propaganda items, which now included radios that were preset to pick up the SOG's own anti-communist radio stations. There were also 11 missions dedicated to ELINT. Meanwhile, the Chinese crews were increasingly tasked to fly airlift missions within South Vietnam.[272]

Back in Taiwan there were two accidents. On 10 May 1967 a C-123B practising single-engine approaches crashed near Hsinchu. Two flight engineers were killed; the pilots were injured. On 22 August 1967 another C-123B on a training flight over the South China Sea developed engine trouble and ditched. Only one pilot and the ECM officer were rescued. The other five crew drowned. On 3 January 1968, another engine failure occurred during a ferry flight from Hsinchu to Nha Trang. The crew made an emergency landing on the small runway of one of the Pratas Islands in the South China Sea, which were controlled by the ROC.

Back in Vietnam, the loss of a Stray Goose C-130 and its 11 American aircrew on the night of 28 December 1967 served to remind all concerned of the risks attached to the SOG's low-level covert missions. The aircraft flew into a 5,000 foot mountain near Dien Bien Phu after a leaflet drop over the Red River delta.[273]

A CIA HISTORIAN REFLECTS

The story of the agents and black teams inserted into North Vietnam is an object lesson in what happens when eagerness to please trumps objective self-analysis, when the urge to preserve a can-do self-image delays the recognition of a failed – indeed archaic – operational technique…anything was worth trying, and something would surely work. - *Thomas L. Ahern Jr, in "The Way We Do Things: Black Entry Operations Into North Vietnam, 1961-1964", Center for the Study of Intelligence, May 2005, declassified March 2009, p1 and p59*

Shocking Conclusion

In early 1968, MACV and the CIA station in Saigon reviewed the long-term agent insertion program and came to the shocking but inevitable conclusion that all of its assets inserted into North Vietnam had been killed, or captured and 'turned.' The solution was to stop dropping fresh agents and step up the propaganda and psychological war instead.

In 1968, the Black Bats flew over North Vietnam only 15 times to drop gift packages, including watches and pre-tuned radios, as well as leaflets. There were also 'deception bundles' of letters that insinuated (for instance) that senior North Vietnamese military officers were in secret contact with Saigon. The FFD also dropped phantom parachutes and resupply loads that were designed to convince the communists that spies and saboteurs were still active in the North. Some of these loads were boobytrapped. There were also a couple of ELINT missions for the C-123s. The last two drop missions of 1968 were flown simultaneously on the night of 25 October. The two C-123s flew up the Gulf of Tonkin at 500 feet, then climbed to 8,000 feet to release their cargo of leaflets and goodies into the prevailing wind, which blew them towards Haiphong.

The reduced activity of the FFD over North Vietnam was offset by ever more airlift work in-country. The Chinese crews found themselves under fire without venturing into North Vietnam, as they flew resupply missions to the besieged U.S. Marines at Khe Sanh.[274]

In common with the C-123s flown by the USAF and Air America, the ones flown by the FFD were converted to the C-123K configuration in 1968 with the addition of small,

A DANGEROUS MISSION

The Air Force Intelligence section telephoned me in July 1968, when they were recruiting new pilots for the 34th squadron. To tell you the truth, I didn't want to go. I knew that they flew a dangerous mission. I had already been asked to join them once before, by my classmate, who was a P2V pilot. That was in the days when officers of the squadron could still do the recruiting. I told him: "Suppose that I end up being killed? Then you'll feel guilty." - *Lt Col Yang Li Shu (楊黎書), C-123 pilot, from Black Bat Squadron Oral History, p279-280*

Many crewmen volunteered to join the 34th squadron, but I was assigned to it by Headquarters. I had heard about their accident rate – it was one per year at that time. Some of my classmates had gone to the 34th squadron before me – and they had all died. I wasn't afraid to die, but I didn't want my children to lose a father. If I died, my wife could probably remarry, because she was young and beautiful. But I worried that my children would be discriminated against. That made me feel bad. - *Lt Col Feng Hai Tao (馮海濤), C-123 navigator, from Black Bat Squadron Oral History, p216*

AIR FORCE OUTSTANDING UNIT AWARD

Detachment 12, 1131ˢᵗ Special Activities Squadron distinguished itself by meritorious achievement in support of the US advisory effort in Vietnam from 1 June 1966 to 31 May 1968. During this period, while operating independently with extremely limited resources, Det 12 flew approximately 4,000 classified combat and combat support sorties, in unarmed aircraft at low altitudes, in all weather conditions at night, over the most rugged terrain in southeast Asia and under the constant threat of hostile ground fire. In spite of these hazards and battle damage sustained on numerous occasions, not a single aircraft was lost nor involved in an accident. This enviable safety record combined with an outstanding utilization rate and operationally ready rate stands in lasting tribute to the superior airmanship and skills of all detachment personnel. - *Department of the Air Force, Washington DC, 1 November 1968*

wing-mounted turbojets. The 2,850lb J85s allowed the aircraft to take off with payload from small airstrips. There was also an ECM upgrade to the planes; they were fitted with the APR-25 radar warning receiver and an ALE-1 chaff dispenser. The Duck Hook designation was changed to Heavy Hook.

In October 1968 President Johnson announced a halt to the bombing of North Vietnam. To SOG's disbelief, the move was extended to all operations north of the 17ᵗʰ parallel. That included the propaganda drops. While SOG was still busy doing rescue and reconnaissance along the Ho Chi Minh trail in Laos and Cambodia, it had no more work for the First Flight Detachment.

In November 1968 the USAF gave an outstanding unit award to "Det 12 of the 1131ˢᵗ Special Activities Squadron" – another cover designation for the Black Bats at Nha Trang. The citation noted that the unit had flown approximately 4,000 classified combat and combat support missions from June 1966 to May 1968.[275]

From now on, the FFD C-123s now became just another part of the tactical airlift mix in the Vietnam War. The Chinese crews flew resupply missions into forward airbases and returned from there with dead soldiers in coffins. They contributed to the new U.S. policy of 'Vietnamization' by training the ARVN's paratroops, and deploying its special forces. Some of the flying was still hazardous; Vietcong gunners lay in wait beneath the approach and takeoff routes to many of the airstrips. The FFD flew 182 missions in 1968 and 283 the following year.

In May 1970 the Black Bats supported the secret U.S. military incursion into Cambodia. In October 1970 flights into Laos began. The FFD logged another 468 airlift missions that year, plus another 123 training flights.

CIA Again Needs the Black Bats
In early 1971, the CIA once again found itself in need of the unique talents and 'deniability' of the Black Bats. The U.S. had been withdrawing troops from South Vietnam since mid-1969, but in an attempt to prevent North Vietnam from taking advantage, a new covert campaign to harass the North was launched from Laos at the request of national security advisor Henry Kissinger. Throughout 1970, these 'Commando Raider' sabotage operations were planned by the CIA and carried out by Hmong tribesmen. The raids were supported by the helicopters of Air America. But the political risks of using American airmen in covert operations against North Vietnam still weighed heavily on U.S. policy makers.[276]

Col Yu Chuan Wen found himself heading for a third time to the top-secret airbase at Groom Lake in the U.S. This time, though, it wasn't to fly the C-130 (see Chapter Seven). Yu and eight other Chinese airmen were taught to fly the De Havilland DHC-6 Twin Otter. This high-wing, twin-turboprop transport had good airfield performance, and could also be used for airdrops in support of the Commando Raider operations. For greater flying accuracy a LORAN navigation set was added to the Twin Otter.

After three months of training in precision nighttime navigation and airdropping over the mountains of Nevada, Yu and his group returned to Taiwan, and the Twin Otter was airfreighted to Hsinchu. After the Chinese pilots received more instruction from an Air America pilot there, the aircraft was fitted with extra fuel tanks in the cabin and ferried to Laos.

During the day, the Twin Otter was flown on routine resupply support missions within Laos by an Air America crew. At dusk, they ferried it to 'PS-44' – an isolated guerrilla base on a mountain plateau in southern Laos. The Chinese crews were based here, ready to fly the aircraft into 'denied territory.' Such missions began in mid-1971, and supported a number of insertions along the Laotian border with North Vietnam that were designed to disrupt movements along the Ho Chi Minh trail. Before he returned to Taiwan to take command of the 34th Squadron from Col Sun Pei Zhen, Yu insisted that a third crewmember be added for these flights to operate the LORAN set. The three Chinese crews rotated in turn to PS-44, each doing a one-month tour at the remote base.[277]

Back on Taiwan, meanwhile, 12 more Chinese pilots were training on helicopters so that they could fly Commando Raider-style operations in Laos. Col Lu Wei Heng (盧維恆), a C-123 pilot and deputy commander of the 34th Squadron, was put in charge of the operation, which was codenamed Golden Strike. The pilots were all from other CAF squadrons, and only a couple of them had previous helicopter experience. After some familiarisation flights in UH-1 Hueys at Hsinchu the group were sent to Fort Rucker, AL, and took the U.S. Army's basic helicopter training course.

Six of them then returned to Taiwan, where they were checked out on the Sikosky S-58T, a twin turboshaft-powered version of the old H-34 troop carrying chopper. It was already being used in Laos. The Chinese pilots deployed to PS-44 later in 1971 and began flying covert missions. They dropped agents and supplies along the border between Laos and North Vietnam. They also hauled some other 'special' cargo – such as an unattended rocket launcher that could be set up on remote hilltops to fire automatically.[278]

The 'Quite One'

The other six Chinese pilots moved on from Fort Rucker to Groom Lake, where they were introduced to the unique Hughes 500P. This was an extensive modification of the OH-6A Light Observation Helicopter to reduce its noise level to the absolute minimum. This was achieved by adding an extra main rotor blade, making changes to the blade tips, providing mufflers for the air intake and exhaust, and providing the pilot with a control to slow the main rotor speed when required.

The modified OH-6A was named 'The Quiet One.' After flight trials and pilot training at Groom Lake, two of them were airfreighted to Taiwan in October 1971. More flight training followed on the unusual choppers, which were now also fitted with sophisticated night navigation avionics. This comprised an AN/AAQ-5 forward-looking infrared (FLIR) system mounted on the nose and cooled by nitrogen supplied by two tanks fixed to the chopper's belly, plus an inertial navigation system and a LORAN-C set carried in pods fixed on each side of the cabin.[279]

Back in Laos, the Chinese crews were still flying out of PS-44, sharing duties on the Twin Otters and the S-58Ts with crews from Air America. But no matter how much effort the CIA and its indigenous irregulars expended against the Ho Chi Minh trail from Laos, or the SOG teams from the Vietnam side, the communists kept on coming south. In April 1972 the CIA concluded that the Commando Raider operations were having little effect, and they were halted. But intelligence gathering missions were still on the agenda.[280]

In June 1972, the two modified Hughes 500P helicopters were collected from Taiwan by an Air America C-130 and flown to Takhli airbase in Thailand. Here the Quiet Ones were re-assembled and flown to PS-44. Five Chinese pilots followed, led by Col Lu.

The CIA was planning a daring mission into North Vietnam, to place a wiretap on a major military telephone line. The U.S. was now negotiating for peace with the North, but what were the true intentions of the communists? Were they preparing for a major conventional military invasion as soon as the final U.S. troops were withdrawn? Henry Kissinger, by now confirmed as President Nixon's Secretary of State, wanted to know.

The North was accustomed to wiretaps being placed along the Ho Chi Minh trail, and guarded its lines of communications well. But from aerial photography, U.S. intelligence identified a weak spot where the line ran through remote terrain, near the town of Vinh. The plan was for two Chinese pilots to fly the quiet Hughes helicopter to this location at night. They would carry two Lao commandos who would secure the tap while the pilots dropped a radio relay antenna in the form of a net on the top of some nearby trees. Meanwhile, two S-58Ts would be hovering across the border in Laos, ready to mount a rescue mission if the Quiet One got into trouble. Above the S-58Ts, the Twin Otter would act as a radio relay and command post. The airmen from the CAF 34th Squadron would be flying all of these aircraft.

But the Chinese helicopter pilots were having difficulties in Laos. They couldn't get used to the night vision goggles that were supplied – a new technology still at the experimental stage. Then they destroyed one of the two modified Hughes choppers during a hard night landing at PS-44. According to Col Lu, the infrared system was not working properly, and the high ground surrounding PS-44 required the two pilots to land the small helicopter downwind at too high an approach speed. The CIA decided to fly the wiretap

---

MORE TAIWAN ASSISTANCE TO SOUTH VIETNAM

Military officers from the ROC taught their political warfare system to Vietnamese troops from 1961. In 1964, the training was formalized by the creation of the ROC Military Advisory Group, Vietnam (ROC MAGV). In 1963, China Airlines (CAL) provided pilots for at least one B-26 mission in Vietnam, under contract to the U.S. From late 1965, CAL provided two C-46s and other aircraft to the SOG for transport flights within South Vietnam. Once again, the aircraft and crews were 'borrowed' from the CAF. One of the C-46s crashed on 5 June 1972 in the Central Highlands, killing 11 Americans, 15 South Vietnamese and the six Chinese crew. This ended CAL's transport contract. The ROC MAGV was disbanded in March 1973, after the Paris Peace Accords. - *The Vietnam War MND Oral History, p10-12; Fu, p51; Conboy and Morrison, "Plausible Deniability"*

TESTAMENT TO THE SOUTH STAR TEAM

The South Star Team's missions were dangerous, but in order to carry out national policies, for which the fees were handsome, they performed them with courage. By the end, we had lost more than 40 personnel and nearly ten aircraft...While the missions in Vietnam greatly increased China Airlines' financial stability, it was paid for with the lives of men who died in the line of duty in a foreign land. Their sacrifice should never be forgotten. - *Gen I Fu En memoir, p186*

mission with American pilots instead. All the Chinese airmen – including those assigned to the S-58T and Twin Otter – were sent home.[281]

Unfortunate End

It was an unfortunate end for the Black Bats in southeast Asia. A few months earlier, on 31 March 1972, the SOG was deactivated. That also meant the end of the FFD and its C-123s at Nha Trang. After nearly nine years the Southern Star operation came to a close.

Four C-123s were formally turned over to the Chinese Air Force. They were flown to Taiwan by the Black Bats crews, and mainly employed on resupply flights to Jinmen Island until the runway there was extended so that conventional airliners could land.

In January 1973 the Paris Peace Accords were signed, signifying a complete U.S. withdrawal from Vietnam over time. The U.S. now clearly had no further use for Chinese crews to fly special operations missions in southeast Asia. On 1 March 1973 the 34th Squadron of the Chinese Air Force was disbanded. The Black Bats and predecessor units had been flying over 'denied territory' for 20 years, serving the Republic of China and the United States. During all that time shootdowns and accidents had claimed no fewer than 142 of the squadron's brave men.[282]

Epilogue

The black P-3s from Taiwan were stored at the Naval Air Depot Alameda during the first half of 1967. They were destined to remain in the classified world of electronic reconnaissance. The Navy made them the prototypes for a new fleet of SIGINT-collecting aircraft, to replace its lumbering EC-121M versions of the early fifties vintage Super Constellation airliner.

But the Navy decided not to use LTV Electrosystems Greenville Division, which had been the CIA's choice for airframe modifications and sensor integration on the black P-3s as a contractor. Instead, the Navy specified a completely different collection sensor suite, and Lockheed modified the airframes. Starting in September 1967, two of the aircraft (669 and 678) were reworked at Burbank, including the removal of most of the CIA equipment. Then they were converted to the EP-3B configuration.

Two large radomes were added under the fuselage. They contained the antennas for an ELINT collection system manufactured by UTL. It was designated ALQ-110 and nicknamed "Big Look," and was already in service on the Navy's old EC-121Ms. A very large canoe-type radome was added along the top of the P-3 fuselage. This contained the antennas for a new communications direction finding system provided by the Garland Division of LTV Electrosystems designated ALD-8. It was part of the 'Deepwell' COMINT system designated ALR-60 and designed by GTE Sylvania to collect communications from Soviet warships.

These EP-3B aircraft acquired the nickname 'Bat Rack' – an interesting echo from their short period of service in Taiwan with The Black Bats. They were issued to the Navy's VQ-1 electronic reconnaissance squadron in 1969 and deployed to Da Nang, Vietnam. Meanwhile, the third 'black' P-3A (673) was converted by Lockheed in 1969-70 to serve as a development aircraft for various electronic programs.

The Bat Rack development led to a larger program; the conversion of ten P-3As to the EP-3E ARIES (Airborne Reconnaissance Intelligence Exploitation System) standard. Hayes Industries underbid Lockheed to get the EP-3E airframe integration contract. The ARIES configuration comprised production versions of the Deepwell COMINT system, plus the Big Look system again for ELINT. The two 'Bat Rack' EP-3Bs were also subsequently modified to the EP-3E configuration.

The EP-3E aircraft is still in service with the U.S. Navy, although the original 12 airframes were replaced during the ARIES II upgrade program from 1986. On 1 April 2000 an EP-3E from VQ-1 collided with a Chinese J-8 fighter off the coast of Guangdong and was forced to land on Hainan Island. The rear crew desperately tried to destroy classified equipment and documents before they taxied to a halt on the Chinese airbase. The crew were released after 11 days, but the Chinese pored over the EP-3E until early July. Then – humiliatingly for the U.S. – the Chinese insisted that the aircraft be dismantled and flown out – on an ex-Soviet An-124 transport!

Kissinger's Secret Mission

On 9 July 1971 Dr Henry Kissinger arrived in Beijing for talks with Chou En Lai and other leaders of communist China. When his secret mission became public the reaction from Taipei was surprisingly muted. In one sense, the security of Taiwan was bolstered by the Sino-American rapprochement. The military balance across the Straits was already tilted firmly in Taiwan's favor, thanks to continued deliveries of American military hardware. The CAF's supersonic F-104 fighters patrolled the airspace, backed up by a growing fleet of F-5s, plus Nike Hercules and Hawk surface-to-air missiles. And now, with politics between the superpowers undergoing a transformation, how could the PRC think of invading Taiwan? Moreover, the ROC was growing stronger by the day, economically. Trade with the U.S. had reached an annual $1 billion.

Soon, though, Taiwan was ejected from the United Nations in favor of the mainland. The U.S. made plans to withdraw its own military forces from Taiwan. The F-4s and C-130s left CCK airbase, and the big aircraft overhaul depot at Tainan was run down and eventually sold to E-Systems. The CIA stopped supporting Taiwan's propaganda war against the mainland in 1973 with radio stations and balloon-borne insertions of leaflets. The joint venture U-2 squadron at Taoyuan was closed in 1974. Ironically, having expended so much energy in tracking mainland China's nuclear weapons programs, the CIA station in Taipei now monitored the ROC's own covert attempt to develop a nuclear deterrent.[283]

Rearguard Action

The ROC was obliged to mount a rearguard action to ensure that U.S. actions did not prejudice Washington's declared aim of ensuring "a peaceful settlement of the Taiwan question by the Chinese themselves." According to one American historian, during their negotiations with the PRC Kissinger and President Nixon "rarely reflected on Taiwan at all," and were quite happy to sacrifice their long-term ally.[284]

Chiang Ching Kuo finally became premier of the ROC in May 1972. Two months later his father, the 'Gimo,' had a heart attack, and was confined to his home. President Chiang Kai Shek died on 5 April 1975 at the age of 87. Mao Tse Tung outlasted his old enemy by 17 months, and his long-serving Premier Chou En Lai by eight months. Mao died on 9 September 1976.

Chiang Ching Kuo succeeded his father as president. The ROC was still a benevolent dictatorship with martial law in place. But economic liberalization was slowly followed by political reform.

However, CCK's actions in respect of compatriots on the mainland were not at all benevolent. When in 1975 the PRC released a large number of KMT prisoners, most dating back to the Civil War, Chiang directed that only those who had been captured during the ROC's raids and agent insertions since 1950 would be allowed back to Taiwan.[285]

Taiwan Relations Act

On 1 January 1979 the U.S. recognized the PRC as the sole legal government of China and broke diplomatic relations with Taiwan. That also meant the end of the Mutual Defense Treaty. President Carter gave vague assurances about Taiwan's future security, but it was the U.S. Congress that firmed them up in the Taiwan Relations Act (TRA). The TRA constructed a new unofficial framework for relations between Washington and Taipei, and "was a political triumph for Taiwan and personally for Chiang Ching Kuo," according to CCK's biographer.[286]

In April 1979 the MAAG in Taiwan was formally deactivated after 28 years. By that time, Taiwan's Aero Industry Development Center (AIDC) was producing F-5 fighters under license, and its own jet trainer (the AT-3, with assistance from Northrop). In the 1980s the U.S. refused to supply F-16s, but allowed General Dynamics to assist AIDC in the design and production of an Indigenous Defense Fighter (IDF).

The military balance continued to favor Taiwan. The PRC adopted a pragmatic policy of economic liberalization and did not invest much in military modernization. The PLAAF was still flying the same MiG-17s that had tangled with the Black Bats 20 years earlier.

In the early 1980s, citizens from the ROC who had been issued a passport were unofficially able to travel to the PRC for the first time, via Hong Kong. Families that had been divided by war and ideology since 1949 were able to resume contact. Although personnel still serving with the ROC armed forces could not travel, military retirees began quietly making the journey to their homeland. Indirect trade between Taiwan and the mainland flourished. In 1987 the ban on travel was formally lifted.

By the time that Chiang Ching Kuo died in January 1988, martial law had been lifted and Taiwan had conducted a democratic parliamentary election. The younger Chiang had presided over the transformation of Taiwan into a modern nation state – in all but name. Now, the rise of a pro-independence party on the island challenged the KMT's central contention that there was only one China, and that Taiwan would eventually be reunified with the mainland. On terms that were acceptable to the Taiwan people, the KMT insisted.

Chiang's chosen successor as president was a native Taiwanese – but still a staunch member of the KMT. President Lee Teng Hui (李登輝) served until March 2000, when the pro-independence candidate Chen Shui Bian (陳水扁) narrowly won the presidential election. Chen served two controversial terms, but was unable to force Taiwanese independence in the face of a divided legislature and population. In the 2008 presidential election the KMT returned to power.

34th Squadron Revived

Although it was deactivated in 1973, the 34th Squadron was revived the following year at Hsinchu to fly the four C-123Ks that had been given to the CAF in 1972. The squadron flew resupply missions from Taiwan to Jinmen. Against all the odds, the ROC had retained control of this island and Matsu, just offshore from the mainland. There was still a hint of the 34th's heritage in special operations. The C-123Ks were fitted with cameras to provide photo reconnaissance of shipping in the Taiwan straits and around Jinmen.

In 1977 the 34th Squadron was also assigned to Anti-Submarine Warfare (ASW) using S-2 Tracker twin-engined aircraft. The C-123s were transferred to the CAF's regular transport squadrons in 1979. Since then, the squadron has been dedicated to the ASW and anti-ship mission. It is currently to be found at Taoyuan airbase, flying the upgraded but ageing S-2T version of the Tracker. Although the unit now belongs to the Naval Air Group and is designated 134 Squadron, it retains the old Black Bats insignia. A small museum in the unit's headquarters displays some memorabilia from the squadron's illustrious history.

Sadly, the larger museum created by the Black Bats at Hsinchu during the 1960s was destroyed when the main squadron building was converted into a dormitory. Some of the other buildings in the old top-secret compound, including the hangar, were demolished. Hsinchu airbase is now home to the ROCAF's three squadrons of Mirage 2000 interceptors, obtained from France in the early 1990s.

Ever-Increasing Threat

The Mirages help defend Taiwan against an ever-increasing threat from mainland China's airpower. As the PRC grew stronger economically it began to modernise its armed forces. In response, the U.S. reversed an earlier policy and agreed to sell F-16s and Patriot surface-to-air missiles to Taiwan. The ROCAF is now a well-equipped and trained air defence force. But in the mid-1990s, the PRC began deploying short and medium-range ballistic missiles opposite Taiwan. According to the latest intelligence estimates, there are now about 1,100 of these Chinese-developed weapons in place. In addition, the PRC has Russian-supplied SA-20 surface-to-air missiles that could shoot down the ROCAF's aircraft almost anywhere in the Taiwan Strait, even over Taoyuan and Hsinchu airbases.

By this offensive military build-up the PRC is intimidating Taiwan and trying to deter potential U.S. intervention in support of the island's right to determine its own future. Few independent analysts believe that Beijing would ever wipe out the compatriots on Taiwan in a massive missile strike or a bloody invasion. But while it remains an authoritarian state, China's inexorable rise as an Asian economic and military superpower threatens the well being of the people of Taiwan – or 'Chinese Taipei' as the PRC would now have us call the island.

Search for Remains

Soon after the restrictions on travel to the mainland were formally lifted, Ge Guang Yu (葛光豫) travelled from Taiwan to the mainland in search of his brother's remains. Ge Guang Liao was a pilot on the last P2V to be shot down in 1964. With help from the mainland authorities Ge Guang Yu found an old farmer who had helped to bury the crews' remains in a field on the Shandong peninsula. There was not even a small tombstone to mark the spot. A ceremony was held there, and Ge Guang Yu returned to Taiwan with some earth from the scene.

In 1992, relatives of two B-17 airmen who were shot down over Guangdong in 1959 decided to try and find the remains of their loved ones. Thanks to an article in a Taiwan national newspaper they got in touch with other families of this B-17 crew. With help from authorities on both sides of the Strait the urns holding the remains were located and brought back to Taiwan. They were reburied with due ceremony in the CAF cemetery near Taipei.

Following this example, relatives of the P2V crew shot down in 1963 travelled to Jiangxi to recover the remains of Lt Col Zhou and his fellow airmen. They even made contact with Wang Wen Li, the eagle-eyed MiG pilot who had shot down the P2V. In 2001 another reburial ceremony was held at the CAF cemetery for this crew.

Memorial Hall

In 2009, the Mayor and government of Hsinchu City decided to recognise the remarkable history of the 34th Squadron. They resolved to build a memorial hall on the vacant ground on Dongda Road, where the downtown dormitory of the Black Bats had once stood. As construction proceeded, advice was sought from the Ministry of Defense, veterans of the squadron, and historians, including author Clarence Fu Jing Ping. The result is a fitting tribute. The single story building tells the story of the Black Bats through memorabilia displayed in cases and information panels on the walls. In the basement below there are rooms where community events can be held. A memorial wall of tempered glass outside the hall introduces the story, and adjoins an open-air space that can also be used by local residents.[287]

On 22 November 2009 The Black Bats Memorial Hall was opened with due ceremony, in the presence of the ROC's Minister of Defence and senior military commanders. Survivors of the 34th Squadron proudly posed for a large crowd of photographers, journalists, and television crews. Relatives sat quietly to one side, perhaps reflecting on how much life has changed since some of their loved ones made the ultimate sacrifice all those years ago.[287]

During the ceremony, the widow of Yin Jin Ding (尹金鼎) presented a large aluminium washing bowl for display in the new hall. Yin was the co-pilot of the P2V that was shot down over the Liaodong peninsula in 1961. Mrs Yin and her son Charles had travelled to the crash site. There, they learnt that local farmers had recovered wreckage from the plane, and recycled it to make useful tools and utensils. They returned to Taiwan with this bowl, a unique memento of their poignant journey 'Back to the Mainland.'

Secondary Sources

Books that are cited in the footnotes by author's name only are fully listed below. Articles and other documents are fully cited in the footnotes.

Accinelli, Robert. *Crisis and Commitment: US Policy Toward Taiwan 1950-55.* University of North Carolina Press, Chapel Hill, NC, 1996

Ahern, Thomas. The Way We Do Things: Black Entry Operations Into North Vietnam, 1961-1964. *Center for the Study of Intelligence, CIA, Washington DC, 2005, declassified 2009.*

Ahern, Thomas *Undercover Armies: CIA and Surrogate Warfare in Laos.* Center for the Study of Intelligence, CIA, Washington DC, 2006, declassified 2009.

Chen, Jian. *Mao's China and the Cold War.* The University of North Carolina Press, Chapel Hill, NC, 2001

China Today series. *Air Force* (in Chinese). Dangdai Zhongguo Kongjun, Beijing, 1989

Cline, Ray. *Secrets, Spies and Scholars.* Acropolis Books, 1981

Cole, Bernard. *Taiwan's Security: History and Prospects.* Routledge, New York, 2006

Conboy, Kenneth with Morrison, James. *Shadow War – The CIA's Secret War in Laos.* Paladin Press, CO, 1995

Conboy, Kenneth and Andrade, Dale. *Spies and Commandos: How America Lost the Secret War in North Vietnam.* University Press of Kansas, 2000

Conboy, Kenneth and Morrison, James. *The CIA's Secret War in Tibet.* University Press of Kansas, 2002

Fu, Jing Ping. *The Secret History of Air Force Special Operations: The 34th Squadron's Heroic Story and Other Units* (in Chinese). Master Books, Taipei, 2006

Gup, Ted. *The Book of Honor.* Doubleday, NY, 2000

Hagedorn, Dan and Hellstrom, Leif. *The Douglas Invader in Foreign Military and US Clandestine Service.* Midland Counties Publishing, UK, 1994

Holober, Frank. *Raiders of the China Coast: CIA Covert Operations during the Korean War.* Naval Institute Press, Annapolis, MD, 1999

I Fu En, *My Memoirs*, Li Ching Cultural and Educational Foundation, Taipei, 2003 (and the edition in Chinese)

Leary, William M. *Perilous Missions: Civil Air Transport and CIA Covert Operations in Asia.* The University of Alabama Press, 1984

Lilley, James. *China Hands: Nine Decades of Adventure, Espionage and Diplomacy in Asia.* Public Affairs, NY, 2004

Lin, Hu Lt Gen. *Fight to Protect Motherland's Airspace* (in Chinese). Beijing, 2002

Liu, Wen Xiao, *Chinese Air Force in Action, Series 3* (in Chinese). Wings of China, Taipei, 1993

Marchetti, Victor and Marks, John. *The CIA and the Cult of Intelligence.* Dell paperback edition, 1975

MND Ministry of National Defence, ROC. *The Vietnam War: An Oral History.* Military History and Translation Office, Taipei, Taiwan, 2008

MND Ministry of National Defence, ROC. *The Brave Men Under The Big Dipper: "Black Bat" Squadron Oral History.* Military History and Translation Office, Taipei, Taiwan, 2004

Weng, Tai Sheng. *The Western Company Story: CIA Secret Activities in Taiwan (in Chinese).* Linking Publishing, Taipei, 1991

Pocock, Chris. *50 Years of the U-2: The Complete Illustrated History of the Dragon Lady.* Schiffer Publishing, Atglen, PA, 2005

Prados, John. *Safe for Democracy: The Secret Wars of the CIA.* Ivan R. Dee, Chicago, 2006

Prouty, Fletcher Col. *The Secret Team.* Prentice Hall, 1973

Reade, David. *The Age of Orion: Lockheed P-3 An Illustrated History.* Schiffer Publishing, Atglen, PA

Shakya, Tsering. *The Dragon in the Land of the Snows: A History of Modern Tibet Since 1947.* Columbia University Press, NY, 1999

Smith, Felix. *China Pilot – Flying for Chiang and Chennault*. Brassey's, Washington DC, 1995

Taylor, Jay. *The Generalissimo's Son: Chiang Ching Kuo and the Revolutions in China and Taiwan*. Harvard University Press, Cambridge, MA, 2000

Thomas, Evan. *The Very Best Men*. Simon and Schuster, 1995

Trest, Warren. *Air Commando One: Heinie Aderholt and America's Secret Air Wars*. Smithsonian Institution Press, Washington DC, 2000

Other Sources and
Author's Acknowledgments

I first became aware of the tremendous story of The Black Bats many years ago, during my research on the history of the U-2 spy plane. I interviewed two veteran managers of the Lockheed Skunk Works, Fred Cavanaugh and Bill Giles, whose references to the 'RB-69' airplane suggested that this subject was worthy of further investigation.

But it was another of my U-2 interviewees who helped persuade me that this episode in Cold War history needed to be properly told. Don Jackson spent the years 1960-62 in Taiwan, and described them as some of the most challenging and fascinating of his career. I am grateful for his encouragement and support. I'm sorry it took so long, Don!

I was finally prompted to begin work when my good friend in Taiwan, Clarence Fu Jing Ping (傅鏡平), decided to write a book on the Black Bats, in Chinese, for the local readership. Clarence is a noted aviation historian in Taiwan, with many years' experience of detailed research. We agreed to collaborate. His book was published in Taipei in 2006, and was the starting point for my further research. Clarence had already interviewed surviving members of the CAF's 34th Squadron in Taiwan to uncover the main outlines of the story. I sought to amplify the story for an English-language readership by concentrating on English-language documentary sources and interviews, mostly in the U.S. Although this is essentially an aviation story, I have tried to provide the context – the fascinating social and political situations that evolved from the eviction of the nationalists from mainland China in 1949.

The usual difficulties arose in trying to shed light on operations that were highly classified at the time from a distance of 40-50 years. Some documents have been released by the U.S. Central Intelligence Agency through the systematic declassification review process mandated by Executive Order 12958. These documents have been redacted (censored) to remove all references to Taiwan, but have nevertheless proven useful. They are identified in the footnotes by the notation CREST (for CIA Records Search Tool). I am grateful to Joe Donoghue and Matthew Aid for helping to trawl the CREST at the National Archives for these documents. However, the CIA refused to declassify an internal history of the joint project to conduct low-level flights over mainland China.[288]

It was indeed fortunate, therefore, that Clarence and myself were able to use some valuable official documents on the joint project from the Taiwan side. Because of certain sensitivities we prefer to specify these documents as 'official Taiwan sources.' I should also note that the Military History and Translation Office of the Ministry of National Defence, ROC, has published an oral history of the 34th Squadron in Chinese that has been very useful. The same office also published an oral history on Taiwan's part in the Vietnam War, in Chinese and English. This also contains some memoirs from crewmembers of the Black Bats squadron. My thanks to Guo Guan Lin (郭冠麟) and Anne Liu Li Xuan (劉力瑄) in that office, which does good work.

The PRC has also not been slow in coming forward. A book by retired Gen Lin Hu (林虎), published in Beijing in 2001, provided significant detail on efforts by the mainland air defence forces to combat the unwelcome airborne intrusions from Taiwan. I am grateful to former Black Bats crewmember Richard Gao Yin Song (高蔭松) for his translation and interpretation of this book, and for his other assistance and encouragement.

I am grateful to the following interviewees who provided personal recollections: Jim Chappell, Ed Connor, Dai Shu Qing, Frank Daly, Hal Ford, Don Grigsby, Paul Herring, Don Jackson, Richard Gao Yin Song, Jerry Kwiatowski, the late Bob Kleyla, Phil Li Chong Shan, Russ Logan, Jerry Losey, Henry Lu Wei Heng, John McCaull, Gordon Raymer, Fred Severo, the late Bob Singel, Norm Stanley, Bud Wheelon, Kent Williamson, Jim Winn, and Yu Chuan Wen.

The author does not read Chinese, and was therefore reliant on others to translate some of the source material for this book. In addition to Messrs Fu and Gao, I must also thank Sun Ya Ming (孫雅明) for many hours of volunteer help during his assignment to the Taiwan Representative Office in London during 2005-7.

I must also thank some more people in Taiwan. Fred Liu Wen Xiao (劉文孝) is the publisher of Wings of China, and has done a tremendous job of recording and publishing the military history of Taiwan (www.wingweb.com.tw). Chang Wei Bin (張維斌) is the author of the website www.taiwanairpower.org, which also records the history and current status of the ROC armed forces. Lu De Yuan (盧德允) is a good friend and former defence journalist who first spotted the Magic Dragon story. Rita I-Wong (衣淑凡) is the chair of The Li-Ching Foundation and a daughter of Gen I Fu En. She has helped to document her late father's long and notable career by publishing his memoirs, and also by sponsoring an extensive documentary film on his life, entitled "The Secrets of the Taiwanese Skies." Gen I's former secretary, Lillian Chu, was also most helpful. Gary Lai Guo Rui (賴國瑞) provided the side view drawings of the Black Bats aircraft. Last but not least, the talented Chang Kuo Cheng (張國徵) kindly provided the cover illustrations.

In the U.S., John Bessette, Rick Burgess, Erik Kirzinger, Al Mongeon, and Hal Weber also provided valuable assistance. Dave and Mary Jo Ostrowski were kind hosts during my research trips to Washington, DC. In the UK, Dave Wilton helped to research the P2V serial numbers. I should also thank the staff of the National Archives at College Park, MD, and of the Air America archive of the University of Texas at Dallas.

Finally, my grateful thanks go to my wife Meng and daughters Nicola and Melanie. None of them really understand this spy plane stuff, but they endure my esoteric preoccupations with patience and humour.

Chris Pocock
Uxbridge, UK
December 2009

A Note on Aircraft Serial Numbers

The aircraft assigned to the 34th Squadron remained the property of the U.S. government, but they carried nationalist Chinese markings and serial numbers when flying operational or training missions from Hsinchu airbase. The CAF applied three-digit serial numbers to the P4Y, B-17s, B-26s, and (from 1961) P2Vs. Four digit serial numbers were applied to the P2Vs (until 1962 and from 1964, when random numbers were used) and to the C-123s.

B-17: 357 (shot down 23 June 1956), 815 (shot down 29 May 1959), 835
B-26: 822, 842 (crashed on mainland 5 November 1957), 844, 862 TB-26: 888
C-46: 210
P4Y: 016
P2V: 5005, 5050, 5055, 5060, 5066, 5070, then 280, 572, 634, 683, 739, then random numbers.
C-123B: 4010, 4020 (crashed 10 May 1963), 5636, 5644, 5652, 5661
C-123K: 0601, 0602, 0603, 0604

The U.S. identities of the P2V-7Us were as follows:

(Lockheed construction number/US Navy serial number/USAF serial number)
7047/135612/54-4037 shot down 11 June 1964
7097/140438/54-4038 crashed 8 January 1962
7099/140440/54-4039 shot down 6 November 1961
7101/140442/54-4040 crashed 25 March 1960
7105/141233/54-4041 shot down 19 June 1963
7286/150283 acquired September 1962, returned to US Navy 1967
7021/135564 acquired December 1964, returned to US Navy 1967
A P2V-5 (128355) acquired for training in 1964, returned to US Navy 1967

The U.S. Navy serial numbers of the P-3As were 149669, 149673, and 149678.
The USAF serial numbers of the C-123Bs were: 54-0641 (crashed 27 June 1965 or 31 August 1965), 54-0643, 54-0657 (crashed 22 August 1967?), 54-0704, 54-0715 (crashed 10 May 1967?), 55-4522 (crashed 24 December 1964), 55-4528, 55-4543, 55-4551 (crashed 10 May 1963), 56-4355, 56-4356 (crashed 27 June 1965 or 31 August 1965), and 56-4528.

Glossary

AAA	Anti-Aircraft Artillery
AAM	Air-to-Air Missile
ADF	Air Direction Finding
ADP	Advanced Development Projects (division within Lockheed, aka The Skunk Works)
AMD	Air-Maritime Division (within CIA)
ATI	Applied Technology Inc
BDO	Bomber Defense Officer
CAF	Chinese Air Force (on Taiwan)
CAT	Civil Air Transport (CIA-owned airline on Taiwan)
CCK	Chiang Ching Kuo (son of Chiang Kai Shek)
CIA	Central Intelligence Agency
COMINT	COMmunications INTelligence
DF	Direction-Finding
DPD	Development Projects Division (within CIA)
DDP	Deputy Directorate for Plans (within CIA, responsible for espionage and covert operations)
DDR	Deputy Directorate for Research (within CIA, responsible for technical intelligence-gathering)
DS&T	Directorate of Science and Technology (within CIA)
ECM	Electronic CounterMeasures
ELINT	ELectronic INTelligence
FFD	First Flight Detachment
FLIR	Forward-Looking InfraRed
GCI	Ground-Controlled Intercept
IBMND	Intelligence Bureau of the MiNistry of Defense (on Taiwan)
KMT	Kuomintang (Chinese nationalist party)
LORAN	LOng Range Aid to Navigation
MAAG	Military Aid and Assistance Group (US aid to Taiwan)
MACV	Military Assistance Command Vietnam
MAD	Magnetic Anomaly Detector
MRBM	Medium-Range Ballistic Missile
NACC	Naval Auxiliary Communications Center (cover name for CIA station on Taiwan)
NCO	Non-Commissioned Officer
NSA	National Security Agency (of the US)
OEL	Office of ELINT (within CIA)
OPC	Office of Policy Co-ordination (within CIA)
PACOM	Pacific Command (of the US military)

PDO	Parachute Dispatch Officer or Operator
PEC	PACOM ELINT Center
PLA	People's Liberation Army (of China)
PLAAF	People's Liberation Army Air Force (of China)
PLAN	People's Liberation Navy Air Arm
PRC	People's Republic of China
RADAN	RADar Aid to Navigation
ROC	Republic of China (Taiwan)
SIGINT	SIGnals INTelligence (used in this book to mean a combination of COMINT and ELINT)
SMG	Special Mission Group (CAF predecessor of 34th Squadron)
SOD	Special Operations Division (within CIA)
SOG	Studies and Observations Group (within U.S. military, responsible for covert operations in Vietnam)
TFR	Terrain-Following Radar
TRG	Technical Research Group (CAF predecessor of 34th Squadron)
UHF	Ultra High Frequency
USAF	United States Air Force
USATG	U.S. Army Technical Group (cover name for CIA station on Taiwan)
USIB	US Intelligence Board
USSR	Union of Soviet Socialist Republics
VHF	Very High Frequency
VIAT	VIetnamese Air Transport (airline)
WEI	Western Enterprises Inc (cover name for CIA station on Taiwan)

Notes

Chapter 1

1 CIA estimate from ORE76-49 "Survival Potential of Residual Non-Communist Regimes in China," 19 October 1949

2 Taylor, p201

3 NIE-10 Communist China, 17 January 1951, p2-3

4 Holober, p8, p14

5 Accinelli, p67. This author provides an excellent account of the policy deliberations within the U.S. government in 1952, as pro-interventionists like CIA Director Walter Bedell Smith argued with neutralists like Secretary of State Dean Acheson.

6 Leary, p129-131; according to Prados, p134, CAT aircraft actually landed at Mong Hsat, the airstrip in Burma that was headquarters for Li Mi's force

7 Holober, p45; Leary p135-6. The only 'new' air defense aircraft available to the PRC at this time were some La-11 piston-engine fighters that were supplied and crewed by the Soviet Air Force, and used to defend Shanghai.

8 Leary, p135-6; airdrop statistics compiled by KC Feng and supplied via Fu email

9 Holober, p177; Fu, p18

10 CAT's first C-54 was chartered from US airline Seabord and Western in March 1952. Three months later, it was replaced with the airline's own C-54, which also did regular international passenger flights as B-1002 on the Taiwan civil register (Leary email to Fu)

11 Leary, p136; Holober, p188-194; Fu, p18

12 Shilling email 23 April 1996, amplified by Tom Cleaver obituary of Shilling at www.warbirdforum.com

13 Shilling email; Leary email to Fu

14 Fu, p17 and Fu email. The American advisors were probably from the MAAG, rather than WEI. The main purpose of these CAF B-25 missions was probably to identify suitable locations for future airdrops of agents and equipment.

15 Fu, p19 and email

16 As noted by Conboy and Morrison 'Tibet' p57-8, in May 1952, the Chinese Air Force sent three pilots, two navigators and two crew chiefs to Tachikawa airbase, Japan, where US airmen trained them on the B-17 and the B-26. But Fu notes that when they returned to Taiwan in October, they were re-assigned to their previous units. Occasionally, however, they were given refresher training on B-17s and B-26s that were specially flown to Xinzhu airbase for the purpose by American aircrew. It is possible that these crews were earmarked for the operations over Manchuria, before the US changed its mind and made this an all-American (eg a CAT) operation. According to Dujmovic (see next reference), the first Third Force insertion was into southern, not northern China, in April 1952. Nothing was ever heard from the four paradropped agents.

17 Nicholas Dujmovic, "Two CIA Prisoners in China, 1952-73", CIA Studies in Intelligence, Vol 50, No 4, 2006. This is the first account of the incident to use official (and still classified) US documents.

18 Leary, p138-140

19 Taylor, p208-9

20 State Dept memo 18 June 1956 "US guidance to GRC on Military Action" in Box 3976, RG59.794A.5, NARA

21 Holober, p199-219. According to Fu, CAF P-47s may also have flown in support.

22   CIA memo from Chief, FI to DDCI on 26 August 1953, reproduced in Early Cold
      War Overflights, p491. According to Dujmovic, op cit, the CIA's local field
      commanders did retain some discretion to send CIA officers on overflights. As for CAT,
      it subsequently flew paramilitary missions in support of the unsuccessful French resistance
      to the communist advance in North Vietnam in 1954. It also staged the airlift that
      repatriated some of the nationalist troops from Burma.

Chapter 2
23   Taylor, p220-1
24   Fu, p27-8. The RB-24 was a 'one-off' conversion of a CAF B-24M, and not the
      RB-24L version as used by the USAF
25   State Dept memo 18 June 1956 "US guidance to GRC on Military Action" in
      Box 3976, RG59.794A.5, NARA
26   Holober, p178; Fu, p28. According to an official Taiwan source, the SMG did not start
      flying B-26s until March 1954
27   NIE 27/1 of 1 April 1952; NIE 80 of 6 May 1953
28   A History of US Navy Fleet Air Reconnaissance, Part 1, in THE Hook magazine,
      Spring 1986
29   Fu, p33
30   Fu, p28
31   Fu, p32
32   Fu, p33
33   Taylor, p228
34   www.TaiwanAirPower.org, ROCAF Combat Losses Since 1950
35   Smith, p269
36   Chen, p168-9; Holober, p156-7; Accinelli, p174
37   Taylor, p231; Accinelli, p175, p180
38   Cole, p26
39   CIA memo from Chief, FI to DDCI on 26 August 1953, reproduced in Early Cold
      War Overflights, p491
40   Li interview; Kleyla interview
41   Fu, p41. According to Conboy, the P4Y2 ELINT mission was codenamed Fox Terrier,
      but this is contradicted by an official Taiwan source
42   official Taiwan source
43   Lin translated by Kao, p79
44   Lin via Fu, p34
45   Ong Tai Shen via Fu, p41
46   Fu, p33; official Taiwan source
47   Kleyla interview
48   official Taiwan source
49   Lin via Fu, p38-9
50   Lin translated by Kao; A Dangerous Business, The US Navy and National
      Reconnaissance During the Cold War, NSA Center for Cryptologic History, 2004, p6-7
51   NIE 13-56 of 5 January 1956. Between 1956 and 1959, the PRC produced 767 MiG-17
      fighters under licence from the Soviet Union. These aircraft were designated J-5 in
      China. License-production of the MiG-19 followed from 1959, and these were designated
      J-6 in China. For ease of reference, this book uses the original Soviet designations.
52   I Fu En, p103-4; Shulinkou veterans website at
      http://members.tripod.com/Shulinkou/Dawg1.html

Chapter 3
53   The CIA has not released any official history of AMD. Fragmentary details can be
      obtained from a number of books dealing with US covert operations in the 1950s, such as
      those by authors Ranelagh, Harclerode, Marchetti and Marks, Prouty and Trest.

54   Bissell's untitled memo dated 20 September 1955 via CREST.
55   Prouty, Chapter 16; Stanley interview
56   Giles interview
57   Prouty, Chapter 16. The CIA acquired two more P2V-7s later, to replace aircraft that were lost on operations from Taiwan.
58   Giles interview; Prouty, Chapter 16; Miller, p57. According to Cavanaugh, interview, the supply container was drop-tested over the El Toro range in southern California. But technical problems meant that it was never used operationally.
59   Cavanaugh interview; Losey interview.
60   DPD memo 28 September 1959 via CREST
61   CIA Memo 8 February 1956, "Meeting at Westinghouse Air Arm," via CREST. Chappell, interview, recalled that the APQ-56 and antenna was fitted inside the bomb bay.
62   official Taiwan source
63   Fu, p53-56; Taylor, p223
64   Lin via Fu, p54; NIE 13-57 of 19 March 1957
65   Fu, p57; Lin translation by Kao
66   Fu, p60; official Taiwan source
67   Prados, p190; Taylor p252-3
68   Conboy 'Tibet' p58-9, Prados, p191-2. However, according to Shakya, p174, the first two Khampa agents were not dropped until 7 December 1957. The dates of the subsequent airdrops also vary by account. The CIA has not declassified any official records of ST Barnum.
69   Prados, p196; Trest, p87
70   Giles interview; DPD memo 10 December 1959
71   7499th wing history, January-June 1957; Cavanaugh interview
72   Fu, p85. He notes that eight of this initial cadre of 12 had been killed in action by 1963, an indication
73   of the high-risk nature of the P2V mission over mainland China note by Richard Kao
74   Hsinchu Base Photo Album, undated, released via CREST
75   undated memo released by CREST, RDP81B00880R000100440013-1
76   official Taiwan source
77   FRUS 1958-60 Vol 19, p509-510 via Taylor, p239
78   interview, source withheld
79   Fu, p85

Chapter 4
80   China Today: Air Force p363-4 via Chang translation; Lin via Kao translation
81   China Today: Air Force p363-4 via Chang translation
82   Lin via Fu p62
83   Fu p64; Lin via Kao translation
84   China Today: Air Force p36x via Chang translation; Fu email; official Taiwan source.
85   NIE-13-58, 13 May 1958, Annex B
86   Fu p64-66; Lin via Kao translation. The pseudonym of the American IP was Major Alexander
87   Fu p66; China Today: Air Force p363-4 via Chang translation. It should be noted here, that the radar-equipped MiG-17PF achieved its first success over China on 18 February 1958, when two aircraft belonging to the PLA Navy air arm shot down a CAF RB-57A at high altitude.
88   Fu, p67
89   official Taiwan source
90   Conboy and Morrison, Tibet, p101
91   Thomas, p192 and 274
92   I Fu En My Memoirs translation via email from Fu
93   Prados, p172-3; Taylor, p240; Fu p46; Jim Cherbonneaux unpublished memoir sent to author.
94   Chen Jian, p171-181

95 SNIE 100-9-58, 26 August 1958
96 Chang Wei-bin website www.taiwanairpower.org
97 SNIE 100-4-59, 13 March 1959; Taylor, p245
98 official Taiwan source
99 State Dept memo "ROC - Paramilitary Activities on the China Mainland", 24 November 1959, in RG59. 794A-5, Box 3976, US National Archives
100 official Taiwan source; KC Feng airdrop data via Fu email
101 Lin via Kao translation; China Today: Air Force p36x via Chang translation
102 official Taiwan source
103 I Fu En, p170-176; Hagedorn and Hellstrom
104 Lin translation by Kao; Fu p67-8
105 NIE-13-59, 28 July 1959, p28
106 Lin via Kao translation; Fu p96-7
107 memo for DDP 12 March 1959, released via CREST
108 DPD Staff Meeting minutes, 24 February 1959 via CREST; memo for Chief FE Division 7 April 1959
109 Memo for DDP 6 July 1959 via CREST
110 official Taiwan source
111 DPD memos 20 April, 7 May and 22 May 1959, via CREST.
112 Giles interview, Jackson interview
113 Kao interview
114 Giles interview; Kao interview; Jackson interview; Williamson interview; DPD memos 18 March 1959, 22 September 1959 and 21 March 1960 via CREST; it is not clear why the ALQ designation - normally used for ECM systems - was applied to the new ELINT receiver.
115 DPD memos 22 and 27 September, and 19 November 1959 via CREST; email from Fu
116 Daly and Giles interviews; Trest, p82; "Robert Fulton's Skyhook and Operation Coldfeet", CIA Studies in Intelligence, Vol 38 No 5 (1995).
117 DPD memos 6 and 7 October, and 3 December 1959, and Monthly Activity Report 19 November 1959, via CREST.

Chapter 5
118 In the absence of firm ELINT data, US intelligence analysts concluded that the RB-57D had been shot down by a fighter-interceptor. In fact, it had been shot down by an SA-2 missile from one of only five batteries supplied by the USSR to the PRC before the Sino-Soviet political split in mid-1959 caused the USSR to suspend further deliveries. U.S. intelligence did not determine that SA-2 missiles had been supplied to the PRC until early September 1961, when a Corona reconnaissance satellite photographed the deployment sites around Beijing.
119 ARC memo dated 22 September 1959 via CREST
120 memo from DDP to Acting Chief DPD 21 March 1960; DPD Staff Meeting Minutes 15 March 1960. The SIGINT specialists at the CIA believed that the K-band receiver could be used to collect intelligence on Soviet ICBM test flights, as they re-entered the atmosphere over the Kamchatka peninsula or further east in the Pacific Ocean. Indeed, a P2V flown by an all-American crew did apparently make one short-notice deployment to Johnston Island in the mid-Pacific to monitor such tests.
121 official Taiwan source
122 Liu Wen Xiao (劉文孝), Chinese Air Force in Action, Series 3, p209. According to a display in the old 34ᵗʰ Squadron museum, this flight lasted even longer – 20 hours and 40 minutes! According to Dai Shu Qing, interview, the long-endurance flights in the B-17 were made possible by the addition of another additional fuel tank in the bomb bay. A similar tank was added to the P2V.
123 Kleyla interview
124 Fu, p97-; Lin via Kao translation

125 official Taiwan source
126 DPD Ops Branch Activity Report, 10 March 1960, via CREST
127 Jackson interview
128 Fu, p94
129 official Taiwan source
130 Giles interview; Raymer, Winn, Jackson interviews
131 Jackson interview
132 Fu, p87
133 email from Kao
134 official Taiwan source
135 official Taiwan source
136 Fu, p94-5; official Taiwan source
137 State Dept memo, 24 November 1959, in RG59.794A.5, Box 3976 at NARA
138 Taylor, p253; State Dept briefing notes for visit September 1965, DDRS
139 Fu, p46. Fu explains that the 3831 Force was created from the remnants of the CAF's 33rd
     Squadron. It was commanded by Col Li Yong Ren (李用仁), and took its orders directly
     from CAF HQ by the J-2, Gen I Fu En. The numbers 3831 represented the date in the
     Chinese calendar when Chiang Kai-shek re-assumed the presidency of the ROC. As Fu
     notes, this event was actually in 1950 – year 39 of the Chinese calendar – so the designators
     of the new force made a mistake!
140 Fu-p46-7; I Fu En memoir, p101
141 I Fu En memoir, p102; Taylor p262; OCI memo dated 17 May 1963, released by
     CIA under FOIA.
142 I Fu En memoir, p183-4; Conboy with Morrison, Laos, p64
143 Fu, p96; Lin via Kao translation
144 Fu, p97-; Lin via Kao translation; Dai in MND Vietnam History. P180-2
145 Kao, "The Unexpected Combat Scores of the 34th Squadron", ROCAF Magazine,
     Taipei, November 2007
146 official Taiwan source; Hsinchu Base Photo Album
147 Fu p101; official Taiwan source
148 CIA cable 6 April 1961 via CREST
149 DPD cable 1 February 1961 via CREST
150 Jackson interview
151 CIA cables 6 April, 1 May and 3 May via CREST
152 official Taiwan source; Lin p145
153 Lin via Kao translation; State Dept background paper for visit September 1965, DDRS
154 ONE memo dated 27 July 1961, released by CIA under FOIA; Taylor, p263; Fu p69
155 Fu p70-72
156 Fu, p102. This was not the NACC's first attempt to make a SIGINT reconnaissance of
     North Vietnam. Some time earlier, a C-54 was temporarily fitted with an ELINT receiver
     and flown by a Vietnamese crew from Saigon. Antennas were taped to the aircraft's
     cabin windows. The COMINT System 3 was also carried. No signals were received.
     (Don Jackson interview)
157 Lin, p122
158 Official Taiwan source; Kao email
159 Lin via Kao translation

Chapter 6
160 NIS39A, January 1961, Communist China Air Forces, in RG263, Job 79-00901A, at NARA
161 AIR40/2726 December 1961 "Air Defence of Communist China" in UK National Archives
162 Fu p103-4
163 NIE 13-2-62, p13
164 Taylor, p265; FRUS 1961-63 Volume XXII, item 94
165 Fu p72

166 SNIE 13-5-62
167 Whiting, p111
168 Mission GRC-126 cable ADIC 6140, released under CREST
169 Fu p74-6. Lu De Qi interview. According to a subsequent PRC statement, only three men were dropped, and the aircraft was mistakenly identified as a P2V.
170 State Dept INR memo 9 January 1963, via DDRS
171 Taylor, p267-8
172 Fu p78; Zai Te Shu Zhan Xian Shang (In a Special Battle), Jilin People's Publication, Jilin, 1988
173 I Fu En memoir, p185; "Plausible Deniability – US-Taiwanese Covert Insertions into North Vietnam" by Ken Conboy and James Morrison, Air Enthusiast Quarterly, November/December 1999. One of the C-123s was destroyed in a training accident on Taiwan before the deployment to Vietnam began.
174 DD/R memo for Executive Director, 13 July 1962, released through CREST
175 Executive Director memo for DDR and DDP, 5 July 1962, released through CREST
176 Raymer, Winn interviews
177 Fu p104; Giles interview. The wing-mounted pods were probably the LASL type, and the gas-sampling system the P52.
178 memo for DDNRO by DDR, 22 July 1963, via CREST
179 Weng Tai Sheng, p138
180 Gao interview
181 Giles interview
182 Official Taiwan source; CIA Air Activities Status Report 20 February 1963, released via CREST
183 Fu p104-5; Lin via Kao translation; official Taiwan source
184 DPD Recap of Air Activties w/e 29 May 1963, released via CREST
185 Flame suppressors were not fully effective when the crew added maximum power to the engine, or changed the mixture control (Daly interview)
186 Lin via Kao translation
187 Fu, p106
188 FRUS 1961-63 Volume XX11, item 86
189 FRUS as above
190 Taylor p269; National Security Archive Electronic Briefing Book 38; Raymer interview

Chapter 7
191 John McCaull email
192 CIA cable 12 December 1963, partially redacted, via DDRS
193 Kleyla interview
194 Fu, p109. Kleyla interview. According to an email to author from a former NACC manager, the PLAAF knew about the fitting of the air-to-air missiles almost immediately. However, since they were intended as a deterrent to interception, it may have been in the CAF/NACC interest to let the new capability be known to the other side!
195 Raymer, Logan, McCaull interviews
196 Fu, p97, Raymer and Winn interviews
197 memo for DDR from DDI, "Requirements for Project STSPIN", 23 May 1963, via CREST
198 Singel interview
199 Kleyla interview; various LTV Electrosystems and E-Systems company publications
200 Naval aircraft records via Rick Burgess; David Reade, "The Age of Orion", p105. According to Reade, the cargo door modification to the first of the Agency's P-3As was done by the U.S. Navy depot at NAS Alameda, CA in mid-1963. A second door was added in mirror image to the existing one, and both swung inwards and back to produce a 53-inch wide opening. Unfortunately, Reade adds, the necessary structural support was inadequate, and "the tail section of the aircraft nearly twisted off during a test flight."
201 I Fu En "My Memoirs" p114

202   Lin via Fu p106; official Taiwan source

203   official Taiwan source. According to a newspaper report in Taiwan, there were nationalist commando raids on the Shandong peninsula in early June, one month after the P2V flight that passed closeby, but offshore.

204   Lin via Kao translation

205   Ong, p146

206   State Dept cable from Taipei 28 July 1964 via DDRS; CIA memo by Office of Current Intelligence, 18 August 1965, via CIA FOIA website

207   History of the Air Force Tactical Applications Center (AFTAC), July-December 1964, Chapter 3, partially released via FOIA

208   background paper for visit of CCK to Washington, September 1965, via DDRS

209   Background Paper on Vice-President's Visit to Taiwan, 23 December 1965, in RG59 at NARA. The Blue Lion joint committee also helped the US to stay abreast of what unilateral moves against the mainland, the MND in Taipei might be planning. In May 1964, the U.S. Embassy reported a big exercise in which the CAF's C-46 transports demonstrated the ability to airdrop a whole regiment of soldiers. (US Embassy Taipei report, RG59.794A box 3717 at NARA)

210   Fu p110, Kao logbook

211   Ford interview

212   Singel interview

213   Connor, Kwiatowski interviews

214   Kleyla interview; Fu, p150

215   Herring interview

216   Fu, p152; Yu interview

217   Herring interview

218   official Taiwan source. Another official Taiwan source suggests that there was a second P2V overflight of the mainland in 1966

219   Connor interview

220   Memo for Sec of State Rusk prepared by CIA, in FRUS 1964-68, Vol XXX, item 222. For reasons unknown, this memo refers to Project Grosbeak, not Goshawk.

221   Kleyla interview. Connor interview. One possible casualty of Chiang's fury was Chinese Air Force General I Fu En, the main contact with the US side for the Goshawk and Razor (U-2) projects until 1964. In July 1966, he was accused of corruption and confined without trial for three years.

222   USATG source; FRUS op cit; Kao logbook

223   State Dept Memo for INR Director Hughes, in FRUS 1964-68, Vol XXX, item 227. CCK was probably referring to the number of aircrew lost in crashes and shootdowns, rather than the number of agents dropped and then killed.

224   Fu email to author

225   Fu p166

226   Marchetti and Marks, p165-7. The ROC already launched balloons from Quemoy into the mainland, carrying 100lb payloads of toothbrushes, toothpaste and portratits of Chiang Kai Shek, that were dropped at fixed intervals (RG59 box 2032 at NARA)

227   NIS 39A "Communist China Air Forces" declassified at NARA in 2001

228   Pocock, 50 Years of the U-2, p246-251

229   NIE 13-8-67, 3 August 1967, Top Secret (Codeword), declassified 2004

230   State Dept memo for the Director of INR, 18 August 1967, via FRUS op.cit. item 278

231   Kleyla interview

232   Fu p170-1

233   Yu interview; TD Barnes email to author

234   It has not been possible to identify the C-130E that was bailed from the USAF to the CIA and used for the Heavy Tea mission. It may have been one of the 14 aircraft that were modified for the support of special forces in the mid-1960s, and designated C-130E(I). However, the author suspects it was one of four more similarly-modified C-130Es that

were flown by the 1198th Operational Evaluation and Test Squadron. This was a USAF squadron based at Norton AFB, CA that supported highly-classified projects, and used the project name Heavy Chain. Certainly, the Norton-based aircraft were used to train the CAF crews at Groom Lake.

235   Fu p172-3; Yu interview; Lu, Black Bats Oral History, p80
236   Kleyla interview
237   Fu p170-174
238   Kleyla interview
239   official Taiwan source
240   Fu p174-6; official Taiwan source
241   MND Vietnam Oral History, p166
242   Fu p176-7

Chapter 8
243   I Fu En memoir, p170-182
244   I Fu En, p184; Conboy "Shadow War" p64
245   Conboy and Andrade, p31-50
246   Dai memoir in MND Vietnam Oral History book, p192-3; Conboy & Andrade, p31-50
247   Fu p114-5; Conboy & Morrison "Plausible Deniability" p31; OSA memos for DDR and the record, 5 and 12 October 1962, via CREST
248   Fu p116; Severo interview
249   Conboy & Andrade p59
250   official Taiwan source
251   Conboy & Andrade p61
252   Conboy & Andrade p63; official Taiwan source. Conboy & Andrade say that the captain of the C-123 immediately quit the program, and flew back to Taiwan.
253   Fu p106; Conboy and Morrison article as above. This was at least the second, and possibly the third time that a P2V was sent from Taiwan to make an ELINT reconnaissance of North Vietnam. The first occasion was 15 June 1961 (see Chapter Five). According to a document released via CREST, a complete survey of North Vietnam was also flown on 23 April 1963.
254   Ahern, p43
255   official Taiwan source
256   Fu interview; official Taiwan source
257   Conboy & Andrade, p84-91
258   The SOG was initially named the Special Operations Group, but this was changed after only a few months. The military-controlled SOG in Vietnam should not be confused with the Special Operations Division within the CIA, which was sometimes mistakenly referred to as a Group (and hence SOG).
259   Ahern p57
260   official Taiwan source. There was apparently another P2V mission over North Vietnam in early June 1964
261   Fu p124
262   Conboy and Andrade p96-7; official Taiwan source
263   official Taiwan source; MND Vietnam War Oral History
264   Conboy & Andrade, p99
265   Jiang Ming Xuan (蔣明軒), in BBOH, p331-2
266   Conboy & Andrade, p158-161
267   Fu p132
268   Official Taiwan source; Conboy & Andrade, p147
269   Conboy & Andrade, p148-9; www.straygoose.org
270   official Taiwan source

271   information via Bill Grimes
272   official Taiwan source
273   John Gargus, "The Last Mission of Combat Talon's S-01 Crew" from www.straygoose.org
274   official Taiwan source; Conboy & Andrade p211-12
275   Fu p144
276   Ahern, "Undercover Armies", p347
277   Yu interview, Conboy and Morrison "Shadow War" p380
278   Lu interview
279   Conboy and Morrison "Shadow War" p382
280   Ahern, "The Way We Do Things" p58. On 25 July 1972, one of the two Twin Otters
      crashed into a mountain on the Plain of Jars, while trying to resupply the Lao irregular army
      led by Gen Vang Pao, who was trying to resist the communist advance. The crew were
      killed, including Ben Coleman, the Air America pilot who had trained CAF crews to fly
      the C-123 and the Twin Otter.
281   Lu and Yu interviews; Conboy and Morrison "Shadow War" p383; James Chiles,
      "Air America's Black Helicopter", Air & Space magazine, March 2008. The wiretap
      mission to Vinh was eventually flown by an Air America crew on 5 December 1972 –
      see Chiles article. According to Ahern, "Undercover Armies" p347 footnote, the tap
      produced a readable signal for only 10 days.
282   In addition to this death toll of squadron members, four agents were killed in the shootdown
      of the B-17 on 26 May 1956, and two more agents in the crash of the B-26 on April 1955.

Epilogue
283   Taylor, p318. Taiwan eventually abandoned the project.
284   Nancy Bernkopf Tucker, "Taiwan Expendable? Nixon and Kissinger Go to China", Journal
      of American History, Vol 92, No 1, June 2005
285   Taylor, p320. None of those who were inserted as agents, captured, and subsequently
      returned to Taiwan, have chosen to speak publicly about their experience. In 1982, the
      PRC released two pilots from the joint CIA/CAF U-2 squadron, who had been shot down
      over the mainland in 1963 and 1965. They, too, were refused re-entry to Taiwan.
286   Taylor, p342
287   The Black Bats Memorial Hall, No 16, Section 2, Dongda Road, Hsinchu City, Taiwan,
      R.O.C. Open 0900-1700 Wednesday – Sunday. Tel +886 (0)3 542 5061.

Other Sources and Author's Acknowledgments
288   "Low-Level Technical Reconnaissance over Mainland China (1955-66)" reference
      CSHP-2.348. It was written in 1972, and was described to me by one CIA official as a
      'draft' history. This official suggested that such histories can often be bettered by
      those working outside the classified system, by virtue of diligent research and
      interviewing. Others can pass judgement on that, with respect to this book. My own
      experience has been that official histories provide a valuable framework upon which
      further work can be based, especially when dealing with the fading memories of veterans.
      I am personally disappointed that the Agency refused to budge on this particular issue
      of declassification, despite my two informal appeals in person to the then-Director of
      Central Intelligence, Gen Mike Hayden.

Index

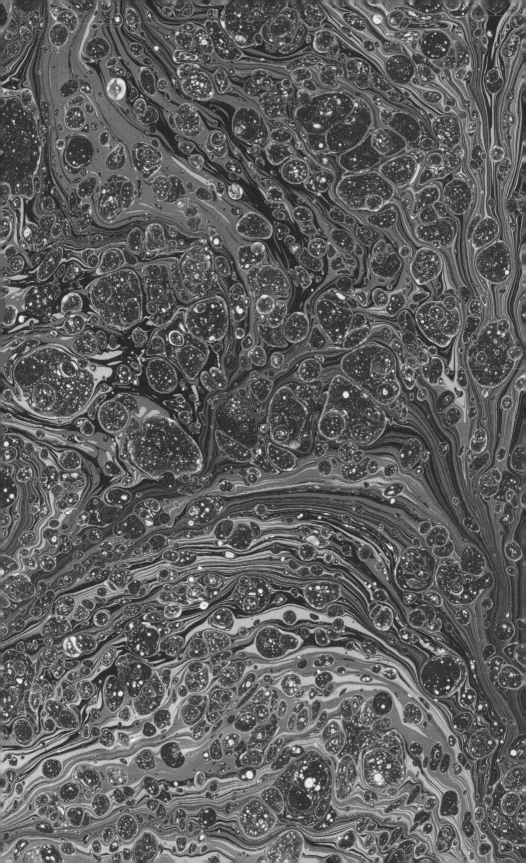